IN PURSUIT OF GOOD ADMINISTRATION

Ministers, Civil Servants, and Judges

In Pursuit of Good Administration

Ministers, Civil Servants, and Judges

DIANA WOODHOUSE

CLARENDON PRESS · OXFORD
1997

Oxford University Press, Great Clarendon Street, Oxford OX2 6DP
Oxford New York
Athens Auckland Bangkok Bogota Bombay
Buenos Aires Calcutta Cape Town Dar es Salaam
Delhi Florence Hong Kong Istanbul Karachi
Kuala Lumpur Madras Madrid Melbourne
Mexico City Nairobi Paris Singapore
Taipei Tokyo Toronto Warsaw
and associated companies in
Berlin Ibadan

Oxford is a trade mark of Oxford University Press

Published in the United States
by Oxford University Press Inc., New York

British Library Cataloguing in Publication Data
Data available

Library of Congress Cataloging in Publication Data
Woodhouse, Diana.
In pursuit of good administration: ministers, civil servants, and
judges / Diana Woodhouse.
p. cm.
Includes bibliographical references and index.
1. Administrative agencies—Great Britain—Management.   2. Public
administration—Great Britain.   3. Civil service reform—Great Britain.
4. Administrative law—Great Britain.   I. Title.
JN318.W65   1997   352.2′9′0941—dc21   97–12928
ISBN 0–19–826036–9

1 3 5 7 9 10 8 6 4 2

Typeset by Hope Services (Abingdon) Ltd.
Printed in Great Britain
on acid-free paper by
Biddles Ltd., Guildford and King's Lynn

CONTENTS

viii *Contents*

PREFACE

This book examines the concept of good administration against the background of civil service reform, an increasingly interventionist judiciary and executive–judicial tension. It looks at administrative and judicial perspectives of good administration in relation to central government. It suggests that the principles which have traditionally been accepted as informing the concept of good administration are being undermined by the philosophy and management style of the new public management, which now dominates the Civil Service, and that it can no longer be assumed that those engaged in public administration support the same values as the courts or the Parliamentary Commissioner for Administration. It therefore argues that now more than ever a code of good administration is essential.

The research for this book was funded by Oxford Brookes University to whom I owe my thanks. I am also grateful to colleagues who read drafts and put forward ideas or asked pertinent questions at research seminars. Similarly, I am grateful to those students who through their questions and responses helped me clarify my ideas and to the civil servants with whom I have spoken. I would also like to thank Richard Hart, now of Hart Publishing, who was so supportive during the early days of writing, and the external reviewers of the initial draft, whose comments and criticisms helped considerably. Thanks are also due to Elissa Soave of OUP who saw the book through its final stages and to the librarians at Brookes University and the Bodleian. However, most importantly my thanks go to Jo Aldhouse who spent long hours at Lexis and patiently trawled through law and Select Committee reports. Without her contribution, this book would not have been possible. However, I alone am responsible for its contents.

Diana Woodhouse
Oxford Brookes University
March 1997

Table of Cases

TABLE OF STATUTES

1

INTRODUCTION

Background

The importance of good administration is frequently stressed by politicians, civil servants and judges. However, as a concept it lacks definition or at least clarity as to its content. At a minimal level administration may be considered 'good' if it achieves the implementation of the policy goals of the Government of the day in accordance with the values underpinning these goals. Thus what constitutes good administration may change as the requirements of Government and the role of the State changes. Good administration in the context of intervention and the Welfare State may be different from good administration in the context of rolling back the frontiers of the State and cutting public expenditure.

This minimalist view of what constitutes good administration is based on the premise that its main purpose is to support the governing party and the political process, and that the principles underlying it have no intrinsic worth. They can therefore vary, according to a government's ideological commitment or economic need. However, this approach would seem to confuse the function of the administrative body with the principles that govern its operation and which support the constitutional position of civil servants as permanent, non-partisan servants of the Crown who are required to serve governments of any political persuasion with dedication and impartiality. This requires the adherence to principles which ensure the legality of administrative action and protect public servants from suspicions of political partisanship and corruption. These principles also provide a base line or blueprint for the way in which decisions are made and services delivered. There may be less (or more) to deliver, but certain key values still attach to the delivery. These act to protect the individual and the wider public from an arbitrary exercise of power or the misapplication of public funds. They also reinforce and inform the concepts developed by the courts in relation to the administrative process.

Thus it is not just the political party in power which has an interest in good administration. Indeed, it could be argued that what constitutes good administration is above government, and certainly outside party, interests. This would accord the concept constitutional authority and suggest that the principles underlying it should not be undermined or dissipated by political requirements born of economic need or ideology. The balance afforded the different values may vary but the base line agreement of what is required of the administrative process needs to be maintained to ensure the system's legitimacy.

The Absence of a Code of Good Administration

Despite the importance of good administration and the benefits which accrue from its practice, British governments have consistently resisted calls for the codification of the principles underlying it. Yet Britain has been involved, through the Council of Europe, in the drafting of Codes laying down minimum standards of good administrative practice. In 1977 the Committee of Ministers adopted a Resolution which detailed five guiding principles which should inform the administrative process.[1] These were aimed at ensuring the 'highest possible degree of fairness', thereby providing protection for an individual whose rights, liberties or interests were affected adversely by an administrative act. They required, firstly, that such a person should have a right to put forward his or her case and to have it taken into account prior to an administrative decision being made. Secondly, he or she should have access to the information used in making the decision, and, thirdly, should be allowed assistance or representation in arguing his or her case. In addition, the Resolution considered that reasons should be given for an administrative act which affects rights, liberties, or interests and that the person affected should be made aware of the available remedies. These principles were concerned with the procedures that should be followed and focus upon the relationship between individuals and administrators rather than on the internal process of administration. They are an extension of the principles of natural justice as developed by the English courts.

Two years later the Committee of Ministers adopted a Recommendation to complement the previous Resolution.[2] This contained eleven principles which the Committee recommended should govern the exercise of discretion. In summary the Recommendation required that power must only be used for the purpose for which it was granted and that any adverse effect of the exercise of discretion upon an individual's rights, liberty, or interests should be balanced against the intended purpose. With regard to decision-making, it stipulated that all relevant factors should be considered and irrelevant factors ignored, and that decisions should be taken within a reasonable time. In addition, it stated that like cases should be treated in like manner, although the particular circumstances of each case must be taken into account, and that administrative guidelines, such as circulars, codes of practice etc., should be applied consistently. It also recommended that if guidelines govern the way in which discretion is exercised, they should be made public, and, if they are not followed, then reasons should be given for the decision. The Recommendation further required that the legality of an administrative act should always be challengeable through a court or other independent body and

---

[1] Resolution (77)31, *On the Protection of the Individual in Relation to the Acts of Administrative Authorities.*

[2] Recommendation No. R(80)2), *Concerning the Exercise of Discretionary Powers by Administrative Authorities.*

that this body must have the necessary powers to obtain information relating to the making of the decision.

Both the Resolution and the Recommendation recognized that there were times when one or more of these principles might have to give way to the interests of third parties, to the public interest, or to the requirements of 'good and efficient administration', by which is meant competing principles necessary to ensure the smooth running of the administrative process, such as cost, speed, and administrative effectiveness.

The combined Resolution/Recommendation had much in common with the Statement of the Principles of Good Administration which had been drafted by a committee of JUSTICE, chaired by Keith Goodfellow QC, in 1971.[3] The Statement encompassed the concepts of reasonableness and fairness which underlie administrative law and which have been developed substantially by the courts since that time. It required that a person 'particularly and materially affected' by a pending decision should be given prior notice of that decision and a reasonable opportunity to make representations, that steps should be taken to ensure that persons likely to be affected by a decision were notified of it, and that decisions should not have retrospective effect. In addition, the Statement imposed a limit of two months on the making of a decision that arose out of a statutory duty and stipulated that a decision arising from a statutory power or discretion should be exercised within a reasonable time. The Statement also incorporated principles requiring all reasonable steps to be taken to ascertain the material facts relating to a decision, any reasonable requests for material information to be dealt with promptly,[4] and, when requested, reasons to be given for decisions.

JUSTICE considered that the Statement provided a necessary framework for those engaged in public administration and that any person 'particularly and materially' affected by a breach of the incorporated principles should have the right of challenge in the High Court. It recommended that the Principles of Good Administration should be enacted. The recommendation was not given effect. The more recent JUSTICE–All Souls Committee had no greater success when it recommended in 1988 that an up-to-date set of principles of good administration should be drawn up and published.[5] It suggested that the Resolution and Recommendation from the Council of Ministers should form the basis of a set of Principles but that account should be taken of the Statement written in 1971, of the findings of the Parliamentary Commissioner for Administration (PCA; more commonly known as the Ombudsman), and of judicial review decisions. The Committee suggested that the PCA was best placed to draw up such a set of Principles because good administration could be seen as the obverse of maladministration. It did not believe that the Principles should be enacted, although it

---

[3] JUSTICE, *Administration under Law*.

[4] Provided the request was made within two months and its release would not be prejudicial to national security.

[5] JUSTICE–All Souls, *Review of Administrative Law*.

recommended that the duty to give reasons should be given statutory form and that there should be a statutory remedy for unreasonable and excessive delay. Otherwise it considered that the Principles should be expressed as 'broad, general principles', so that they would retain the 'sensitivity and flexibility . . . essential to good administration'.[6]

The reluctance of the Government to adopt such a Code accords with the British tradition of government by convention and understandings rather than law and codes, and with the customary arrogance which holds that Britain, unlike other countries, does not need formal documents to safeguard the rights of individuals or ensure good administrative practice. For JUSTICE the call for a Code or Statement of Principles arose out of concern at the unstructured expansion of administrative law, its apparent lack of a theoretical base, and judicial uncertainty regarding the relationship of the courts with government. It saw the principles incorporated in such a Code as providing a basis for the review of administrative decisions with a breach of the Code in some cases being grounds for judicial review. The Committee looked enviously towards Australia where the grounds on which judicial review can be sought have been given legislative form.[7] It noted that 'many of them [the grounds] could be established only by proving a breach of one of the principles of good administrative practice adopted by the Committee of Ministers' (and supported by JUSTICE).[8]

Reform of the Civil Service

The lawyers' call for a Code of Good Administration remains undiminished. Moreover, it has since been supplemented by calls from past and present civil servants, Parliamentary Select Committees, ex-ministers, and Whitehall-watchers, all of whom want the principles underpinning public administration, on which such a Code is based and supported, to be agreed and provided with a degree of permanence. Their concern arises from the reforms of the 1980s and 1990s, which have transformed public administration. These have been motivated by the drive towards efficient government, by which is meant less government, both in functions and cost. The aim, wherever possible, is to transfer functions to the private sector, either permanently or under contract, where, it is argued, they will be performed more efficiently, offering better value for money and improved quality. This transfer serves the economic requirement to reduce public expenditure and the ideological commitment to reduce the role of the State. Where transfer to the private sector is not possible, at least in the immediate future, Next Steps executive agencies offer an alternative location.

Such agencies are an extension of the Financial Management Initiative instigated in 1982 to improve efficiency. They remain within government departments

---

[6] JUSTICE–All Souls, *Review of Administrative Law*, 7.   [7] See ch. 9.
[8] JUSTICE–All Souls (above, n. 5), ch. 2, para. 2.20.

and are staffed by civil servants. Thus they are protected, or more usually confined, by the convention of ministerial responsibility, being responsible first and foremost to the minister. However, they operate at a distance from the minister under framework agreements which set out their responsibilities and provide targets and performance indicators, and their organizational and management methods owe more to the private than the public sector. They are headed by chief executives, often appointed from outside the Civil Service, who are on fixed term contracts and performance-related pay and who have considerably more financial and operational autonomy than has previously been accorded civil servants.

Agencies, like their parent departments, are governed by the Competing for Quality Programme, which was launched by the Government in November 1991. The Programme demonstrates the Government's commitment to the market and underlines its belief that 'competition is the best guarantee of quality and value for money'.[9] It introduced market testing, the purpose of which is 'to establish for activities where it is possible for them to be performed either by public servants or by the private sector, which alternative represents the best long-term value for money'.[10] Thus the public sector is required to 'compete' with its private counterparts for the business of fulfilling public functions. However, in many cases in-house competition is excluded and services have been contracted out without the public sector being permitted to tender, despite, or perhaps because of, its overwhelming success when it does.[11] This suggests that the ideological commitment to reduce the role of the State, or to change it from provider to enabler, may at times be more important than the economic requirement to reduce public spending. This seems to be borne out by Mr William Waldegrave, who, when Minister for the Public Service, stated that his aim was to relocate the activities of government so that less than 40 per cent of 'public' services would be carried out by the public sector.[12]

'Public' administration has therefore developed a hybrid form. It may be undertaken by traditional civil servants within departments of government, by temporary civil servants, still within government departments but operating under the private-sector controls and incentives adopted by executive agencies, and by private sector contractors. Alternatively, it may be undertaken by quangos or non-departmental public bodies, established to operate at arm's length from the minister in a regulatory, advisory or executive capacity.[13] The decision as to what type of organization fulfils a particular function depends on the assessment made by the Government, firstly, as to whether the job needs to be done at all; secondly, if it does, whether the Government needs to be responsible for it; thirdly, whether this means that the Government has to carry out the task itself, and, fourthly, if so,

---

[9] Cm. 1730 (1991) p. i.   [10] Ibid.

[11] Up to 70% of the value of the completed Competing for Quality Programme has been won by the private sector without in-house competition (TCSC, HC 27–I, (1993–4), para. 133).

[12] Ibid., II, Q1824.

[13] For discussions on quangos see Cmnd. 7797 (1980); A. Barker (ed.), *Quangos in Britain*; R. Baldwin & C. McCrudden (eds.), *Regulation and Public Law*; L. Pliatzky, 'Quangos and agencies' (1992) 7 *Pub. Admin.* 4.

whether the organization is properly structured and focused on the job to be done.[14] Thus the check-list runs through whether the function or service can be abolished, privatized, contracted out or market tested, fulfilled by a body outside the department, and, if none of these is appropriate, consigned to an executive agency with the necessary framework agreement and performance targets. Finally, if all else fails, then the function remains a departmental one.

Constitutional Concerns

The nature of public administration and the way in which services are delivered have therefore undergone a fundamental change. This has taken place without public debate or involvement, despite the nature of public services 'which are a matter of general public concern and public interest',[15] and without regard for the constitutional consequences. Indeed, William Waldegrave, Minister for the Public Service, expressed impatience with matters constitutional. He asserted that 'By leaving our reforms half-finished and diverting our energies for years to come to legal constitutional mongering, designed to close a non-existent democratic deficit, we would be helping neither the public service itself, not those long suffering residents of Cleveland or anywhere else.'[16] The tone of this statement, if not its content, accords with the response generally received from politicians, particularly those in office, when a constitutional issue is raised. It also reflects the way in which institutional change is undertaken in Britain. The reasoning is pragmatic not constitutional and the process is incremental. The constitution arrangements are required to auto-adapt to accommodate the changes as best they can.

It is perhaps not surprising that reservations have been expressed from a number of quarters about the consequence of the reforms, as evidenced by the investigation undertaken by the Treasury and Civil Service Committee (TCSC) into the role of the Civil Service. At the outset of its investigation, the TCSC set out five concerns it intended to investigate. These related to the 'fundamental implications' of the management changes (most notably the Next Steps initiative), the impact of market testing and the possible privatization of some Civil Service functions, the suitability of the higher Civil Service for management tasks and the provision of policy advice, the 'alleged deterioration in standards of conduct in the Civil Service', and the implications for the Civil Service of the continuation in office of the same political party.[17] These effectively translate into concerns about the constitutional position of the Civil Service, both with regard to its relation with ministers and the public, and they also raise questions about accountability, the private operation of public services, the role of senior civil servants, the perceived decline in probity and integrity, and the politicization of the Civil Service. The

---

[14] Cm. 2627 (1994) para. 2.25.
[15] D. Faulkner, C. Crouch, M. Freeland & D. King, Memorandum to TCSC, HC 27–III, (1993–4).
[16] W. Waldegrave, *Reality of Reform*. [17] TCSC, HC 390–I, (1992–3).

overriding thesis from which these concerns arise is that the search for efficient government is undermining the key characteristics of the Civil Service. These are generally agreed to be impartiality, integrity and objectivity, selection and promotion on merit, and accountability[18] and any reduction in the weight accorded to them has a bearing on the concept of good administration to which they lend support. They represent the 'constitutional principles that underlie the Civil Service'[19] and concern about them informs the argument for a Code of Good Administration.

Accountability

In its Report *The Role of the Civil Service* the TCSC stated that accountability may be regarded as 'the logical concomitant of the other characteristics of the Civil Service'. This is

> [b]ecause the Civil Service is largely funded by the taxpayer and through the public spending process, it has to control and account for the use of money to Parliament on behalf of the taxpayer. Because the Civil Service is responsible for administering laws passed by the Parliament equitably and impartially, it should be held to account to Parliament both for general administration and for particular cases. Because the Civil Service serves a Government which is democratically elected and answerable to the electorate, the Civil Service should be accountable to Ministers for developing and implementing the Government's policies.[20]

The importance of political accountability within the British constitution suggests that any changes in the structure of this accountability are likely to impact upon the other characteristics of the Civil Service and thus upon administrative practice. Moreover, effective accountability through the appropriate channels is a fundamental aspect of good administration. The way in which accountability is exercised, and the effectiveness of the mechanisms for accountability, have frequently been the subject of debate. In constitutional theory, Ministers alone are accountable to Parliament not just for their own actions but for the actions of their departments. Civil servants, who have no legal personality, are considered to be an extension of the Minister and, as such, speak not for themselves but on his or her behalf. Thus the personal accountability of civil servants is limited to an internal or managerial accountability up the hierarchical chain to the Minister and they are protected from public accountability by the constitutional requirement of anonymity. There are exceptions. The Accounting Officer, usually the Permanent Secretary of the department, is directly accountable to Parliament through the Public Accounts Committee (PAC) for the probity and rectitude of his Department's spending, and officials are required to account for their own actions

---

[18] Sir Robin Butler in evidence to TCSC, ibid., II, Q101.   [19] Ibid., Q102.
[20] TCSC, HC 27–I, (1993–4), para. 70.

to the Comptroller and Auditor-General (C & AG) and the PCA, both of whom report to appropriate Select Committees.

In addition, the requirement of anonymity has not always been met. Officials have at times been associated with particular policies[21] and the establishment of the office of the PCA in 1967 had notable consequences for anonymity. His investigations are largely uninhibited by the convention of ministerial responsibility and thus civil servants are unprotected, a matter which was raised in the House when the PCA's Report on his inquiry into the *Sachsenhausen* case was received.[22] Mr George Brown, the responsible minister, was concerned that his officials rather than himself had been blamed in the Report and that the convention of ministerial responsibility had therefore been undermined.

Similarly inquiries such as those into Crichel Down (1954) and Vehicle and General Insurance Company (1972), whose Reports 'named and blamed' officials, have consequences for Civil Service anonymity which is fundamental to the traditional operation of the convention. More recently, the inquiry chaired by Sir Richard Scott into Matrix Churchill, which reported in 1996, exposed officials to public scrutiny to an extent that some Whitehall supporters found intrinsically unfair.[23] However, most significant with regard to the public exposure of civil servants has been the increased role of Select Committees since the reform of the system in 1979. Whilst officials appear before these Committees on behalf of the Minister and are protected and restrained by the convention of ministerial responsibility, they are identified and may be exposed to compromising questions, sometimes in the glare of the television cameras.

Yet despite these developments, the exposure and public accountability of officials has still been exceptional and limited. The establishment of executive agencies would appear to alter this position. Anonymity is greatly reduced, both with regard to the chief executives of the agencies, who are known to the public and adopt a higher profile than is traditionally expected of civil servants, and those officials who deal directly with the public. They are required by the Citizen's Charter to wear name-badges and to give their names when answering the telephone to aid identification and foster good public relations.

This removes the protection afforded by anonymity for 'front-liners' and for chief executives and suggests a change in the arrangements for public accountability. These arrangements, which centre on the convention of individual ministerial responsibility, have frequently been criticized as an over-simplification of a complex division of responsibilities between ministers and civil servants and a 'very unsatisfactory sledge-hammer to crack a nut somewhere down the executive chain'.[24] Any change to the accountability structure could therefore be a welcome

[21] E.g. when the Govt. was forced to delay its pit closure programme in 1992, Robert Priddle was identified as the senior civil servant in charge of energy policy in the Dept of Trade. His sideways move was also widely reported (see *Guardian*, 28 Oct. 1992).

[22] HC Debs., cols. 107–12, 5 Feb. 1968.

[23] See, e.g., G. Howe, 'Procedure at the Scott Inquiry' (1996) *PL* 445.

[24] W. Plowden in evidence to TCSC, HC 390–II, (1992–3), Q528.

development. However, it needs to provide a coherent set of arrangements which takes account of the constitutional implications. This the changes so far have failed to do.

Accountability now operates at two levels. First, agency officials are required to be accountable to the customer or client for meeting the Charter standards which have been set by the agency or parent department. Such accountability, which is concerned with the agency's response to the individual, is an important additional aspect of accountability. However, by itself it is insufficient as it does not provide the mechanism whereby an agency can be held accountable for the provision of services in accordance with public policy.[25] Indeed, there is a danger that public attention will be distracted from this provision and that the concentration on easily measurable standards will result in more important ones being ignored or neglected. The agency's responsiveness will thus be misdirected and accountability will suffer. Moreover, accountability to the individual ignores the loyalty of the public service to 'the larger moral enterprise which is the state'[26] and suggests a downgrading of the national or public interest and thus of collective interests.

At the second level, the chief executive of an agency bears overall responsibility for the performance of the agency and is accountable to the Minister for it. He is also accountable, as Agency Accounting Officer, to the PAC, either directly or through the Accounting Officer of the parent department. However, there is a degree of confusion over the extent to which the chief executive is otherwise publicly accountable. In constitutional terms, the Minister retains ultimate responsible for the agency. Moreover, this is a direct responsibility in line with departmental responsibility, rather than the indirect responsibility that is exercised with regard to the nationalized industries and non-departmental public bodies.

However, accountability is in many ways no clearer. Written replies to questions from MPs, which are now answered by the chief executive in his name, appear in Hansard under a general ministerial heading but it is not known whether the reply has been approved by the Minister or come directly from the chief executive, the practice varying from agency to agency.[27] Either way the tendency is for the Minister to operate on the lower slopes of responsibility, as if his or her responsibility were indirect, wherever possible redirecting questions from Members of Parliament to chief executives and exercising informatory responsibility — simply reporting to Parliament what the chief executive has told him. There is therefore a difference in theory and practice. In theory, agencies come under the umbrella of ministerial responsibility. In practice, responsibility seems to lie with the chief executive.

The Government has sought to justify the practical distancing of the minister from responsibility by drawing a distinction between responsibility and

---

[25] J. Stewart, Memorandum to TCSC, HC 27–III, (1993–4).
[26] N. Lewis & D. Longley, 'Ethics and the Public Service' (1992) *PL* at 603.
[27] Pub. Serv. Cttee, HC 313–I, (1995–6), para. 93.

accountability, wherein responsibility 'implies direct personal involvement in an action or decision, in a sense which implies personal credit or blame for that action or decision'. It follows from this that 'a Minister is *accountable* for all the actions and activities of his Department, but is not *responsible* for all the actions in the sense of being blameworthy; a civil servant is not directly accountable to Parliament for his actions, but is responsible for certain actions and can be delegated clearly defined responsibilities.'[28] This distinction was accepted by Sir Richard Scott in his report into the export of arms to Iraq.[29] However, the Public Service Committee, inquiring into ministerial accountability and responsibility, was less convinced.[30]

The distinction suggests an increasing diminution of ministerial responsibility to the point where no blame is attributable to the minister, except for matters of high policy, but a retention of the constitutional position that those who are responsible, in this context the chief executives of agencies, cannot be held personally accountable before the Select Committees of Parliament. The protection of officials from public scrutiny therefore continues but such protection also has the effect of preventing civil servants from defending themselves fully from accusations of incompetence or error, or from revealing ministerial misjudgements or meddling. The distinction between responsibility and accountability could therefore be beneficial to ministers but detrimental to accountability, particularly as there has so far been a 'failure to ensure that delegation of responsibility is accompanied by clear lines of control and accountability'.[31]

Thus while chief executives find themselves thrust into the front line when their agencies are the subject of public criticism, the Government still insists that chief executives, as civil servants, operate under the convention of individual ministerial responsibility. This means that although they appear before select committees to account for the operation of their agencies, they, like departmental officials, are bound by the Osmotherly Rules.[32] These Rules uphold the conventional position that civil servants speak on behalf of the minister and instruct them as to the type of questions they should refer to him or her. These include matters of policy, the disclosure of advice they have given to a minister, and communications with other departments. The Rules are explicit about the position of agency chief executives appearing before select committees. They state: 'Where a Select Committee is investigating matters which are delegated to an Agency in its Framework Document, evidence will usually be given by the Chief Executive. Like other officials, Agency Chief Executives give evidence on behalf of the Minister to whom they are accountable and are subject to that Minister's instruction.'[33]

[28] Cab. Off., Memorandum to TCSC, HC 27–II (1993–4).

[29] Sir Richard Scott, HC 115–IV, (1996), K8.15.

[30] Pub. Serv. Cttee, HC 313–I, (1995–6), para. 21.   [31] PAC, HC 154, (1993–4), Annex 1, vii).

[32] Cab. Off., *Departmental Evidence and Response to Select Committees* ('Osmotherley Rules').

[33] Ibid., para 42. In 1996 the Pub. Serv. Cttee recommended the Rules should be amended to indicate a presumption that CEs would give evidence on matters delegated to them (Pub. Serv. Cttee, 313–I, (1995–6) para. 113). In its Response (HC 67, (1996–7)) the Govt. maintained there was this presumption. However, it reiterated that CEs gave evidence on behalf of the Minister.

The way in which the Rules can be used to limit the information given by civil servants to select committees was demonstrated during the TCSC inquiry into the role of civil servants. The Committee had wanted to conduct an attitude survey among civil servants but Mr William Waldegrave, Minister for Public Service, had refused permission. It was pointed out to him at the Select Committee hearing that the Committee could call a sample of civil servants to appear before it and ask them the questions proposed for the questionnaire. Mr Waldegrave, replied, 'You are entirely free and it is your right to send for anyone you want. It would be for the civil servants of course to answer the questions rather carefully so that they did not involve themselves in the controversy over policy.'[34]

The consequence for chief executives is therefore that they account in public for the operation of their agencies. Yet if they consider that shortcomings in policy or a lack of resources has contributed to any under-performance within the agency, they may not raise the matter in their defence nor answer questions on policy put by the Select Committee. Policy remains the responsibility of the minister. This division between operations and policy reawakens the problems of accountability associated with the nationalized industries and suggests the blurring of responsibilities between ministers and chief executives. Moreover, the consequence of this blurring is potentially more serious where agencies are concerned because of the official status of chief executives. The head of a nationalized industry may have considered it politically expedient not to dispute a ministerial dictate on what constituted 'operations' and what 'policy', but he was not constitutionally restrained from doing so. The danger as far as agencies are concerned is that 'there will be a bureaucratic Bermuda Triangle'[35] into which accountability disappears with neither minister nor chief executive responding to troublesome questions. Alternatively, 'ministers might pass the buck for policy failures, and disclaim responsibility for operational activities'.[36]

The latter concern has arisen in relation to the resignation of the Chief Executive of the Child Support Agency in 1994 and the dismissal of the Director-General of the Prison Service Agency in 1995. Ms Ros Hepplewhite resigned after a disastrous first year for the Child Support Agency. The Agency had been the subject of constant criticism in the media, protest marches, and a damning Select Committee Report. On the surface the main faults were administrative or managerial. The Agency had been £112m short of its savings target and nearly 50 per cent short of its target for the child maintenance payments it was required to arrange. In addition, there had been gross inaccuracies in maintenance calculations, serious delays in responding to queries, cases of misidentification of absent fathers, and a concentration on 'soft targets', that is on those fathers who were easy to locate. However, these faults should not be considered in isolation from the policy that the Agency was required to operate nor from the resources it was

---

[34] In evidence to TCSC, HC 27–II, (1993–4), Q2358.

[35] V. Bogdanor, Memorandum to TCSC, HC 390–II, (1992–3).

[36] P. Greer, Memorandum to TCSC, HC 27–III, (1993–4).

given. The policy, which was Treasury-driven, was perceived by many to be inherently unfair and unworkable. Moreover, it was the need to meet the savings targets stipulated by the Treasury that resulted in the Agency adopting a policy of going for soft targets, as an internal memorandum indicated: 'The name of the game is maximizing the maintenance yield—don't waste a lot of time on non-profitable stuff.'[37] In addition, the resources allocated to the Agency were inadequate, as demonstrated by the subsequent increase from £114m to £184m. Nevertheless it was Ms Hepplewhite who took total responsibility.[38]

Similarly, it was the Director-General of the Prison Service Agency, Mr Derek Lewis, who was held to be culpable after the Learmont Report into the Whitemoor Prison breakout blamed operational and management errors.[39] The Home Secretary, Mr Michael Howard, insisted that these matters were the responsibility of Mr Lewis and dismissed him. For his part Mr Lewis contested some of the conclusions of the Report and in particular refuted the allegation that the responsibility was his. He alleged that the Home Secretary had intervened directly and regularly in the running of the prison service and thus could not abdicate responsibility for it. The Home Office subsequently settled an action brought by Mr Lewis, accepting that his dismissal had breached his terms of employment and was thus unfair. However, there was no acceptance of responsibility by the Home Secretary for the expenditure of taxpayers' money incurred in the settlement. Responsibility was thus removed from the public arena, becoming a private law matter with no constitutional consequences for ministers—perhaps the ultimate privatization.

The problem lies in making a clear distinction between policy and operations. Below the surface 'policy and administration are largely indistinguishable' with all policy decisions being influenced by considerations of implementation, and implementation involving policy decisions.[40] The separation is therefore false, for in practice the worlds of politicians and administrators are 'closely integrated' and 'the possibility of distinguishing the ends which politicians want to reach from the means to achieve these ends is a remote one'.[41] The existence of a 'grey area' between policy and operations was recognized by the Next Steps Project Manager, who suggested that where it is unclear, the Minister should reply.[42] Ministers, however, are only likely to do so when it suits their political interests.

This indicates that 'finding departmental structures' which make the sharing of power 'explicit and hence introduce meaningful accountability' should be an

[37] Soc. Sec. Cttee, HC 69, (1993–4), para. 28.

[38] It is interesting to note that Ms Hepplewhite's successor, Ms Ann Chant, who was a career civil servant, was only in office for two years before leaving the Civil Service to join a charity in Nov. 1996. Moreover, whilst Ms Chant and Govt ministers insisted the agency 'had turned the corner', in Nov. 1996 the CSA was criticized by the Chief Child Support Officer for the fact that in more than a quarter of cases it made an incorrect assessment.

[39] Cm. 3020 (1995).

[40] J. Greenwood & D. Wilson, *Public Administration in Britain Today*, 139.

[41] A. Lawton & A. Rose, *Organisation and Management in the Public Sector*, 18.

[42] R. Mottram in evidence to TCSC, HC 390–II, (1992–3), Q970.

'urgent priority'.[43] The only solution may be for chief executives to have a direct constitutional responsibility to account for those areas where they have delegated responsibility as determined in the framework agreement and to be able to draw attention to misguided policies or to a mismatch between the expectations for the agency and the resources given. They should also be able to indicate attempts by ministers to interfere in areas of delegated responsibility. The consequence otherwise is that chief executives will be obliged to make statements that are 'rather more opaque than open'.[44]

An additional concern regarding accountability is the extent to which agency accountability is focused solely on framework agreements, performance indicators, and an agency's success in fulfilling its targets. These present an 'off-the-peg' package which is easy to assess but discourages an examination of the appropriateness of the indicators and targets or of other factors which are less easy to measure (what have been termed 'value-added' factors). They may also present a false perspective of what constitutes success and failure. For example, Derek Lewis' angry reaction to his sacking was in part because he did not believe he had failed. He had, after all, met all his performance targets.

Such a focus for accountability also disguises the fact that output measures or targets are political choices. It is for political reasons that the take-up of benefit by those entitled to it is not a target of the Benefits Agency. If benefits were really analogous to 'products' for sale in the private sector, as suggested by terms like 'Benefits Shop' and 'DSS customers', this would be the most obvious target to set. Moreover, as a package provided by Government, accountability concentrates on outputs, steering clear of policy and resource issues and the means by which results are achieved. It thus represents a limited agenda for accountability which is set by the accountees rather than the accountors and suggests managerial rather than political responsibility. It is also meaningless unless there 'is sound performance data, subject to validation'.[45] In any case, its emphasis on 'value-for-money' audits means that it may be better attuned to accountants than to Members of Parliament (other than perhaps those who sit on the PAC), who may not have the expertise nor the inclination to probe an agency's performance.

The establishment of executive agencies may therefore act to de-politicize accountability and in some cases remove it from the political arena, a trend encouraged by ministers through the redirection of Members' questions on agency matters to the chief executive concerned and by the exercise of only informatory responsibility with regard to agency affairs. Such de-politicization may be appropriate where agencies are delivering a non-political service, for example issuing vehicle licences. However, other agencies, such as the Benefits Agency, Employment Agency, Prison Service Agency and Child Support Agency, are implementing policies which involve political choices, and it is important that

---

[43] G. Mather, Memorandum to TCSC, HC 27–II, (1993–4).
[44] W. Brett in evidence to TCSC, ibid., Q1698.
[45] Sir John Bourn, C & AG, quoted in *The Independent*, 8 May 1996.

they do not become detached from political and public opinion, to which they may be required to respond. Ministers, therefore, need to retain political control and ultimate responsibility.

It is not only the establishment of executive agencies that would seem to be affecting the nature of public accountability. The change from 'administration' to 'management' throughout government departments is producing changes in internal accountability which inevitably impact upon the external or public accountability of politicians. Thus the decentralization of decision-making undermines the hierarchical chain of control necessary for the channelling of responsibility to, and through, the Minister. Moreover, managerial accountability is concerned with rational decision-making and takes little account of the values and needs of political accountability. The cult of managerialism may also result in managers seeing themselves as more accountable to their professional bodies than to politicians. This has proved to be the case with other professionals, such as lawyers and accountants. Thus just as these groups do not see it as appropriate for their judgements to be subject to political scrutiny, so managers may likewise eschew the processes through which public accountability is achieved.

A further challenge to public accountability arises through market-testing and contracting out. The Government has insisted that the presence of a contract increases accountability because of its legal enforceability. However, many of the terms and conditions within a contract are protected by commercial confidentiality, and, as a consequence, the standards of performance that are contractually required may not be known. Moreover, whilst the Minister is still politically accountable, very often the chain of responsibility passes through an agency to the contractor, and is therefore diluted. Lord Bancroft expressed the concern of many when he asked, 'How can one have effective accountability to Parliament if hundreds of functions are to be contracted out, or otherwise separated off into agencies which are deliberately placed at arm's length from Ministers responsible for them?'[46]

This raises questions about the relationship between the Minister and the private contractor, particularly in view of the provisions for delegation to private contractors contained in the Deregulation and Contracting Out Act 1994. Part II of the Act removes statutory obstacles to the contracting out of public services and provides for ministers and office-holders to nominate others to carry out their statutory functions. This nomination is achieved by what the Government describes as an extension of the *Carltona* principle, the principle accepted by the courts as an exception to the general rule against the delegation of statutory functions.[47] *Carltona* is a recognition of the constitutional relationship between ministers and civil servants, whereby civil servants are merely an extension of the minister with no legal personality of their own. However, the extension of the principle to the private sector has no constitutional validity for 'a contractual relationship between the minister

---

[46] HL Debs., col. 970, 6 June 1994.
[47] *Carltona Ltd* v. *Commissioner of Works* [1943] 2 All ER 560.

. . . and a private enterprise with its own separate life to lead and commercial aims to pursue' is hardly compatible.[48] Moreover, whilst the minister remains accountable and legally liable for the statutory functions which are contracted out, the exercise of these functions is the responsibility of the private contractor, thus raising once more the problems associated with the policy/operations divide.

The reform of the Civil Service and the way in which services are delivered clearly has considerable implications for accountability and there is concern that the changes are producing 'an uncontrollable, unaccountable public service, which is impossible to scrutinize by Parliament, in other words it is progressively escaping Parliamentary scrutiny'.[49] This may be most obviously the case with contracting out which seems to 'dramatically reduce the accountability of service provision to the public and Parliament' by severing the direct administrative link between the providers of the service and ministers.[50] If this is so, then one of the fundamental principles on which the Civil Service is based is being eroded. This will inevitably effect the ethos of the Service and the way in which it interacts with the public, and have implications for good administration.

A decline in standards

A second concern relates to the 'ethical environment' in which those who hold public office operate. This is 'the mix of law, regulations, culture, attitudes and traditions, procedures and controls which govern the behaviour of those in public life'.[51] The fear is that the search for efficient government is adversely affecting this environment and undermining the essential characteristics or 'constitutional principles that underlie the Civil Service'.[52] Sir Robin Butler conceded in evidence before the TCSC that maintaining the high standards they represented was 'a challenge'.[53] However, he considered the challenge was being met and that the characteristics 'remained unchanged'.[54] This is not a view shared by all.[55]

The concern about the public service characteristics, particularly as they inform the principles under which civil servants operate, arises from the diversification of service delivery, such that the Civil Service is no longer 'the exclusive vehicle for performing functions'.[56] Even where it is, the structure under which it operates is now federal rather than unitary. Thus the Civil Service is increasingly fragmented, and, as a consequence, it may be losing its sense of identity and purpose. Despite revolutionary changes, the Government has not 'sufficiently defined what it wants from a Civil Service and what they expect its role to be'.[57]

---

[48] J. Aldhouse, *Waiving the Rules* (unpub. research paper, Oxford Brookes Univ. (1995)).
[49] J. Garrett MP in evidence to TCSC, HC 27–II, Q1612.
[50] Council of Civil Service Unions, Memorandum to TCSC, HC 390–II, (1992–3).
[51] A. Doig, 'From Lynskey to Nolan' (1996) 23 *JLS* at 36.
[52] Sir Robin Butler in evidence to TCSC, HC 390–II, (1992–3), Q102.   [53] Ibid., Q201.
[54] Ibid., Q102.   [55] See, e.g., B. J. O'Toole, 'The Loss of Purity' at 1–6.
[56] P. Barberis, Memorandum to TCSC, HC 27–III, (1993–4).
[57] Lord Callaghan of Cardiff in evidence to TCSC, 390–II, (1992–3), Q588.

Associated with this possible loss of identity and purpose is concern that morale and commitment are being adversely affected, most obviously by the introduction of short-term contracts and the making of appointments from outside the Service amd more subtly by a general denigration of those who work within the public sector. The TCSC noted that 'if civil servants no longer have a sense of a job for life, it is hardly surprising if they find it difficult to offer a lifelong commitment in return'.[58] Moreover, the fragmentation of the Civil Service, together with the move away from common systems of pay, grading, recruitment and promotion, may undermine 'the sense of being a public servant and all that entails',[59] suggesting instead that the Civil Service is 'just a collection of jobs, with tenure uncertain'.[60] Coupled with this is the 'importance of performance and efficiency targets and the inducements offered by performance-related pay'.[61] These shift the emphasis from 'that of a vocation to the point where self-interest is positively encouraged. Instead of loyalty to altruistic ideals, there is every encouragement to disregard altruism if altruism is not in an individual's own interests.'[62]

Consideration of these factors leads to concern that the public service ethos, which stems from the underlying characteristics of the Civil Service, is being undermined by the ethics of the market-place and by the different requirements and objectives of the private sector. Changes in the approach to work and performance, brought about through the development of a managerial culture, may result in an undermining of integrity, in part because of 'inaccurate perceptions of private-sector values and practices'.[63] Moreover, the preoccupation with a managerial ethos may in the long term attract people with little commitment to 'values that ought to underpin the democratic process'[64] and, in addition, as 'business methods' spread, there may be fewer and fewer officials and ministers 'who put the interests of society above their personal and political interests'.[65] This raises questions about the extent to which 'serving the public good' will remain a motivating factor of public administration. The inter-change between public and private also suggests that it is necessary to consider whether, and how, the notion of public service should apply to those in the private sector who are contracting for public work.

Defence contractors already have the requirements of official secrecy imposed upon them. It would therefore not be revolutionary to devise contractual terms which require an adherence to principles such as integrity, fairness and honesty[66] for those who contract for work in the public sector. Moreover, in the United States model clauses are attached to contracts with private contractors and a condition of the contract is that the standard of provision can be upgraded. Such terms

---

[58] TCSC Report, HC 27–I, (1993–4), para. 36. [59] Ibid., para. 75.

[60] R. Chapman, Memorandum to TCSC, HC 390–II, (1992–3). [61] Ibid.

[62] Ibid.

[63] J. Harrow & R. Gillett, 'The proper conduct of public business' (1994) 14 *Pub. Money and Man.* at 5.

[64] J. Boston, 'The problems of policy co-ordination' (1992) 5 *Governance* 1 at 328.

[65] B. J. O'Toole, Memorandum to TCSC, HC 27–III.

[66] See draft Civil Service Code, TCSC Report, HC 27–I, Annex 1.

require careful definition and may be less easy to enforce than secrecy but they would help to diminish concern about the delivery of public services by private enterprise, although if the contractual impositions are too heavy, they could result in private sector tenders being less cost-effective. This could reduce the effectiveness of contracting out and market testing policies and be counter to current political ideology. Nevertheless, ironically, it may be easier to introduce appropriate public sector principles contractually to the private sector than it is to sustain them internally, the organizational upheaval that has taken place within the Civil Service casting doubts over the reliability of the Civil Service culture to instil and reinforce the traditional values of the public service.

This doubt is given substance by the appointment of those outside the Service to managerial positions. They may be unfamiliar with the public service ethos, even failing to recognize its existence,[67] and have no protective instincts towards it. If the public service ethos is to be sustained, it may therefore be necessary for adherence to it to be part of a manager's job description, or at least for external appointees to know 'from the outset that their responsibilities change as [they] ... come into the public service'.[68] This view, expressed by the Chairman of the PAC, was supported by the C & AG, who, in evidence to the TCSC, argued that it was right to draw the attention of such appointees 'to these traditional values, to these traditional methods of work' and to require that they maintain 'the values and proper standards of probity that have developed in the public service'.[69] The point was also made by Mr William Plowden in a memorandum to the TCSC in which he supported the making of external appointments, providing they were of people 'who understood government *is* different (different from business in particular), and who can help preserve a "public service ethos" against all encroachments.'[70]

There would, however, seem to be a dichotomy between making appointments, aimed at fostering high-performance management, and requiring that the appointees adhere to the core values of the Civil Service. The two are not always compatible. Indeed, it may be that 'genuine managerialism stretches Civil Service principles, perhaps to breaking point'.[71] Thus, the insistence that such principles remain unaltered may act as a constraint upon management performance, while, on the other hand, the downplaying of the principles may lead to a slow erosion of the standards they support. It thus seems inevitable that as 'managerialism' takes over from 'administration' in the Civil Service, there will be a change in the ethos of the Service.

Some consider that this erosion is underway. The PAC, in its Report *The Proper Conduct of Public Business*, noted 'a departure from the standards of public conduct which have mainly been established during the past 140 years'.[72] Moreover,

---

[67] E.g. Chief Executive of Driving Standards Agency in interview with Sheena McDonald on *Inside the Civil Service: a Quiet Revolution*, Radio 4, 7 Jan. 1994.

[68] R. Sheldon MP in evidence to TCSC, HC 27–II, (1993–4), Q1576.

[69] Sir John Bourn in evidence to TCSC, ibid., Q1602.

[70] W. Plowden, Memorandum to TCSC, HC 390–II, (1992–3).

[71] S. Richards, Director, Public Management Foundation, Paper to TCSC, ibid.

[72] HC 154, (1993–4), para. 1.

according to the Chairman, the Committee thought that there was 'some co-relation between what we saw as failings and what we saw as the changes in governmental administration'.[73] He also noted that a common thread linking recent incidents had been that they concerned people from outside the public service.[74]

The Report of the PAC detailed a number of 'serious failures in administrative and financial systems and controls within departments and other public bodies, which have led to money being wasted or otherwise improperly spent.'[75] It reported inadequate financial controls at the Foreign and Commonwealth Office, the Department of Employment, the Property Services Agency, the Insolvency Agency, the Ministry of Defence and the Department of Social Security, as well as outside departments in the National Rivers Authority and Wessex Regional Health Authority. The Ministry of Defence was also criticized for incurring irregular expenditure, totalling £1.2m, on a scheme designed to reward groups of staff for their contribution to efficiency, and the Department of Employment was brought to book for wasting £11m on consultants for a computer system which proved to be unsatisfactory.

The PAC also listed a number of instances where the C & AG had found a failure to comply with the rules. For example, the Department of Employment had made 'doubtful and incorrect payments' to training providers and to Training and Enterprise Councils.[76] These payments amounted to some £55m in 1989–90 and £24.5m 1990–1. The Forward Catering Service was also criticized, the PAC noting. 'This case, involving poor control, mismanagement, irregularities, malpractice and fraud, represented a serious failure in the proper conduct of public business in what was—or should have been—a straightforward trading operation.'[77] The Treasury, which has responsibility for overseeing the Forward Catering Service, acknowledged 'a serious breakdown in financial control'.[78]

The PAC's severest criticism was reserved for the Welsh Development Agency (WDA) and the Welsh Office, the latter being admonished for failing to keep the WDA under control. The Agency committed a catalogue of misdemeanours. These included making dubious recruitments, paying out large sums of redundancy money from its redundancy scheme, which it had failed to submit to the Welsh Office for approval, and allowing senior executives to use Agency cars for private motoring without payment. The PAC considered that the standards applied by the Agency had been well below those that Parliament had the right to expect. Indeed, in evidence before the TCSC, the Chairman of the PAC stated.

> The Welsh Development Agency just did things that you would never assume could ever be done by civil servants. They went to America, they hired a conman, who had three sentences in the United States, they brought him back, they put him in charge of publi-

[73] R. Sheldon MP in evidence to TCSC, HC 27–II, (1993–4), Q1572.
[74] Ibid., Q1576.   [75] HC 154, (1993–4), para. 1.
[76] Ibid., Annex 2, x, from C & AG, HC 172, (1991–2). The Cttee noted that procedures had subsequently been tightened.
[77] Ibid., Annex 2, xii, from C & AG, HC 558, (1992–3).   [78] Ibid.

city, he entertained seven model girls in his hotel room on Sunday afternoon to see which was suitable; this is the sort of conduct you do not expect from a public service.[79]

In the light of this and other instances, the PAC, whilst supporting the drive to provide improved services at reduced cost, noted that it was 'even more essential to maintain honesty in the spending of public money and to ensure that traditional public sector values are not neglected in the effort to maximize economy and efficiency'.[80] The PAC's catalogue of incidents is not the only evidence which suggests that standards need reaffirming. Other incidents have also given cause for concern. For example, the Foreign Affairs Committee was highly critical of the way in which the cost of fitting out M.I.6's new headquarters in London (some £86m) had been 'buried' in Foreign Office expenditure totals, thus making it difficult for Parliament to ascertain the true costs. There was also concern over the Treasury payment of £4,700 to meet the legal costs of the Chancellor of the Exchequer, at that time Mr Norman Lamont. This concern was twofold and related, firstly, to the propriety of the payment, and, secondly, to the way in which it was recorded. The much-criticized payment was made to the libel lawyer, Mr Peter Carter-Ruck, in connection with media coverage of Mr Lamont's letting of his London home to a 'sex therapist'. Civil servants defended the payment as necessary to support Mr Lamont's position as Chancellor. The PAC, whilst expressing some reservations, accepted that there had been no impropriety.[81] However, civil servants did not really give an adequate explanation as to why the payment was not recorded as a separate item, thereby making it clear to Parliament that the payment had been made.

Home Office officials were also accused of acting improperly when they ran checks on the President-elect, Bill Clinton, at the request of journalists. However, it was the arms to Iraq saga, culminating in the Matrix Churchill prosecution in 1992, that caused the most concern as it became apparent that civil servants had helped ministers get round the arms embargo and had colluded with them to keep the information from the public, press, and Parliament. Three big Departments were involved, the Ministry of Defence, the Foreign Office and the Department of Trade and Industry, and it would seem that no official within any of the departments was prepared to say 'no' to ministerial requests or to blow the whistle when ministers were misleading Parliament.

The apparent complicity of civil servants with ministers to deceive the public provides some evidence of 'unhealthily close relationships between ministers and their civil servants'[82] which may have been the product of one party being in office for seventeen years. Indeed, ministers may no longer have understood or accepted the traditional division between officials and themselves. Their tenure of office and the certainty (until the latter year or two) that it would last may have

[79] TCSC Report, HC 27–II, (1993–4), Q1572.   [80] HC 154, (1993–4), para. 6.
[81] C & AG, Memorandum to PAC, HC 386–i), (1992–3), para. 22–4.
[82] TCSC Report, HC 27–I, (1993–4), paras. 78.

resulted in a tendency to conduct themselves as if they were the permanent or 'official' government or at least to ignore any distinction between themselves and their civil servants.

It also suggests that the emphasis on 'can do' civil servants resulted in few officials hesitating over ministerial requests, even those that were unethical. Even where there was hesitation, in practice, the action an official could take if unhappy with instructions was limited. Moreover, it was inhibited by fear that making a complaint could reflect badly on performance or result in him or her being unpopular with the minister. The procedure by which civil servants could appeal was laid down until 1996 in the Armstrong Memorandum.[83] It provided for complaints to be made to the Permanent Secretary, with the Head of the Civil Service acting as the final appellate authority. Many, including the Civil Service Unions, considered this to be inappropriate, for officials were limited to making complaints up the same chain of command down which the instructions causing problems had come in the first place.[84] In addition, it was seen as unsatisfactory for the Head of the Civil Service to consider such complaints when he or she is also the Cabinet Secretary and thus adviser on the appropriateness, or otherwise, of ministerial behaviour. Sir Robin Butler, holder of this dual position during the 1990s, consistently denied that the appeals mechanism was inadequate. However, in 1996 the Government yielded to pressure and introduced a revised procedure which allows an appeal to the Civil Service Commission (see below).

A further concern, relating to a perceived, or actual, decline in standards, has been that observance of the principles of impartiality and objectivity is not as strict as it used to be. This is not to say that the Civil Service has become 'politicized' in the sense that appointments are made on a political basis, but that officials at times cross the line between explaining Government policy and defending it. This may be particularly the case with executive agencies, where chief executives may feel that it is part of the job to support and defend the policy which they are being paid to implement.[85] However, even within mainstream departments, there has been a noted trend to attribute certain views on policy to particular civil servants.[86]

Whether the public support of a policy by an official breaches the requirement of impartiality depends on whether 'impartiality' embraces 'objectivity', usually associated with giving advice, and 'serving the national interest', or whether it is confined to the ability of civil servants to adapt to governments of any political persuasion. If the latter is the case, then it may be acceptable for officials to be 'partial' to the government of the day, providing they are equally 'partial' to a new

---

[83] Note by Head of Home Civil Service, Sir Robert Armstrong (Feb. 1985).

[84] TCSC Report, 27–I, (1993–4), para. 98.

[85] Thus in the run-up to the 1992 election a CE entered a party political argument to defend reform in the   health service, and it was evident that the CE who first headed the controversial CSA, personally supported its policy objectives.

[86] V. Bogdanor, Memorandum to TCSC, HC 27–II (1993–4); E. Symonds, FDA, in evidence to TCSC, HC 390–II, (1992–3), Q247.

government. This, of course, is difficult to test when the same party is in office for more than seventeen years, but suggests that impartiality would be breached when official support could be construed as favouring a political party. Much therefore depends on the way support is given and on the policy concerned. Particular care has to be taken in the lead-up to a general election and officials are instructed not to do anything that 'might make it appear that they were seeking to influence the outcome of the election either way'.[87] General elections aside, any act which helps a minister in a party political way will be seen as inappropriate. Thus, when it became known that a senior official in the Department of the Environment was advising ministers how to use 'the political network' to rebut criticisms of the Government's Green Paper on homelessness, new guidelines were issued by the Department, together with a statement confirming the principle that 'no civil servant should act in a way that might be seen to be in favour of a political party'.[88]

Traditionally, impartiality has been supported through the principle that appointment and promotion are on merit and sustained by the central control of appointments by the Civil Service Commission. This prevents political patronage and also accords the Civil Service a special status in relation to the private sector and other parts of the public sector. However, recent changes have removed the central control over appointments and Government policy has resulted in a significant increase in the size of 'quangoland' with a corresponding increase in the number of appointments made by ministers. This presents the danger that not all of these appointments will be accepted by an incoming government of a different political persuasion. More significantly, the appointment of chief executives of Next Steps executive agencies from outside the Civil Service may undermine the principle of appointment and promotion on merit, if these appointments are in any way suspect. There was, for instance, concern over the appointment of Mr Derek Lewis, an outsider, as Director-General of the Prison Service Agency when the internal candidate had been recommended by the Civil Service Commission for the job.

There is also concern that the principle of objectivity will be undermined by the use of short-term contracts. These may not provide the incentive for officials to give advice that is impartial and objective. Instead, because 'the extension of these contracts and the amount of performance pay due is in part influenced by his or her ability to please the minister', civil servants may be inclined to present ministers 'with what they want rather than informed assessments of all political options'.[89]

Although the evidence to date is not overwhelming, there have been sufficient recorded incidents to support the concern that there has been, or is likely to be, a

---

[87] Sir Robin Butler, *re* his Memorandum 'Guidance to Departments', in evidence to TCSC, HC 27–II, (1993–4), Q2038. In Nov. 1996 he stipulated that departmental officials should not comply with the request of the Deputy PM, Mr Heseltine, to draw up lists of individuals outside Govt who could be called upon to endorse Govt policies in the run-up to the general election.

[88] *Guardian*, 24 Mar. 1994.   [89] P. Greer, Mem. (above, n. 36).

decline in the standards of public administration, as upheld by the principles of integrity, impartiality, and objectivity. Moreover, these incidents are amplified by the widely held view that there has been a general decline in standards in the body politic. The 'sleaze factor', used mainly with reference to politicians, inevitably raises questions beyond Parliament, as the terms of reference of the Nolan Committee, set up in October 1994, indicated. The Committee's remit was 'to examine current concerns about standards of conduct of all holders of public office'.[90] The concern with regard to both politicians and civil servants was the apparent use in certain instances of public positions for private gain. This manifested itself in Members of Parliament taking on multi-agency consultancy work and accepting payment for asking specific questions in the House and in ex-ministers and, to a lesser extent, ex-officials taking up paid employment, shortly after leaving office, in industries that their departments had been regulating.

Such instances raise the possibility of a conflict of interest and the statement made by Nolan that '[p]eople in public life are not always as clear as they should be about where the bounds of acceptable conduct lie' casts a shadow over the integrity of the public service.[91] Confidence in the public service is also diminished by ministerial admissions that they do not always tell Parliament all they should,[92] for although this concerns the ministerial evasion or half-truth, it reflects on civil servants and the extent to which they connive with ministers to conceal information from Parliament.

Any decline in the standards by which public administration operates may be a reflection of a general moral malaise, an unconscious redefining of the principles under which the Civil Service operates to bring it in line with other sectors of public life. This would mean that the fact that it coincided with the reform of the public service was accidental. Such a conclusion stretches coincidences too far, hence the TCSC's concern that the principles should be clarified and presented in such a way that they can be sustained. They should not be gradually eroded or undermined by practices and requirements which are alien to public service.

A Civil Service code

In response to the TCSC the Government refused to accept that there has been a decline in standards, insisting that the principles underlying the Civil Service are not in danger, and that in any case current documentation (in the form of the Armstrong Memorandum, the Civil Service Management Code, and Questions of Procedure), provides adequate guidance for Civil Servants and Ministers as to the principles that should inform behaviour and decision-making. This was not accepted by the TCSC which stated, 'None of the documents examined states the essential values of the Civil Service with sufficient clarity' nor 'communicates a

---

[90] HC Debs., col. 758, 25 Oct. 1994.   [91] Cm. 2850–1 (1995) Summary, para. 2.
[92] TCSC Report, HC 27–II, (1993–4), Q1841.

clear and simple message to all civil servants and to the wider public about the standards to be upheld.'[93]

The Committee recommended that a new Civil Service Code should be drafted, which should have 'some clear public status, public endorsement, going beyond the government of the day'.[94] Indeed, it saw 'the preservation of the principles and values of the Civil Service . . . [as] too important to be left to Ministers and civil servants alone' and suggested that the drafting of a Code should involve public debate, possibly culminating in a Resolution of Parliament.[95] This would seem to accord a Code constitutional status, its contents to be constant and to take precedence over conflicting principles or values. Moreover, the Committee considered that a Code should apply to all civil servants, whether in departments or agencies, and thought that it might be appropriate to extend the principles in such a Code to those working in quangos, and even to private-sector organizations contracting for public work.

To support its conclusions the TCSC provided an initial draft of a Civil Service Code which might form the basis of discussion. Perhaps feeling vulnerable ahead of Sir Richard Scott's Report on Matrix Churchill, which at that time was pending, the Government accepted the draft Code. The Code states that the 'constitutional and practical role' of the Civil Service is, 'with integrity, honesty, impartiality and objectivity, to assist the duly constituted Government of whatever political complexion . . .'.[96] It is to this government that civil servants owe their loyalty. However, this loyalty is not absolute but 'subject to the provisions' of the Code, which also provide the principles under which civil servants should operate. Thus 'civil servants should conduct themselves with integrity, fairness and honesty in their dealings with Ministers, Parliament and the public.' They 'should endeavour to deal with the affairs of the public efficiently and without maladministration' and 'to ensure the proper, effective and efficient use of public money under their control.'[97]

The Code also presents a revised procedure for a civil servant who 'believes he or she is being required to act in breach of this Code or in a way which is illegal, improper, or in breach of constitutional conventions, or which may involve possible maladministration'.[98] The official first reports the matter 'in accordance with procedures laid down in Government guidance or rules of conduct'.[99] However, thereafter representation can be made to the Civil Service Commissioners, who take on an appellate role.[100] Thus the Code provides civil servants with clear grounds for a resolution and a more satisfactory means of seeking it.

The Code establishes principles which inform the concept of good administration and could aid its codification, a codification which would seem to have become increasingly necessary as the revolution within the Civil Service suggests the development of an underlying tension, not just between administrators of the

---

[93] TCSC Report, ibid., I, para. 101.   [94] Ibid., para. 103.
[95] Ibid., para. 102.   [96] Ibid., Annex 1, Draft Code.
[97] Ibid.   [98] Ibid.   [99] Ibid .   [100] Ibid.

'old' school and those of the 'new', but also between public administration on the one hand and the courts and the PCA on the other. This tension arises because of a divergence in the weight accorded to competing principles of good administration and because of a perceived decline in the importance accorded the public service ethos. The following chapters will examine this tension, the principles supported by the different models of good administration, the relationship between public administration and the courts, and judicial perspectives on good administration.

Part I

ADMINISTRATIVE PERSPECTIVES ON GOOD ADMINISTRATION

Public administration is concerned with fulfilling recognized social needs. What these are may vary from time to time, as will the resources allocated; both may be the subject of debate and political conflict. Traditionally such conflict has not arisen with regard to the way in which services are delivered and it is the essence of good administration that the public, the administrators themselves, and their political masters are satisfied with the values and principles which underlie service delivery. The Government stresses the importance of good administration, which it recognizes as necessary to legitimate the implementation of its policies and the goals they are intended to fulfil. Bad or corrupt administration undermines Government policy, reflecting on the party in government and reducing its popularity. Good administration therefore benefits those in office and is essential for continued success at the ballot box.

However, what constitutes good administration is now not necessarily agreed. The fundamental reform of the Civil Service means that for the first time the principles underlying the way in which services are delivered are the subject of political debate. The result is that two distinct models of good administration can be discerned, a traditional or public service model and a New Right or new public management model. Such 'models' represent the extremes in position. On the ground public administration is not, of course, so black and white and to this extent presenting models as separate and discrete is misleading. The models do not represent an accurate description of public administration, past or present. Rather they are reflections of their political and constitutional basis. As such, they provide a useful means of determining the extent to which the reforms in the Civil Service suggest a divergence from the Civil Service principles which have traditionally informed public administration.

The next two chapters consider these models. They are constructed from a constitutional perspective. However, they are informed by perspectives of the sociology of organizations, political economy, and public administration and they include key features of the models emanating from these disciplines. The third chapter in this Part examines the perspective of the PCA, a key player in relation to good administration.

2

THE PUBLIC SERVICE MODEL OF GOOD ADMINISTRATION

Introduction

The public service model of good administration reflects the traditional 'public service' view of administration and the constitutional principles upon which the Civil Service is based. It therefore has its origins in the latter part of the nineteenth century when the characteristics of the modern Civil Service were established, but it also embodies values from the culture of intervention and the Welfare State that developed during the twentieth century. A starting-point for reflection is provided by the five key principles which are generally accepted as underpinning the Civil Service. These are impartiality, integrity and objectivity, selection and promotion on merit, and accountability through ministers to Parliament.[1] To these could be added 'a sense of public service' and 'a commitment to the public interest'.[2] It is from these principles, which both inform the administrative process and reinforce the constitutional position of civil servants, that the requirements of good administration can be distilled.

The Administrative Process

To maintain public confidence in public administration it is necessary for administrators to exhibit certain characteristics, some of which are more usually placed in a political rather than an administrative context. These include probity, integrity, and impartiality. The importance of these characteristics as administrative concepts is at times overlooked but in essence they are 'duties imposed by the nature of the work' and they can therefore be seen as 'implicit in the delivery of services within a statutory framework'.[3] Also essential for public acceptance of the system is the fair and equitable treatment of individuals. Taken together these characteristics suggest an adherence to 'rationality, consistency and justifiability'.[4] Thus decisions must have a rational basis and not be made in an arbitrary manner and they must be consistent, with like cases being treated in the same way. This enables them to be justified retrospectively for the criteria used will be clear and the decision will have been recorded.

[1] Sir Robin Butler in evidence to TCSC, HC 390–II, (1992–3), Q101.
[2] D. Faulkner, C. Crouch, M. Freeland & D. King, Memorandum to TCSC, HC 27–III, (1993–4).
[3] TCSC Report, HC 27–I, (1993–4), para. 69.
[4] R. G. S. Brown & D. R. Steel, *Administrative Process in Britain*, 199.

These characteristics have much in common with models based on Weber's concept of bureaucracy.[5] This is concerned with a system of administration which is carried out by trained professionals in accordance with prescribed rules. The system is centralized and hierarchical, enabling the wishes of those at the top to be carried out by those at the bottom and ensuring the equitable application of departmental rules. The structure also allows for complex administrative problems to be broken down into repetitive, manageable tasks, which are co-ordinated by the centre. The model is characterized by impersonality. This is reflected internally by appointment and promotion procedures that are based on merit not patronage, and externally by a system of categorization. This ensures the uniform treatment of like cases, prevents the arbitrary use of power, and produces a model that is rule-governed and essentially mechanistic.

Weber's concept of bureaucracy may be seen as identifying some of the structural features of traditional public administration and therefore informs the public service model of good administration. Like the Weberian concept, public administration is rule-governed. Although some departments, for example the Inland Revenue, are given considerable discretion, such power is more usually exercised in accordance with rules laid down in regulations, guidelines and circulars, these rules being used to 'structure and confine discretion'[6] so that decision-making is consistent and uniform.

However, the public service model extends further than the Weberian concept of bureaucracy, recognizing that good administration is also underpinned by values that arise from the constitutional position of civil servants and from the culture of public service.

The Constitutional Position of Civil Servants

The constitutional position of civil servants is more apparent in the higher echelons of the Civil Service than it is at the front line of administration. Officials who advise ministers on policy matters clearly have a constitutional role, which is not evident in those staffing benefit or employment offices or manning customs posts. Yet the principles that support this position apply to and affect all levels. Civil servants form the permanent, non-political arm of government which ensures continuity in the administration of policies and the delivery of public services. The centralized nature of the Civil Service also ensures 'unity, identity and common culture'[7] and allows for the development and preservation of a collective memory or 'inherited wisdom'[8] of the way in which the system and the institutions of government work. This is particularly important in a country without a written

[5] E.g. the control model (see R. C. Mascarenhas, 'Reform of the Public Service in Australia and New Zealand' (1990) 3 *Governance* 1 at 77).

[6] P. Cane, *Introduction to Administrative Law*, 385.   [7] D. Faulkner *et al.*, Memo. (above n. 2).

[8] W. Waldegrave, Minister for Public Service, quoted by P. Riddell, *The Times*, 7 Dec. 1993.

constitution as it provides the State with 'a certain continuity and sense of its own past'.[9] On a more practical level, it ensures that a department's 'previous achievements and disappointments' are used to inform the administrative process.[10]

In constitutional theory, if not in practice, there is a strict separation between the functions of civil servants and those of the minister. Ministers, who are the elected representatives, are concerned with policy decisions, whilst civil servants, as appointed officials, are concerned with the implementation of policy and with providing advice to ministers on policy options. It follows therefore that impartiality, neutrality, and objectivity are important principles which must be adhered to if Civil Service advice is to be trusted and confidence in the ability of civil servants to serve governments of any political persuasion is to be maintained.

The separation of elected representatives and appointed officials is further demonstrated by the appointment and promotion system which distances politicians from the process. As a consequence ministers do not appoint civil servants, are not responsible for their promotion (although in the higher levels of officialdom they, or at least the Prime Minister, have the final say), and cannot dismiss them. Civil servants are therefore free from the corrupting influence of patronage, being both selected and promoted solely on merit in competition with their peers.

The separation of officials and politicians is also reinforced by the fact that civil servants owe their allegiance to the Crown. There is general acceptance that the Crown in this context does not mean the personage of the sovereign in whom 'efficient' powers no longer reside.[11] Thereafter there is disagreement as to the definition that should apply. Successive governments have argued that as executive power has transferred to government, the Crown should be translated as 'the government of the day'.[12] Others prefer something less tangible, such as 'the state as a representation of the people' or as a 'symbol of the public interest' to which civil servants owe a loyalty 'higher and more lasting than that they owe to the government of the day'.[13]

However defined, allegiance to the Crown encapsulates the non-political nature of the Civil Service and its ability to serve governments of any political persuasion. It also embodies the principle that officials act in the public interest (although this in itself is a somewhat slippery term) and thus are required to divorce themselves from private and sectional interests, to be above the political process, and to act as guardian of the public purse. These requirements place great importance on the need for high standards of integrity, non-corruptibility, and probity.

[9] Ibid.

[10] D. Faulkner *et al.*, Memo. (above, n. 2).

[11] For distinction between the 'efficient' and 'dignified' functions of the Crown, see W. Bagehot, *English Constitution*.

[12] See, e.g., the Armstrong Memorandum (ch. 1).

[13] D. Faulkner *et al.*, Memo. (above, n. 2) and see, Pub. Serv. Cttee Report, HC 313–I, (1995–6), paras. 168–9.

Accountability

Accountability to Parliament and its Select Committees

Accountability to Parliament is the overriding principle of the public service model of public administration, firstly, because it distinguishes the position of civil servants from that of their private sector counterparts, and, secondly, because it has determined the prime characteristics of public administration. It has resulted in a system in which there is 'detailed record-keeping so that decisions can be justified retrospectively'[14] and put a 'premium on probity, impartiality, rectitude, and the fair and equitable treatment of individuals'.[15]

The constitutional requirement that ministers and through them their officials are accountable to Parliament not only affects decision-making processes, it also has an impact on working priorities and departmental structure. The need to attend to a Parliamentary Question, whether written or oral, takes priority over any other work. It must be dealt with at once, regardless of competing claims upon a civil servant's time which may be made by members of the public, and regardless of the requirements of efficiency. 'It is the business of [a minister's] . . . civil servants to help him defend himself, since in defending himself he is defending them'.[16] The responsibility for composing appropriate responses lies with senior civil servants but even the most lowly official may be required to provide relevant information, hence the need for detailed record-keeping and for guiding principles which affect the operation of public administration and make it look upwards towards the minister as 'client', rather than outwards towards members of the public and other interested or affected parties.

Similarly, accountability to select committees reinforces a Civil Service culture which is based on hierarchical principles. It also supports the ethos of mutual protection and 'back-covering' engendered in the convention of ministerial responsibility. Civil servants are frequently required to write memoranda for submission to Select Committees and appear before the Committees to give evidence, although, in practice, appearances before Select Committees are mainly by senior officials. It is rare for junior officials to be engaged in giving evidence. Nevertheless a Select Committee inquiry can impact upon even the lowest reaches of a department, particularly if it is concerned with the implementation of a controversial policy and its outcome. Officials at all levels may be required to provide information. In addition, if the subsequent report is critical of the administrative process, new procedures may need to be established, different methods of reporting introduced, and in serious cases an internal inquiry may be necessary and appropriate disciplinary action may be taken against individual officials.

---

[14] Brown & Steel (above, n. 4), 199.   [15] Ibid.
[16] W. J. M. Mackenzie & J. W. Grove, *Central Administration in Britain*, 379.

Accountability to the Public Accounts Committee and the role of the Comptroller and Auditor-General

The Accounting Officer of each department, usually the Permanent Secretary, is also required to account to the PAC for the financial rectitude of his department. This responsibility overrides his conventional responsibility to the minister and enables him to minute any disagreement with the minister over proposals for spending which he feels he will be unable to justify before the PAC. Such minutes are rare but not unknown.[17] The PAC works in conjunction with the C & AG, basing its inquiries on his audits of government departments, which are undertaken in a more or less systematic cycle, and upon his reports on investigations into particular aspects of government spending. The role of the C & AG in the public service model is to ensure that all monies are accounted for and have been spent and recorded in accordance with financial practice.

The certainty that financial audits will be undertaken by the C & AG, and the possibility that there will be an investigation into an aspect of departmental spending or that the PAC will inquire further into the cost of the administrative process, encourages strict rules with regard to departmental expenditure and the avoidance of extravagance. These rules require that any expenses incurred are passed upwards for approval. Thus even very small amounts paid to an individual as recompense for an error that has been made have to be passed up the organizational hierarchy for approval.[18] Financial accountability therefore reinforces the culture of the public service model, which is rule-based and is supported by the belief that civil servants work in the public interest and thus act as guardians of the public purse.

Accountability to the PAC and C & AG also retains the link with Parliament. Thus whilst such accountability is restricted to the scrutiny of departmental expenditure, critical reports by the Committee or the C & AG may have political implications. They may raise questions which reflect on Government policy or on the actions of particular ministers and may result in a debate in the House.[19] Ministers cannot therefore afford to be too remote from the administrative process and its associated costs, and officials once more are concerned not to embarrass their minister. This once again supports a hierarchical system in which decisions are pushed upward, in case they have political implications.

Accountability to the Parliamentary Commissioner for Administration

Departments may also be investigated by the PCA. The PCA, like the C & AG, is concerned with administration not policy, although investigations are into the

---

[17] E.g., in 1975 Peter Carey, 2nd Permanent Sec. in DTI, submitted an Accounting Officer's Minute relating to Tony Benn's decision to provide funds for the Kirby Workers' Co-operative.

[18] Citizen's Charter Task Force, Discussion Paper No. 6, para. 2.6.11.

[19] E.g. Pergau Dam (see HC Debs., cols. 773–86, 13 Dec. 1994).

process rather than the financial rectitude of departmental decision-making. His remit is to investigate allegations of maladministration which have resulted in an injustice. Thus investigations undertaken by his Office are directly relevant to officials and affect the way in which they operate. Such investigations may also have political implications, resulting in a further investigation by the Select Committee for the PCA to whom the PCA reports or, exceptionally, being the subject of a debate in the House.[20]

Investigations frequently concern instances where officials have given members of the public wrong information or advice, for example, about their tax liability, or their entitlement to disability payments or various pensions. In such cases the PCA seeks compensation for complainants and may also require changes in administrative practice and the review of all similar cases to ensure that the same error has not been made. Thus whilst the number of investigations undertaken is small,[21] the possibility of investigation focuses the attention of departments on administration and procedures and reinforces the characteristics of the public service model of good administration.

Accountability and control

The requirements of public accountability mean that officials must not only adhere to the standards of administration expected by the PCA and the C & AG but must also be sensitive to political opinion as expressed in Parliament, in the media, and through letters to the minister. Administration may in theory be separated from policy, but this does not remove it from the political agenda. The minister is constitutionally accountable for the actions of his department and its effectiveness. Moreover, in the public service model of good administration, effectiveness is a qualitative or political judgement. It is therefore essential for public administration to be under political control.[22] This is most easily achieved through a hierarchical structure which ensures a chain of command. Instructions can then be passed downwards whilst decision-making is directed upwards. The accountable minister is therefore in control of his department, or so the story goes.

The Public Service Ethos

The hierarchical structure of departments does more than ensure the political control of public administration. It acts as a conduit through which the public service ethos can pass, enabling it to permeate the department. Thus whilst those at the bottom of the structure may have little or nothing to do with the higher echelons

---

[20] See ch. 4.

[21] In 1994, 226 investigations were completed; 1,322 complaints were received (A. Bradley, 'The Parliamentary Ombudsman again' (1995) *PL* 345).

[22] Brown & Steel (above, n. 4), 201.

of policy advisers and deciders, they are nevertheless affected by the presumptions and attitudes of those at the top from whom the ethos of service emanates.

The public service ethos is central to the public service model of good administration and is an amalgam of beliefs and norms or conventions of behaviour. All organizations have cultures and sets of values which develop over time and which reflect the history of the organization. These cultures specify goals and objectives, suitable behaviour, and the qualities that the organization see as particularly valuable.[23] The values may change as 'the external and internal environment of the organisation changes',[24] and thus different things are expected from the organization, but such changes are likely to be gradual and incremental. A sudden change in the value system on which an organization is based would be tantamount to a revolution.

The public service ethos, which constitutes the value system of the Civil Service, is, like all value systems, to some extent intangible. However, it is largely responsible for 'the distinctive character of the British Civil Service'.[25] It supports the idea of service as a vocation rather than just a job and thus of officials being hard-working, conscientious, disciplined and non-corruptible. It demands an adherence to the law and due respect for the legally enforceable rights of individuals, and is also concerned with commitment to the public interest, rather than narrower sectional or private interests, and to the collective 'public' nature of the administration. It also embodies values and principles arising from the culture of intervention and the Welfare State. Indeed, the vast increase in the size of the Service was a response to the development of the Welfare State, while, at the same time, welfarism flourished in response to an interventionist administration, the Civil Service being part of the 'culture of state intervention'.[26]

The culture or ethos therefore supports 'public service values' which require public services to be 'accessible to all . . ., free of bias, discrimination and unnecessary red tape, properly resourced and consistently maintained, delivered efficiently, effectively and to a high standard, accountable to the citizen through Parliament, provided with great attention to confidentiality and security of information, [and] free of corruption, patronage and conflict of interest.'[27] The culture therefore encourages adherence to constitutional principles and to principles which protect the individual. It also supports a system of welfarism, having arisen, in part, as a response to it. Thus the public service ethos provides 'its own norms and procedures' or professional standards for the effective delivery of services.[28]

Because of its nature, the public service ethos cannot easily be translated into a set of rules to be learnt by rote by new recruits to the Service. Rather it is passed on from generation to generation in the form of a 'genetic code', which,

[23] A. Lawton & A. Rose, *Organisations and Management in the Public Sector*, 27.   [24] Ibid.
[25] W. Plowden, 'What prospects for the Civil Service' (1985) 63 *Pub. Admin.* 4.
[26] Sir Robin Butler, 'Evaluation of the Civil Service' at 395.
[27] Council of Civil Service Unions (CCSU), Memo. to TCSC, HC 390–II, (1992–3).
[28] D. Beetham, *Bureaucracy*, 40.

according to Peter Hennessy, produces certain characteristics identifiable in senior officials.[29] These include probity, a care for evidence and respect for reason, the willingness to speak truth to power, a capacity not just to live with the consequences of what is conceived to be a mistaken course but to pursue it energetically, an awareness of other people's life chances, equity and fairness, constant and careful concern for the law and for the needs and procedures of Parliament, and concern for democracy.

Such a code may be seen as applicable to all levels of the public service[30] and contributes to an understanding of the concept of good administration as concerned with two sets of relationships. Firstly, it is concerned with the interaction between public administration and politicians and the political process. This relationship is based on constitutional principles and requires civil servants to protect the public interest and respect the democratic process. In other words, to recognize a duly elected government as master whilst at the same time recognizing that it is the interests of the public (usually as expressed in an election), and not party interests, that they serve. Arguably, there is also a requirement for civil servants to respect the European Convention on Human Rights and to ensure that ministerial policy and departmental administration accord with it.[31]

Secondly, the code is concerned with the relationship between public administrators and the public. It is particularly applicable to the lower ranks because they deal face-to-face with the public. Indeed, 'they *are* the face of the Civil Service' and so 'their decency and incorruptibility is absolutely crucial to the system'.[32] This is particularly the case when they are exercising discretionary judgement. Such decisions cannot all be subject to appeal, 'so taking proper care over decisions of this kind and balancing the interests of the individual against the national interest is an important part of the Civil Service ethic.'[33]

The requirements of the 'genetic code' in this context are easier to list and they may be translated into more solid, legalistic-type principles, namely, probity, taking relevant considerations into account and ignoring irrelevant ones, reasonableness, honesty, taking account of an individual case, equity, fairness, and legality. Thus Hennessy's code supports the view that a public service or traditional model of good administration is underpinned by constitutional principles and liberal values, centring upon fairness, equity, and reasonableness.

[29] 'Genetic Code inherited by Mandarins', *The Independent*, 5 June 1989.

[30] D. Falcon, 'Public Administrators and Constitutional Reform', Conference paper (Sheffield Univ. 1990).

[31] As supported by Questions of Procedure and see Lord Lester, 'Government's compliance with international human rights law' (1996) *PL* 187.

[32] P. Hennessy in evidence to TCSC, HC 390–II, (1992–3), Q351.

[33] O. MacDonald, *Future of Whitehall*, 130.

Efficiency

The public service model is also based on the expectation of efficiency.[34] Efficiency does not, of course, operate in isolation but in relation to the goals to be achieved. So, for instance, if the goal is the equitable distribution of funds, then the service is efficient if equity is achieved. In the public service model efficiency is defined in terms of the proper and best use of public funds, and interpreted to mean that such funds must not only be used in a cost-effective way but also as fairly and equitably as possible and within the context of probity, honesty, and integrity. The aim is 'to provide services at the minimum cost to the taxpayer but not at the cost of effectiveness'.[35] Thus the administrative methods employed must be consistent with the public service ethos and departmental culture, and are concerned not just with cost but with the quality of performance, including speed and predictability but also fairness and equity. They are also concerned with the level of provision and with the underlying values of the policy itself, administering it 'in accordance with the values which have determined it, among which considerations of cost efficiency may have a smaller or a larger place'.[36]

Efficiency in the public service model is therefore not just about the end result in terms of translating input into output but about the means by which it is achieved. 'Ends and means interconnect' and this interconnection ensures the preservation of the 'substantive values' of the administrative system.[37] Thus the public service model may be a rule-based system, but 'rule keeping is not a means to the end of profit, to be varied if the occasion demands, but a value in itself'.[38] Indeed, it is one of the key requirements of good administration because it underpins the values of equity and fairness.

The public service model is therefore concerned with the balancing of principles which serve the public interest, and whilst value for money — can we deliver the same (or a better) service cheaper — is an important factor, it has to be balanced against other parameters. This means that unlike the private sector, public administration cannot be measured simply in terms of market share or profit. Complex and often conflicting principles come into play and the weight they are given varies according to the nature and purpose of the activity. It also depends on who is operating the scales, for the administrative balancing exercise has to stand up to public scrutiny by Parliament, the Audit Commission and the PAC, the PCA, select committees, and the courts. These bodies may use different criteria in their measurement of efficiency. Moreover, they are not measuring the performance of public administration just in terms of cost-effectiveness, important though this may be, but are concerned with 'whether money is spent for the purpose and on

---

[34] As recognized by the CCSU in its statement of public service values (see n. 27).
[35] J. Ellis, CCSU, in evidence to TCSC, HC 390–II, (1992–3), Q450.
[36] Beetham (above, n. 28), 36.   [37] Ibid.   [38] Ibid.

the terms for which it was voted, and administration conducted in accordance with legally defined powers, and the legally established rights of the citizen.'[39]

The public service model of good administration is therefore concerned with efficiency but this is defined in a broad way to include many parameters which have competing claims. Cost-effectiveness is not seen as an objective, neutral requirement but as a value, the requirements of which need to be balanced against competing values. These concern 'equity, justice, citizenship, [and] democracy'[40] and thus relate to the quantity and quality of services and not just their cost.

A Summary of the Public Service Model

The public service model of good administration is therefore based upon adherence to the law and the constitutional conventions of accountability, both of which may require the retrospective justification of decisions. It is also founded upon values embodied in the public service ethos which inform the conduct and attitudes of officials. The model supports the requirements of probity, impartiality, equity, fairness, reasonableness, consistency, and rationality; recognizes the need for cost-effectiveness; and is concerned to balance the interests of the individual with the wider public interest. At the front line good administration requires officials to develop systems of categorization so that like cases are treated alike, thereby removing the possibility of favouritism or partiality, but it also requires that each individual is treated fairly. This may include being given the opportunity to show that his or her case is an exception and should be dealt with accordingly. The public service model of good administration has developed within a hierarchical, rule-based system in which the processes are valued for their own sake, not simply as a means to an end, and in which central control and co-ordination is assured.

Criticisms of the Public Service Model

In general terms the public service model of good administration can be criticized on the grounds that it is based on an idealized, outdated view of public administration, of the role of the Civil Service and of the relationship of officials with ministers. As a consequence the theory does not accord with either administrative or constitutional practice. In addition, the model ascribes characteristics to civil servants which may no longer be valid (if they ever were), accepts systems of control which are ineffective, and assumes that the underlying principles upon which it is based have positive rather than negative effects.

[39] Beetham (above, n. 28), 37.
[40] J. D. Stewart, 'Management in the public domain'(1989) 15 *Loc. Gov. Studies* 5 at 14.

Parliamentary accountability

Many of the criticisms of the public service model centre upon its dependence on ministerial responsibility. The convention is the key principle on which the public service model is based. Departments are structured and procedures ordered on the premise that public accountability is exercised by ministers not civil servants and that ministerial responsibility provides the mechanism for civil servants to be accountable through ministers to Parliament. However, critics argue that the convention of ministerial responsibility does not provide accountable government but rather a black hole through which responsibility escapes, neither ministers nor officials being held accountable. Under the system that operates ministers are able to evade accountability, which they do wherever possible, and in this, it would seem, they are aided and abetted by their civil servants who see their own interests, as well as those of the minister, best served by withholding as much information as possible from Parliament.

For the New Right the ability of civil servants and ministers to side-step the requirements of accountability is evidence that Parliamentary accountability is an inappropriate mechanism for ensuring an efficient public service. Others, whilst upholding the principle of ministerial responsibility, suggest that by itself 'it is not a sufficient way of getting at the minutiae of administration'.[41] Moreover, the addition of the PCA and the C & AG, which operate outside the protective cloak of ministerial responsibility, is not seen as sufficient compensation because of their relatively low-key role within the public service model. The PCA is seen as having insufficient resources and inadequate enforcement powers. There is also criticism from the New Right that his investigations are concerned with subjective concepts such as reasonableness and justice rather than objective or measurable matters.

The C & AG offers a better prospect of accountability for the New Right but is seen as having had only a small impact upon government efficiency in terms of the management of public funds, partly because of a lack of necessary resources to undertake extensive investigations into all areas of government spending, and partly because, when evidence is found that funds have been mismanaged, the C & AG lacks the power to impose, or direct the imposition of, a penalty on the responsible Permanent Secretary.[42]

More generally, critics argue that accountability to Parliament actually inhibits efficiency because the mechanism through which it is supposed to operate, ministerial responsibility, focuses departmental attention on the political needs of the minister rather than on the delivery needs of the customer. In addition, it encourages, even demands, a culture of secrecy and back-covering, a culture that is reinforced by the Official Secrets Act 1989, the thirty-year rule, the guidance for civil servants appearing before select committees,[43] and Questions of Procedure (the

---

[41] W. Plowden in evidence to TCSC, 390–II, (1992–3), Q528.   [42] C. Ponting, *Whitehall*.
[43] Cabinet Office, *Departmental Evidence and Response to Select Committees*.

document given to incoming ministers). A further criticism is that the hierarchical structure it engenders results in a system that is bureaucratic and bound by red tape, and, as a consequence, unresponsive. Thus, critics suggest, the public accountability of ministers to Parliament is an unsatisfactory principle upon which to base a modern model of good administration.

Public service ethos

Critics from both sides of the political spectrum are suspicious of the public service ethos, contesting the view that 'there is a single ethos or equity for the public service'[44] and disputing the notion that civil servants serve the public interest. Rather they argue that those in the Civil Service are concerned with forwarding their own interests, be these class or personal interests. The argument from the Left is that civil servants are part of the Establishment. As such they belong to an élite class and it is the interests of this class, not the public interest, that they serve. This thesis is used to support the alleged obstruction by officials of socialist policies which Labour wished to implement when it was in office.[45] The Right also cites a resistance to radical policies, particularly by the Foreign Office and the Home Office. Such resistance to policies from both the Left and the Right, if resistance there has been, supports the view that the Civil Service has its own political agenda; the maintenance of consensus politics. It will therefore seek to avoid dramatic changes in policy, for such changes make administration more difficult, cause alarm in the City and big business, and generally upset the equilibrium of the governing classes.[46]

A further argument from the Right is that public officials, like those in the private sector, are motivated by self-interest. As a consequence, they will work to ensure their own financial gain and increased personal power. To this end they will seek to expand the role of their department and will therefore resist attempts to reduce public expenditure, not because they believe it to be against the public interest but because it is contrary to their own interests.

Both theses suggest a model of a powerful—indeed over-powerful—Civil Service which uses this power for its own purposes. Sometimes these purposes coincide with, or are served by, government policy. At other times, where this coincidence is lacking, policies may be undermined or frustrated. Such arguments are mainly directed against the senior echelons of the Civil Service, for this is where the power to frustrate most obviously lies. However, if self or sectional gain is the motivating force amongst senior civil servants, this will inevitably impact on all levels of administration, for the value-system of the Civil Service is largely

---

[44] P. Kemp, first Project Manager of Next Steps, in evidence to TCSC, 390–II, Q408.

[45] See, e.g., B. Castle, *Diaries 1974–76* and *1964–70*; T. Benn, *Diaries*.

[46] See, e.g., B. Sedgemore, *Secret Constitution*; J. Dearlove & P. Saunders, *Introduction to British Politics*.

top driven and officials at the bottom of the departmental hierarchy are thus affected by attitudes at the top.

Civil Service characteristics

A further criticism relates to the characteristics which the public service model claims are exhibited by the Civil Service. The Civil Service is characterized as impartial and objective. These are considered important characteristics because they enable officials to serve governments of any political persuasion and ensure that the administrative process is fair. However, critics suggest that the requirements of impartiality have resulted in the public face of the Civil Service being impersonal, unsympathetic and remote. Moreover, 'the systems and procedures developed for one set of circumstances [have] tended to become obstacles when circumstances [have] changed'.[47] As a consequence, officials are at times ineffectual and unresponsive to either individual needs or public concerns. Responsiveness is further inhibited by the bureaucratic nature of the system, caricatured by red tape and form-filling and by the possibility of the rules becoming ends in themselves with the actual objectives forgotten. In addition, there is a belief that the close supervision, which is engendered by the hierarchical, centralized system, results in a lack of motivation. As a consequence, officials perform poorly, feel frustrated and have a poor relationship with the public.

More generally, critics suggest that characteristics which are portrayed as virtuous have often had a negative effect, particularly with regard to the relationship between officials and members of the public. Moreover, for the New Right, these characteristics, together with the mechanisms for accountability, have resulted in a public service which fails to meet modern-day requirements for efficiency. They do not, therefore, provide a suitable basis for a model of good administration.

In summary, the public service model of good administration is criticized for its insecure foundations. It is based on the convention of ministerial responsibility and on the public service ethos, neither of which are considered capable of supporting a modern system of public administration. Indeed, critics claim that they have a negative, rather than positive, effect upon public administration, providing a non-accountable, inefficient bureaucracy which perpetuates its own interests rather than those of the electorate.

[47] Mascarenhas (above, n. 5) at 75.

3

THE NEW PUBLIC MANAGEMENT MODEL OF GOOD ADMINISTRATION

Reform of the Civil Service

Criticisms of the public service model of public administration have been long-standing. However, any proposals for fundamental reform were by and large ignored. Thus the far-reaching recommendations made by Fulton remained unimplemented.[1] In addition, whilst there have always been some, particularly economists, who have questioned the size of the public sector and the cost of the Welfare State, they were on the fringes of the debate. 'Institutions such as the Institute of Economic Affairs, a right-wing think tank, was outside the mainstream of policy-making and considered somewhat eccentric'.[2] This was to change as reform of the Civil Service was put on the agenda and by the end of the 1980s such institutions 'were at the centre of government thinking'.[3]

The impetus to undertake structural change came with concern about ever-increasing public expenditure. The consideration was how to reduce, or at least prevent, costs from continuing to rise. Such a consideration brought into question the role and nature of government. The ensuing drive towards efficient government, by which was meant less government, both in functions and cost, was therefore economically driven and saving (even making) money was the motivation behind the privatization of public enterprises and, where this was not possible, in the establishment of executive agencies.

The reforms also accorded with the desire of the Prime Minister, Margaret Thatcher, to reduce the size of the Civil Service and with the ideological commitment of the New Right to roll back the frontiers of the State. Subsequent reforms, which centred on contracting-out and market-testing and on the citizen as 'customer', continued to seek reduction in cost, although they also carried a commitment to improving quality, thereby suggesting a tension between the Treasury—concerned to reduce public expenditure—and the Efficiency Unit within the Office of Public Service and Science (OPSS)—engaged in providing value for money, defined in terms of quality as well as cost. Such tension aside, the principles behind the reforms, as expressed in Reports such as *Competing for Quality* (1991), *The Citizen's Charter* (1991), and *The Civil Service: Continuity and Change* (1994),[4] suggest they were informed not by constitutional relationships but by theories of efficiency. Such theories 'which questioned state inter-

---

[1] Cmnd. 3638 (1966–8).   [2] N. Flynn, *Public Sector Management*, 9.
[3] Ibid.   [4] Cm. 1730 (1991), Cm. 1599 (1991), and Cm. 2627 (1994) respectively.

vention and reasserted the importance of market forces were clearly going to have a sympathetic hearing among politicians who were looking for reasons for curbing state expenditure and intervention'.[5] Indeed, they have provided a rationale for reducing State-provided services, seen by the New Right as encouraging a dependency culture, and increasing the role of the market, thereby restoring freedom to the individual and hence encouraging individual responsibility.

The Contracting State

Along with concern about individual responsibility, the theories argue that the size of government and the lack of competition has produced a bureaucratic, wasteful, and inflexible system which is impossible to manage effectively and which, by its nature, is inefficient. It follows that to ensure efficiency the size of government needs to be reduced, bureaucratic constraints need to be removed and the system opened up to the competitiveness of the market-place. This constitutes a 'reinvention' of government, whereby policy-making (service provision) and implementation (service delivery) are severed.[6] The government's function thus changes to enabler and regulator. Its role is to ensure that services are provided and financed appropriately but thereafter it acts only to regulate the quality of services, the delivery of which is no longer a government responsibility.

A reduction in government responsibilities has the effect of substantially reducing the size of government; for some 90 to 95 per cent of civil servants are engaged in policy implementation or service delivery.[7] Public administration thus becomes confined to a small core of policy advisers and managers, whose main function is to contract with other organizations for the delivery of services and to oversee the operation of these contracts. The benefit for government and therefore the taxpayer of 'government by contract' lies not only in a reduction in the size of the Civil Service, but in the promotion of competition, the minimization of the use of bureaucratic mechanisms, and the encouragement of innovation and entrepeneurialism. The result is a system which is market-led and thus more efficient and cost-effective.

The reforms in Britain have moved some way down the road towards this 'contracting State'. The 1991 Report, *Competing for Quality: Buying Better Public Services*, introduced compulsory competitive tendering (CCT) to central government and to those services delivered by civil servants.[8] The Report drew heavily on experiences of the private sector where, it claimed, large companies were responding to the need to be more efficient by reducing the size of their labour

5 Flynn (above, n. 2), 9.   6 D. Osborne & T. Gaebler, *Reinventing Government*.
7 Efficiency Unit, *Next Steps*.
8 Cm. 1730 (1991). CCT had already been imposed upon local authorities by the Local Government Act 1988 and the list of services to which it applies was extended by the Local Government Act 1992.

force and concentrating on 'core activities'. As a consequence, many of the services which were previously provided in-house were now bought-in, as and when required, from outside contractors. This, the Report stated, had two benefits. Firstly, it allowed the organization greater flexibility in responding to change. It did not have to undergo expensive and disruptive internal restructuring to respond to market changes. It merely had to reconsider its contracts. Secondly, it provided opportunities for cost-saving, engendered by the competition for contracts. The end result, according to the Report, was a leaner, fitter organization which was better able to respond to changes in demand and, as a consequence, was more efficient.

Competing for Quality applied the private enterprise experience to the governing process, arguing that competitive tendering in respect of some government functions would provide better value for money. It would lower costs, increase efficiency and encourage innovation. Contracting-out would also enable the core management in departments and agencies to concentrate on overall strategy, thereby improving its own performance. The implementation of the Competing for Quality strategy means that, wherever possible, service delivery is contracted out or 'privatized', and support services, such as office cleaning, building maintenance, catering, legal and accounting services, and less obvious services like prisoner escort, are bought-in. This reduces the Civil Service staff requirement, ensures competition, and enables management to be more effective. Moreover, it provides the opportunity for private sector innovation and thus opens the way for alternative ways of service delivery to be tried.

Competition

One of the functions of the reforms is to provide the competition of the marketplace. To this end contracting-out is not a static, one-off process, whereby a decision is made as to which services are suitable for delivery by the private sector and which should remain the function of the public service. Rather it is an ongoing process with agencies and departments required to go through the rigours of market-testing, which measures their work against that of other potential suppliers. This generates constant competition and may result in contracting-out to the private sector for specific services, or in a management buyout, where those civil servants already doing the job contract to provide the service at a competitive cost. Competition is further generated by allowing departments and agencies to put out to tender services which have previously been provided in-house by other parts of the Civil Service. Thus, for instance, the Civil Service College no longer has a monopoly on the provision of management training courses but must compete with private enterprise.

The link between competition and efficiency is also evident in the growth of a competition culture which uses open competition for the appointment of chief executives and for some senior departmental positions and encourages personal competition through performance-related pay. It also introduces an element of team competition through the publication of league tables of performance by different districts or areas within an agency or department, and fosters competition between agencies and other public sector bodies, such as health authorities, through the award of Chartermarks, gained for meeting Charter objectives.

The emphasis given to competition assumes that there is a correlation between the competitiveness of the market-place and high productivity or efficiency. In other words, the more competitive the market becomes, the more efficient industry has to be to survive. It also assumes that private enterprise is more efficient than the public service and that this efficiency can be captured by using the private sector wherever possible. Where it is not, then it is assumed that efficiency will be improved by importing its management methods.

Managerialism

Since the publication of *Improving Management in Government: the Next Steps*,[9] public administration has largely been replaced by public management.[10] The establishment of Next Steps executive agencies[11] to carry out 'the executive functions of government within a policy and resources framework'[12] has created discrete units of management. These are strongly focused on performance, both in relation to the quality of service received by the customer and in terms of efficiency. The units are managed by chief executives who have delegated management responsibility for the operation of their agencies, which enables them 'to design organizational structures and processes which match the needs of their particular task'.[13] Such delegation allows a considerable variation between agencies. Moreover, management autonomy now extends in many cases to the recruitment of staff and the development of schemes for performance-related pay. It also makes cost-saving, market-testing, and subsequent decisions on the buying-in of support services largely the responsibility of chief executives. The agency is also responsible for setting and publishing appropriate Charter standards.

The Citizen's Charter, which was launched in 1991, has been a 'powerful tool' in the management reforms.[14] It requires agencies to provide objectives or standards against which they can be measured and has therefore forced them 'to examine their processes to improve efficiency and effectiveness and to enable standards to be raised over time'.[15] In line with management theory, there is recognition that for optimum performance the targets need to be 'owned' by those who are

---

[9] In 1988.   [10] See C. Hood, 'Public management' (1991) 69 *Pub. Admin.* 1.
[11] There are now approximately 100 Next Steps executive agencies, covering about 2/3 of the Home Civil Service.
[12] Efficiency Unit (above, n. 7).   [13] Cm. 2627, (1994) para 2.21.
[14] Ibid., para. 3.8.   [15] Ibid.

committed to delivering them. Thus 'top-level targets' need to be 'linked to, and informed by, lower-level internal management targets'.[16] There is therefore a correlation between Charter standards and performance indicators.

Charter standards provide only one set of targets or performance indicators. Objectives are also set by departments as part of the framework document. These include stringent financial controls and cost-saving objectives. Some agencies, who sell their services, either to other parts of government or to the public, have Trading Fund status and their targets for financial performance are similar to those used by equivalent service-providers in the private sector.[17]

The Next Steps initiative has not just concerned the management of service delivery within executive agencies. It has impacted upon the core departments, bringing into focus the way they manage the agencies and their other tasks, even those relating to policy advice, all of which are subject to performance measurement. Thus the initiative has 'fundamentally altered the way in which the Civil Service is managed'.[18] Moreover, the move towards a managerial culture, in which competition, targeting, and increased efficiency dominate, continues to be informed by private sector practices. Hence further management information systems have been developed to 'enable managers to take soundly-based decisions reflecting a better understanding of the relationship between inputs and outputs in their organizations and to allocate resources more efficiently and effectively,' and, importantly, to 'help ensure that departments and agencies plan effectively to achieve the efficiency increases required'.[19] In addition, resource-accounting systems 'based on commercial accounting principles'[20] have been introduced.

Departments and agencies are also encouraged to make use of 'the range of available management techniques',[21] such as those concerned with 'priority-based cost management', 'bench-marking', and 'process re-engineering',[22] and the delegation of management functions continues with its extension to pay and grading of civil servants, below senior level, such that as of April 1996 existing national pay arrangements were no longer applicable. Departments, and through them agencies, therefore have responsibility for their own staffing structures and for pay. This has been presented as an opportunity for restructuring, by which is meant the cutting out of layers of management, perceived as being unnecessary. Such a process has already taken place in companies in the private sector and contributes to the 'leaner and fitter' image that is presented. It also signifies the end of the Civil Service as a centralized, unified organization with uniformity of pay and conditions across the grades.

---

[16] Ibid.
[17] Ibid., para. 3.10. Examples of such agencies include the Royal Mint, Companies House, the Fire Service College and HM Land Registry, some of which would seem to be candidates for privatization and set to go the same way as HMSO, a Trading Fund which was subsequently privatized.
[18] Ibid., 2.23.   [19] Ibid., 3.15.   [20] Ibid., 3.16.   [21] Ibid., 3.31.
[22] Ibid.

The Fragmenting State

The reforms of the 1980s and 1990s have been revolutionary. One of their prime effects has been to blur the lines between public and private. The traditional position, whereby public administration was concerned with the implementation of policies whilst private sector management was involved with the delivery of a service or product, has all but gone. Civil servants are now 'managers' and they 'manage' the delivery of those services which are not considered suitable for delivery by private enterprise or by other non-governmental agents of the State. Even then, supporting services may be provided by the private sector, and the 'manager' may well be someone appointed from outside the Civil Service.[23] Thus service delivery and its supporting framework has become fragmented and a mix of public and private.

This fragmentation feeds through into the entire governmental or departmental structure. Departments are no longer whole units but the sum of various and varied parts. These may include a core of departmental staff, who are concerned with advising on policy, controlling the budget, regulating contracts, dealing with personnel matters, and overall strategy and management; departmental units or divisions, which are not themselves agencies but are run on Next Steps principles; Next Steps executive agencies with varied extents of autonomy; non-departmental public bodies (or quangos) for which the Minister has indirect responsibility; and a range of private-sector contractors. The exact mix will obviously vary from department to department. Moreover variation will be further encouraged as departments are given autonomy over most areas relating to pay, grading and recruitment, and further powers are delegated to executive agencies.

The New Public Management Model of Good Administration

The reforms clearly have implications for the concept of good administration. They support a new public management model which is underpinned by different values from the public service model, or at least places a different emphasis on these values. Most significant is the domination of efficiency which is supported by the language of consumerism[24] and the values of the competitive market. The mechanisms of control and accountability also have an emphasis which accords more readily with management theory and with accountability to the market rather than to the public interest.

---

[23] Out of the 94 CEs in post in 1994, 34 came from outside the Civil Service.
[24] J. Stewart & K. Walsh, 'Change in management of public services' (1992) 70 *Pub. Admin.* 4 at 499.

Efficiency

The new public management model of good administration centres upon value for money, measured in terms of efficiency, effectiveness and economy. The '3Es' are given simple definitions. Economy is concerned with cost-cutting,[25] whilst effectiveness is concerned with 'the extent to which objectives have been met'.[26] In determining whether objectives have been met, no account is taken of cost, unless, as is usually the case, the objectives are related to cost performance. Efficiency, upon which most emphasis is placed, is concerned with the input–output relationship, that is with looking at how the resources have been used to obtain the end result and whether they could have been used better. Thus an 'efficient' programme is one 'where the target is being achieved with the least possible number of resources'.[27] This suggests that the emphasis has changed from the 'quality and quantity of services to the cost at which, and efficiency with which, they are provided'.[28] There is little recognition of possible points of conflict between efficiency and other values and no suggestion of the need to balance efficiency with effectiveness. Indeed, in contrast to the public service model, this is not seen as necessary because effectiveness is concerned with meeting measurable, quantifiable objectives, many of which will be concerned with cost-efficiency. Efficiency and effectiveness are thus linked together. Moreover, the new public management model takes little account of competing requirements which traditionally arise from the administrative process. Its rationale is efficiency, and this does not yield to other administrative requirements.[29] The characteristics of the model follow from this guiding principle.

The new public management model is characterized by its reliance on the methods and procedures of the private sector and upon theories of management practice. It is based on the premise that individuals are motivated by self-interest and it sees this interest fostered by the devolution of management responsibility and by competition. Particularly important is performance-related pay, which requires clear, quantifiable objectives and targets, concerned with how much, how many, how quickly, etc. Objectives and targets also play a part in the frameworks provided for the executive agencies and management units within departments. They lay down responsibilities and overall performance indicators. As a consequence, there is little discretion as to the end result. However, within the confines of the framework, there is discretion as to how this is achieved. Administrators or managers are therefore able to be flexible and responsive in securing their targets. Moreover, in contrast to the public service model, those at the front line are encouraged to be innovative and to take personal responsibility. The aim is therefore more targeted objectives but greater management and budgetary freedom to achieve them.

---

[25] Treasury, Memorandum to TCSC, HC 236–I, (1981–2), para. 52.   [26] Ibid., para. 33.
[27] Ibid.   [28] P. Cane, *Introduction to Administrative Law*, 387.
[29] N. Johnson, 'Change in the Civil Service' (1985) 63 *Pub. Admin.* 4 at 428.

Accountability

The new public management model equates responsibility with accountability at least at managerial level if not constitutionally. This is reflected in the increase of accountability of chief executives in line with their delegated responsibilities. Furthermore, staff who are in contact with the public are now frequently identifiable by name badges, thereby suggesting a more direct accountability to the public than has previously been the case. Such public exposure also emphasises the importance placed on 'individual initiative and personal responsibility', one of the hallmarks of the reforms.[30] The reduction of anonymity has been accompanied and encouraged by the publication of a Code of Practice on Access to Government Information. The Code came into force in April 1994 and is intended to make government more open and transparent, and thus more easily held to account. The 'presumption is in favour of disclosure of information, subject to specific tests where confidentiality is justifiable'.[31] The move towards more open government is intended to make citizens better informed of the reasoning behind Government policies, actions and decisions, but it is also seen as another weapon in the armoury for improving efficiency. The opening up of policy making and service delivery to greater public scrutiny should encourage the streamlining of processes and ensure that inefficiencies become less easy to hide.

There have therefore been significant changes in the way accountability is exercised. These have been accompanied by other changes which effect the type of accountability and its location, and as a result provide a different emphasis. The new public management model favours controls which are oriented towards the market and which are more attuned to the professional standards of accountants and managers than to the requirements of political accountability. The model therefore accords a bigger role to the C & AG. In addition, the accountability of civil servants to the minister takes the form of a more formalized managerial accountability. The market approach to accountability is also apparent in the shift from accountability to the public interest to accountability to the individual customer in the form of the Citizen's Charter. This alters the emphasis from public service to customer relations. Similarly, the model supports the control of discretion by internal review bodies, which share the same objectives of economy, efficiency and effectiveness, rather than by external tribunals which are guided by principles such as reasonableness and fairness.[32]

Management accountability

The manager, or chief executive, of an executive agency is personally accountable to the minister for the agency's responsibilities as laid down in the framework

[30] Cm. 2627, (1994) para. 2.29.   [31] Ibid., para. 2.31.
[32] P. McAustlan, 'Public law and public choice' (1988) 51 *MLR* 699.

agreement, a document which is seen as being quasi-contractual. The ways in which this accountability is exercised, for instance through quarterly reports and performance targets, is also detailed in the framework document, and the chief executive is measured on his success or otherwise against these targets. In the short term this affects his monetary reward. In the long term, career advancement may depend on a successful period as a chief executive, and the promotion prospects for a failed chief executive, particularly one who spends over budget, are unlikely to be good.[33]

Comptroller and Auditor-General and the National Audit Office

The C & AG's role was extended by the National Audit Act 1983. This set up the National Audit Office under the C & AG and gave it a remit to undertake value-for-money audits, that is to examine 'economy, efficiency and effectiveness', in addition to routine audits. The chief executive, as Accounting Officer (AO) or Agency Accounting Officer (AAO),[34] appears before the PAC in response to these audits, being either directly answerable to Parliament, or answerable through his or her department head, for the 'economy, efficiency and effectiveness with which the Agency has used its resources in discharging the functions given to it in the framework document'.[35] Thus financial accountability is structured in accordance with the main objective of the new public management model: that is, to provide value for money.

Citizen's Charter

In 1991 the Prime Minister, John Major, launched the Citizen's Charter initiative. He told the House, 'I want the people of this country to have services in which they as citizens can be confident and in which public servants themselves can take pride.'[36] The Citizen's Charter establishes six principles of public service. These are listed as 'standards, information and openness, choice and consultation, courtesy and helpfulness, putting things right, and value for money'.[37] Public services are required to set, monitor and publicize the standards that a customer can reasonably expect. The emphasis is therefore on identifiable and measurable standards, such as speed, frequency, politeness, and the provision of relevant information rather than on vaguer, less-easily assessed concepts such as fairness or equity. It is also on the individual as customer rather than as 'the object of an administrative procedure' and, as customer, the individual is 'undoubtedly at an

---

[33] Sir Robin Butler indicated that s/he should be replaced (*Analysis*, Radio 4, 31 May 1990).
[34] AO if a trading company, otherwise AAO.
[35] P. Kemp, Project Manager Next Steps, Memorandum to TCSC, HC 348–II, (1988–9).
[36] HC Debs., col. 765, 22 July 1991.   [37] Cm. 1599, (1991) 1.

advantage in terms of courtesy, access to information and the recognition of minimum standards of efficiency in such matters as response to letters'.[38]

Central to the Citizen's Charter is an effective complaints procedure. This is seen as an integral part of the process of raising the standards of public service and making them more efficient. It is also recognized that 'being able to complain effectively is particularly important in public services where dissatisfied users often cannot go elsewhere'.[39] Thus an effective complaints procedure contributes to the legitimization of public services whilst also compensating for the deficiencies of 'the market'. In addition, it provides management with information as to how the service can be better run. It therefore benefits both sides, an important factor that needs to be fed into any equation regarding cost.

In order to determine what constituted an 'effective' complaints system, the Government set up the Citizen's Charter Complaints Task Force (CCCTF) team in June 1993. The Task Force was required 'to undertake a wide-ranging review of public service complaints systems, to ensure that they operate in line with Citizen's Charter principles'.[40] It concluded that systems should be 'easily accessible and well-published . . . simple to understand and use . . . [and] provide an effective response and appropriate redress.'[41] To this end the Task Force recommended that the standards of service which an organization seeks to provide are published so that people know what standards to expect and thus the grounds on which they can complain, and that 'complaints . . . [are] dealt with in accordance with clearly set out procedures which are easy to understand.'[42] In addition, it recommended that the procedure should guarantee a full reply and explanation, together with suitable redress. This might range from an apology (suitable in all cases) to financial compensation. It further suggested that if others had suffered in the same way, they should receive the same redress, even if they had not complained—echoes here of the PCA.[43]

The Task Force also stated that a complaints system must provide for 'speedy handling' of complaints with the customer being kept informed as to what was happening. It must respect customer confidentiality and the investigation must be 'full and fair'. Thus 'all complaints should be thoroughly and objectively investigated' and 'procedures should include independent review within the organization where appropriate (i.e. review by someone within the organization but separate from the direct line management of the person or section complained about).'[44] The complaints procedures recommended accord with the new public management model. Their internal nature means that the process is retained within the organization or agency, making the use of external grievance procedures exceptional. In addition, a system which allows, even encourages, complaints based on the performance or Charter standards of the agency works to support those

---

[38] D. Faulkner, C. Crouch, M. Freeland, & D. King, Memorandum to TCSC, 27–III, (1993–4).
[39] CCCTF, *Effective Complaints Systems*, 1.   [40] CCCTF, *Access to Complaints Systems*, 1.
[41] CCCTF, (above, n. 39), 3.   [42] Ibid., 5.
[43] See ch. 4.   [44] CCCTF (above, n. 39), 7.

standards. Thus for the new public management model an effective complaints procedure is integral to improved performance, cost-effectiveness and good customer relations.

The Citizen's Charter therefore provides direct accountability to the individual for the service he or she receives. Again—like the accountability of chief executives to the minister—this accountability is quasi-contractual and reflects the influence of the market-place. It can also be articulated in the terms of contracts with private suppliers to ensure adherence to minimum standards of delivery. Indeed, the Charter is so fundamental to the thinking of the new public management model that the Treasury and Civil Service Committee considered that it could 'be argued that Citizen's Charters effectively redefine the notion of public service by pointing to the features which unite services used by the public, whether they are in the public or private sector.'[45] This suggests that Charters could become a linking mechanism between those public services which have been contracted out and those which continue to be delivered by public servants.

A Summary of the New Public Management Model

The Next Steps initiative and the Citizen's Charter have been at the forefront of a fundamental reform of public administration within central government. The New Right or new public management model of good administration that emerges is one based on value for money, of which the key indicator is cost-efficiency. It is concerned with measuring the transfer of inputs into outputs and with being flexible and responsive. It therefore encourages competition and personal responsibility and allows considerable delegation and personal initiative. As a consequence the model is not rule-governed in the same way as the public service model. Rather rules and procedures are adopted to improve efficiency not because they have any intrinsic value. The model also favours controls which measure its performance against quantifiable objectives. Thus effectiveness and efficiency are inter-related.

Good administration in relation to the new public management model therefore means 'efficient, effective and economic' administration when all the 'Es' are quantifiable. The administration is 'good' if performance targets are fulfilled. The orientation is towards the customer, to whom the administrator is accountable for the service he or she gives, and for whom there should be an effective complaints mechanism, and the principles upheld by the model centre on flexibility and responsiveness, innovation and initiative, speed and accuracy. This view of good administration is largely uncluttered by notions of public service or concepts such as fairness, equity and reasonableness. These are not pursued in their own right but only as a means to an end, the end being customer satisfaction as measured against the standards promised and efficiency in terms of cost.

[45] TCSC HC 390–I, (1992–3), para. 12.

Criticisms of the New Public Management Model

Many of the criticisms of the model relate or lead to the concerns expressed in Chapter 1, namely that the reform of the Civil Service has resulted in confused accountability, a decline in standards, and a changed culture within the Civil Service. However, there are also criticisms of the premises on which the model is based.

The assumed compatibility between public and private sectors

The introduction of methods and techniques from commerce and industry, which are aimed at increasing efficiency, presupposes that public and private sectors are compatible and takes little account of the difference between running a country and running a company.[46] Yet they have different objectives to meet and different problems to overcome. Thus public administration is required to have characteristics that are not shared by private enterprise. These were recognized by the Royal Commission Report of 1914, which noted: 'the administration of Government differs, and must necessarily differ, from the activities of the business world, both in the objects to which it is directed, in the criteria of its success, in the necessary conditions under which it is conducted, and in the choice of instruments which it employs.'[47]

The TCSC considered that this statement was still true today, although reformists might argue that the 'objects' and the 'criteria' have changed because of the need for greater efficiency. Nevertheless, whilst a business has the 'overriding objective or constraint . . . of profitability', public administrators 'have a multiplicity of objectives, often conflicting'.[48] These cannot always be broken down into simple performance targets against which administrators can be measured, for some of the tasks are complex and ambiguous. Moreover, their implementation may be complicated by other factors which have a higher profile than in the private sector. Thus public administration needs to be 'seen to be held to stricter ethical and legal standards so that it engages in activities with a greater symbolic significance'.[49] Administrators must also 'respond to issues of fairness and equity before the law', 'appear to operate in the public interest', and 'maintain minimum levels of public support above those required in private industry'.[50]

The requirement that the public interest is served and public support maintained is fundamental to the notion of public service. Thus whilst private business is concerned with satisfying shareholders (through making a profit) and responding to individual customers (thereby ensuring the profit), the public sector has different and additional concerns—hence the importance of the 'constitutional principles'

---

[46] L. Pliatzky, 'Mandarins, ministers and the management of Britain' (1984) 66 *Pol. Quart.* 1 at 25.
[47] Cited in TCSC, HC 27–I, para. 67.   [48] Pliatzky (above, n. 46) at 25.
[49] A. Massey, Memorandum to TCSC, HC 27–III, (1993–4).   [50] Ibid.

or Civil Service values. Yet these principles may be in danger of dilution as a consequence of 'the imposition of supposed private sector ethics, which are irreconcilable with those associated with the British public service'.[51] This is not to suggest that the private sector lacks consideration of ethical responsibility, but rather that this responsibility is different from that required in the public sector. Moreover, whilst 'business is a very broad church where the ethical standards vary',[52] variation is not acceptable in public administration. There is in any case 'a difference in ethos between management on the one hand and administration on the other. . . . The consequence of actions, the degree of accountability and responsibility in the private sector is far more direct than in the public sector.[53]

Critics also see the assumption of the New Right that 'the market' will resolve conflicts between different interests as misguided. '[I]t tends to respond only to those wants that are either most easily satisfied or affect most people.'[54] The consequence may be that those needs which are difficult and expensive to fulfil and which affect a minority of society may be sidelined. Thus, for example in the National Health Service 'improvements in minor surgery may be at the expense of chronic patient care'.[55] Moreover, the encouragement of a culture of self-interest through the emphasis on the market may result in a resistance by taxpayers to fund services from which they receive no direct benefit. This would result in a deterioration in public services to the obvious detriment of the poor. It would also be an implicit acknowledgement that the existence of an underclass was acceptable.

The reorientation towards 'the customer'

Closely linked with the assumption that 'private' and 'public' are compatible is the emphasis upon 'customer satisfaction'. This shift to the customer has largely come about through the Citizen's Charter. On the positive side, Charters have made public administrators look outwards and focus more on those who use their services. However, the 'stress on customers might lead to a lack of appreciation of the extent to which public services . . . [are] concerned with more than the services to individual customers'.[56] The criticism is that the wider public interest will be neglected. In addition, the need to identify 'a customer' may result in other stakeholders affected by, or interested in, the service being forgotten. Thus whilst the convicted criminal, magistrates and judges, the general public and the victim all have an interest in the prison service, the nomination of the convicted prisoner as 'customer' may reduce the claims of the other parties. 'Customer' is in any case a misleading label to attach to someone who has no choice about using the service

---

[51] Charter 88, Memorandum to TCSC, ibid.
[52] W. Brett in evidence to TCSC, ibid., Q1739.
[53] C. Cox, Hoskyns Group plc, in evidence to TCSC, ibid., Q1524.
[54] R. Bellamy & J. Greenaway, 'New Right conception of citizenship' (1995) 30 *Gov. and Oppos.* 4 at 485
[55] Ibid.   [56] TCSC, HC 390–I, (1992–3), para. 14.3.

and could more appropriately attach to judges and magistrates. At least they may have a choice of sentencing options, including fines and probation, with which, in a sense, the prison service is in competition.[57]

The problem is that the use of the term 'customer' is artificial in the context of many public sector services. The prisoner, for instance, is unlikely to see himself as a 'customer' of the prison service. Similarly, whilst those who choose to use the court system to settle private disputes might be viewed as 'customers', those who are being prosecuted for alleged offences cannot be seen in the same light. At times denoting someone as the 'customer' stretches credibility to the extreme, as when the term is used to describe an individual undergoing the Habitual Residence test to determine his or her right to benefit.[58]

Effectiveness as quantifiable

A further criticism concerns the distortion that arises because of the need for measurable objectives and indicators in order to determine performance-related pay and to provide Charter standards upon which customers' expectations are based. The Government has stressed that objectives and targets are set 'not just in terms of cost but in quality of service', and points to the results 'in the speed and accuracy of Social Security benefits, the time people have to wait for the delivery of passports; the time they have to wait for driving tests . . .'.[59] However, measuring 'quality' in quantifiable terms can undermine the service provided because it may introduce 'distorted incentives into the system'.[60] This is evident with regard to law enforcement where only the end results that can be counted are used as performance indicators. Thus the number of crimes committed, the crimes solved and the convictions obtained assume greater importance and, as a consequence, an increased share of resources than crime prevention and a good relationship with members of the public. This encourages the manipulation of crime figures and means that important aspects of police work that cannot be measured go unrewarded. The manipulation of figures has also been evident in the Employment Agency where, in order to satisfy the 1993 performance target of 'getting clients off the employment register', clerical staff placed them on the invalidity register instead.[61]

The consequence of using quantifiable targets has been particularly evident in relation to the CSA, where the most significant objective was concerned with saving money. In order to save the £530m required, the Agency targeted those fathers who were already paying maintenance or who had been involved in 'clean break' settlements rather than the 'absent fathers' who had never contributed to the

---

[57] Flynn (above, n. 2), 146.

[58] See Adjudication Officer's *Guidance on the Administration of the Habitual Residence Test* (Benefits Office).

[59] Sir Robin Butler in evidence to TCSC, HC 27–II, (1993–4), Q1354.

[60] Bellamy & Greenaway (above, n. 54), at 485.   [61] Ibid.

upkeep of their children and were less easy to trace. Absent fathers were seen as 'non-profitable' when 'the name of the game . . . [was] maximising the maintenance yield'.[62]

The actions of the CSA caused public concern largely because they were seen as unfair but the performance of an agency is not assessed in terms of how it has achieved its objectives but with regard to the extent to which it has achieved them. This gives rise to a related concern, namely the objectives chosen. Even if performance is quantifiable and thus lacks a subjective judgement, the determination of the objectives remains subjective. The targets that are set therefore reflect political preferences. However, the way in which they are presented fail to reflect this and political argument may therefore be deflected, with targets being seen as an administrative mechanism rather than a policy choice. The consequence may be that the weakest sections of society may be disadvantaged even further. This can be demonstrated with reference to the Benefits Agency, whose performance indicators do not include take-up rates of benefit,[63] and the Immigration Service, the Charter for which targets routine waiting time at Immigration Control but is silent on the treatment of those detained in custody.[64]

Quantifiable objectives and targets have a part to play in ensuring that services are delivered efficiently. However, critics see them as inadequate and inappropriate as the measure of effectiveness, which they consider is a qualitative, and therefore a political, judgement. Thus what constitutes 'effective' is far more complex than meeting objectives related to speed, cost and quantity. It is determined in relation to objectives which are 'provided for the most part as a matter of public policy on the basis of law and administrative practice, embodying for the citizen a variety of claims, entitlements and expectations. There are considerations of equity, fair treatment and reasonableness, the duty of care and attention, and the proper exercise of discretion conferred by Parliament . . .'.[65]

The failure to recognize fairness and equity

A major criticism of the model is its failure to recognize the importance of fairness, equity and reasonableness within the public service and to accept that at times efficiency needs to give way to them. The concentration of the new public management on outputs significantly shifts attention from the process by which these outputs are achieved. This produces concern that the processes, intended to ensure equity and fairness, may be bypassed. Programmes like the Benefit Agency's Bias for Action, which give 'the front line staff more power and . . . [encourages] them to concentrate on their output rather than so much on the way

[62] Social Security Sel. Cttee, HC 69, (1993–4), para. 28.
[63] M. Bichard, CE Benefits Agency, in evidence to TCSC, HC 27–II, (1993–4), Q2243.
[64] J. Garrett MP, Memorandum to TCSC, ibid. III.
[65] N. Johnson, Memorandum to TCSC, ibid.

they do things',[66] may enable an official to respond to an individual's specific needs but carry the danger of arbitrary decision-making.

The extension of discretion without a confining and defining framework of rules would seem to open the way for inequity and unfairness. This is demonstrated with regard to the Social Fund which provides loans and grants for people in need. It is administered locally according to a centrally determined and fixed budget. Local officials must therefore prioritize the use of the Fund, rather than allocate it to everyone who is entitled to it. This principle departs from the idea of entitlement according to a set of universally applied criteria; 'any claimant's probability of receiving assistance is dependent on the level of take-up by other people in the same area'.[67] This clearly offends against principles of equity and fairness and results in inconsistency or arbitrary decision-making, neatly translated into 'flexibility' in the Social Fund Manual. This 'flexibility of the Social Fund and the wide variety of individual circumstances covered mean that a decision in one case will not be a binding precedent for others'.[68] Thus decisions are made on an *ad hoc* basis and cannot be challenged for inconsistency.

Moreover, the focus on responsiveness to the customer suggests that the concern is not to treat all who use the service in the same way, but to respond to the complaints of the dissatisfied customer. Thus while the new public management model probably 'looks after the articulate customer very well . . ., the old notion of being fair to the awkward or the ignorant has been sacrificed'.[69] This was a point of concern for the Citizen's Charter Task Force who recognized that some people might need help in making a complaint. However, its concern was accompanied by a recognition that the provision of help, whether by the public service organization itself or an outside organisation, was costly,[70] and its final checklist, designed to help agencies fine-tune their grievance procedures, confines itself to suggesting that customers should be made aware that help may be obtained from some outside bodies (such as the Citizens' Advice Bureaux), from a relative or friend, and from designated staff within the organization.[71] Indicating sources where help may be obtained goes a little way to addressing the concern about the fairness and equitable nature of public services as delivered by the new public management model. However, it still treats fairness and equity as an 'add-on' not as a fundamental requirement of the public service. Moreover, it is only concerned with the fairness of grievance procedures not with the fair delivery and distribution of services.

The problem for the new public management model is that the concepts of fairness, equity and reasonableness do not sit comfortably with innovation and initiative, and may not enhance performance in terms of efficiency. They are unlikely to be value for money. Indeed, 'equity of treatment may reduce profitability'.[72]

---

[66] M. Bichard, (above, n. 63), Q2188.   [67] Flynn (above, n. 2), 39.
[68] Ibid., 41.   [69] According to 'some DVLA people' (*The Economist*, 31 Oct. 1992).
[70] CCCTF (above, n. 41), para. 2.   [71] CCCTF (above, n. 40), para. 2.
[72] Flynn (above, n. 2) 109.

However, unlike private enterprise, public administration cannot, or should not, be governed by profitability or by requiring there to be a tangible benefit for any financial outlay. 'The search for the "3Es", economy, efficiency and effectiveness should be accompanied by a fourth "E", equity'.[73] Moreover, value for money and customer service should not be at the expense of the integrity of the public service but 'should take [their] . . . place alongside the ethics of probity and steward-ship'.[74]

Accountability

The new public management model seeks to shift the location and type of account-ability from public and collective to private and individual, hence the develop-ment of the 'contracting State' and the introduction of the Citizen's Charter. Proponents of the model assert that 'government by contract' will result in better accountability because of the customer's right to litigate. However, such an asser-tion presupposes that all 'customers' will have the ability, as well as the desire, to engage in litigation, an erroneous supposition. It also fails to take account of the frustrating effect of commercial confidentiality which enables the standards to which a private company is expected to perform to be kept secret and makes a mockery of the reformers' claim of openness or transparency. In any case, in many instances, particularly those concerned with social welfare policies, the parties to any contract would be the minister and the contractor. The customer would have no contractual rights—unless, of course, Charter standards are to become legal obligations, a possibility not accepted by the Government on the grounds that this would result in inflexibility. Even then, a problem arises in that contractual rights do not protect the public interest. Indeed, their existence may be inhibitory to pub-lic law actions, which can have this function.

The model also supports the 'transparency' or openness of government, hence the introduction of the Code of Practice on Access to Government Information, again not justiciable, and the commitment towards more open government. However, critics argue that, whilst more information is publicly available, much of it is of little substance and does little to make the government more account-able. Indeed, the presentation of much of the documentation released suggests a public relations exercise rather than an opening up of the governing process. The publication of Charter standards and framework documents may be useful but in themselves are of little significance in forwarding accountability, unless there are independent checks on whether standards are met[75] and sufficient clarity in frame-work documents and other publicly available information 'for outsiders to

---

[73] Ibid.

[74] M. Holmes & D. Shand, 'Management reform' (1995) 8 *Governance* 4 at 552.

[75] Only 4 out of 15 Charters in existence in early 1994 were subject to independent checking regard-ing the meeting of targets (*Financial Times*, 14 Mar. 1994).

determine the allocation of responsibility'.[76] Particularly important is a clear statement on the extent to which ministers interfere behind the scenes in the running of agencies.[77]

Conclusion: Where Are We Now?

Public administration in the 1990s does not precisely conform to either the new public management model of good administration or the public service model. Rather characteristics of both models are evident. However, evidence suggests that a predominantly public service model is giving way to a model which accords largely with a new public management model. At the moment it retains, albeit rather uncomfortably, elements of the traditional model. Thus it still operates under the convention of ministerial responsibility although this reduces the effectiveness of the Civil Service reforms by limiting, even confusing, the accountability of chief executives for Next Steps executive agencies. It is also accountable to the PCA, whose powers are extended with the Code of Practice on Access to Government Information, and the courts. Moreover, the public service ethos is still evident, at least in the core departments if not always in the agencies, and the Government has insisted that the attendant values will be preserved, hence its acceptance of the TCSC's draft Civil Service Code.

All this suggests that the individual and customer relations have not quite replaced the community and public interest and that value for money and efficiency are still compromised by other considerations such as fairness, equity and reasonableness. The difference thus lies in the weight given to the component parts and this seems to have shifted away from the softer concepts towards harder, more easily measurable ones. Moreover, this process seems likely to continue as public services are increasingly delivered by private enterprise or by a mix of public and private. Good administration would thus seem to be in transition, between models which are based on different foundations and informed by different values.

The next chapter will examine the PCA's perspective of what constitutes good administration and the extent to which this accords with the preceding models of good administration.

[76] The TCSC in its investigation into the role of the Civil Service found clarity to be insufficient (TCSC, HC 27–I, (1993–4), para. 165).

[77] Ministerial interference was an aspect of the complaint made by Derek Lewis after he had been sacked from his position as DG of the Prison Service in Oct. 1995.

4

THE PARLIAMENTARY COMMISSIONER FOR ADMINISTRATION: PERSPECTIVES ON GOOD ADMINISTRATION

Common to both models of public administration is the part played by the PCA. Indeed, his role in relation to the administrative process has increased in the 1990s. There are several reasons for this. Firstly, the internalization of appeal procedures means that in many cases the PCA has become the only external mechanism for the redress of grievances. Secondly, the Citizen's Charter has contributed to the development of a complaints culture. It has also provided the PCA with a possible further checklist as to what constitutes maladministration, and, thirdly, the PCA now has a remit to accept grievances with regard to the operation of the Code of Practice on Access to Government Information.

Maladministration

The powers of the PCA are determined by the Parliamentary Commissioner for Administration Act 1967 (the PCA Act). This legislation gives the holder of the office the discretion to investigate grievances concerning administrative action taken by, or on behalf of, a government department or other public body named within Schedule 2 of the Act. Grievances must be referred through a Member of Parliament, must constitute maladministration and must have given rise to an injustice.[1] In 1983 the Select Committee on the PCA voiced its concern about the number of quangos or non-departmental public bodies which were outside the jurisdiction of the PCA yet were carrying out the functions of government. It considered that 'when the wrong is alleged to have been committed by a body discharging functions which might just as appropriately be those of central government, we think there are occasions when an appeal to the PCA is as appropriate as when it is alleged against central government itself.'[2] As a result, in 1987 the Parliamentary and Health Service Commissioners Act extended the PCA's powers in relation to non-departmental bodies.[3] However, those bodies whose functions are predominantly commercial in character are still excluded from his jurisdiction.

---

[1] PCA Act 1967, ss. 4(1) & 5(1).   [2] Sel. Cttee on PCA, HC 619, (1983–4).
[3] S. 1 of the 1987 Act provides a new s. 4, PCA Act 1967. Sched. 1 lists depts. and public bodies within the jurisdiction of the PCA.

The PCA Act provides no definition of what constitutes maladministration, thus giving special importance to the description provided in the House of Commons by Richard Crossman, the minister responsible for the passage of the Act. He suggested that maladministration included 'bias, neglect, inattention, delay, incompetence, ineptitude, perversity, turpitude, arbitrariness, and so on.'[4] This list was soon supplemented by a recommendation from the Select Committee on the PCA that maladministration should also include decisions that were 'thoroughly bad in quality' or 'clearly wrong'.[5] The PCA was also encouraged by the Select Committee to examine the substance of departmental rules to determine whether the rules themselves constituted maladministration, although it accepted that where delegated legislation was concerned, such an examination was, under the terms of the PCA Act, limited to the operation of the rules.[6] Further suggestions were subsequently made by JUSTICE which considered maladministration should extend to actions which were 'unreasonable, unjust or oppressive'.[7]

The reports of the PCA provide evidence of the application of many of the above ideas as to what constitutes maladministration. However, aware that his jurisdiction is limited to the administrative process, the PCA has avoided impugning decisions on the basis that they are 'thoroughly bad' or 'clearly wrong'. Such a finding would suggest a questioning of the merits of the decision, and thus the policy on which it was based, and would result in a rejection of the PCA's conclusions by the government department concerned on the basis that the PCA was acting outside his jurisdiction.

The line between policy and administration is not, however, always easy to draw, as was apparent in the PCA's investigation into the Channel Tunnel Rail Link in 1995. This concerned complaints that properties in certain areas had been unsaleable between 1990–94 because of uncertainty as to the route of the rail link. The hope of the Government had been to attract private money to the scheme but this was not forthcoming and the Secretary of State for Transport announced that the route was to be reconsidered. This reconsideration took four years. The PCA was of the opinion that 'the effect of the Department of Transport's policy was to put the project in limbo, keeping it alive when it could not be funded. That increased uncertainty and blight in the period from June 1990' and, as a result, '[p]ersons not covered by the compensation schemes may have suffered as a result of the delay in settling the route.'[8] He believed that '[t]he [Department of Transport] had a responsibility to consider the position of such persons suffering exceptional or extreme hardship and to provide for redress where appropriate.'[9] However, he found that 'no specific consideration was given to that aspect of good administration.'[10]

The Government argued that it was not its policy to compensate for generalized blight and that to determine criteria in relation to the compensation of individuals

[4] HC Debs., col. 51, 18 Oct. 1966.   [5] Sel. Cttee on PCA, HC 350, (1967–8), para. 14.
[6] Sel. Cttee on PCA, HC 385, (1968–9).   [7] JUSTICE, *Our Fettered Ombudsman*, para. 66.
[8] PCA, HC 193, (1994–5), para. 46.   [9] Ibid.   [10] Ibid.

was too difficult. Moreover, the PCA's Report was rejected by the Permanent Secretary on the basis that the PCA had acted outside his jurisdiction by examining and criticizing ministerial policy not administration. Both contentions were refuted by the PCA who did not accept that it was beyond the department's capability to establish relevant criteria.[11] Moreover, he held that he was not commenting on policy but on its effects and his finding of maladministration was based on the failure of the department to mitigate these effects by devising a compensation scheme for those individuals suffering 'exceptional or extreme hardship'.[12] The PCA was supported by the Select Committee who believed that there was 'an expectation that when an individual citizen is faced with extraordinary hardship as a result of strict application of law or policy, the Executive must be prepared to look again and see whether help can be given.'[13] Such an expectation clearly constitutes an important principle of good administration.

Nevertheless, the PCA has generally been cautious with regard to the line between ministerial policy and administration. Likewise, he has exercised restraint in the examination of departmental rules. He has acknowledged the distinction between rules that amount to delegated legislation, which cannot be questioned as to their substance, and those that do not have this status, and made a further distinction in the latter category between rules which are concerned with departmental policy and those concerned with procedure. Where policy rules are concerned, the PCA is unwilling to question the substance of the rules. However, procedural rules are not shown the same respect. They, after all, 'provide the nucleus of the concept of maladministration',[14] and their substance has on occasions been examined and found wanting. The office of the PCA, equipped with the necessary statutory powers and administrative experience, is in fact in 'a unique position to determine whether particular pieces of procedural guidance . . . conform to accepted minimum standards of administrative procedure.'[15] In particular its right of access to departmental papers means that it is not hindered in its determination by the guidance or rules being unpublished.

The most common instances of maladministration are those concerning unreasonable delay or a failure of communication.[16] Both these failures of administration take a number of forms which vary in severity and extensiveness. Cases of delay which the PCA has held to be unreasonable include delay in answering letters or queries, in processing applications or claims, and in paying out benefit,[17] all of which were found to constitute maladministration. Maladministration has

---

[11] Sel. Cttee on PCA, HC 270, (1994–5), Q1. The refusal of the department to accept the Report's conclusions resulted in the PCA using his power under s. 10(3), PCA Act 1967, to lay a special report before Parliament. This was only the second time the power had been used.

[12] Ibid.   [13] Ibid. para.20.

[14] A. Mowbray, 'Parliamentary Commissioner and administrative guidance' (1987) *PL* 570 at 579.

[15] Ibid.

[16] Sel. Cttee on PCA, HC 480, (1975–6) and PCA, HC 257, (1982–3).

[17] See, e.g., PCA, HC 62 (1989–90), para. 12, regarding delay both in paying benefit to a pregnant young woman and in seeking a ruling from headquarters on 'severe hardship provision'.

also arisen in relation to investigations where the PCA has found unreasonable delay in concluding an investigation into tax liability[18] and in the communication of the outcome of an investigation to the individual concerned, something that the Select Committee on the PCA considered to be contrary to 'an obligation, under the principles of good administration, to convey their decision with reasonable dispatch.'[19]

In addition, the PCA has criticized as unreasonable delays in dealing with representations made on behalf of an immigrant who was being investigated[20] and in the investigation of a miscarriage of justice.[21] Unreasonable delay is particularly disturbing where the liberty of an individual is concerned. It is also disturbing when it relates to appeal cases. Here the PCA has found that departments have been tardy in sending the necessary papers for appeal and have delayed making, or in some instances failed to make, a formal decision regarding appeal.[22] Such actions, or rather inactions, conflict with the right of the individual to justice, as does a delay or failure to give effect to tribunal findings, of which the PCA has also been critical in his investigations.[23] These delays or failures are also contrary to any implied right the individual may have to good administration.

The other most common finding of maladministration, a failure of communication, provides an extensive range of failures which in terms of the Crossman list may be attributed to neglect, inattention, incompetence, ineptitude or turpitude and may amount to actions which, in accordance with JUSTICE's recommendations, can be described as unreasonable or unjust. In many instances such a failure arises from giving 'inaccurate or inadequate advice', or making 'incorrect or inadequate replies to letters'.[24] More specifically, the PCA has been critical of failures to give sufficiently detailed explanations,[25] to publish rules in reasonable time,[26] to make publicly available any existing provisions for compensation,[27] and to advise of possible changes to compensation schemes.[28]

The PCA has also expressed concern about telephone conversations that give the wrong impression,[29] forms and leaflets written by the department which are not as helpful as they should be,[30] and a failure to give sufficient notice of proposed changes in the distribution of grants.[31] Further criticisms have been levelled at the failure to keep information leaflets up to date,[32] to answer questions fully,[33] to provide prisoners with comprehensive information on their rights,[34] and

---

[18] PCA, HC 257, (1982–3), paras. 26–8.   [19] PCA, HC 116 (1976–7).
[20] PCA, HC 301, (1988–9), para. 59.   [21] PCA, HC 191, (1983–4), para. 67, and above, n. 16.
[22] PCA, HC 62, (1989–90), para. 27.   [23] Ibid.
[24] Sel. Cttee on PCA, HC 480 (1975–6).
[25] Sel. Cttee on PCA, HC 322, (1983–4), paras. 38–9; failing to explain in sufficient detail how to qualify for foreign income tax deduction.
[26] PCA, HC 116, (1976–7) paras. 27–30.   [27] PCA, HC 666 (1977–8).
[28] PCA, HC 275, (1985–6), para. 44.   [29] PCA, HC 257, (1982–3), para. 14.
[30] Ibid.   [31] Sel. Cttee on PCA, HC 64 (1993–4); housing grant repairs.
[32] PCA, HC 275, (1985–6), para. 18.   [33] Ibid., para. 80.
[34] Particularly their right to have their case reviewed for release on licence; PCA, HC 307, (1994–5).

to communicate to a claimant that an investigation has been concluded or dropped.[35] Failures of communication which constitute maladministration are not confined to external situations. They can also occur within a department, as when an office of the then Department of Health and Social Security took a restrictive view of departmental instructions without seeking clarification or checking with other departmental offices as to how they should be interpreted.[36] The lack of communication produced inconsistency and injustice to those claimants using the office concerned.

Whilst delay and failure of communication provide the main categories of maladministration, they are not exclusive. Cases brought to the PCA also include 'individual errors, mistakes and oppressive behaviour',[37] a failure to apply the rules[38] or to take account of legal advice,[39] and breaches in confidentiality. The PCA has also reported instances of bias, where, in concurrence with the courts, he has held that it is 'not enough . . . that officials' actions should be free of bias. They need to be seen to be free of bias.'[40] Similarly, he has been critical of a denial of natural justice in regulatory or licensing situations, where an individual's livelihood is at stake, requiring, like the courts, that the person affected should know the case against him and be provided with 'a full and fair opportunity of answering the case.'[41]

These instances of maladministration demonstrate a close affinity between the expectations of the PCA and the courts with regard to the administrative process. They are based on considerations of equity, fairness, justice and reasonableness. However, whilst the individual examples of maladministration can frequently be accommodated within the grounds for review used by the courts—illegality, irrationality, and procedural impropriety—the standard sought by the PCA goes beyond that upheld as law by judges and would seem to be 'an amalgam of administrative and legal norms'.[42] Meeting this standard may therefore require administrators not simply to apply the relevant statute but, in addition, to be prepared to mitigate its effect if it produces an unjust result in an individual case.[43] It may also require the giving of reasons, explanations, information, and accurate advice as well as a level of behaviour which is considerate and polite. Many of these requirements would not be given legal effect by a court but '[t]he concept of maladministration and the Office of the Ombudsman exists precisely to deal with executive actions, which, whilst not illegal, manifestly fail to provide the standards of service which the public expect.'[44]

---

[35] Sel. Cttee on PCA, HC 290, (1994–5), Q19.

[36] PCA, HC 248, (1986–7), para. 14–17.   [37] PCA, HC 205, (1978–9).

[38] PCA, HC 116, (1976–7), para. 25.   [39] Sel. Cttee on PCA, HC 544, (1977–8).

[40] PCA, HC 569, (1992–3), para. 57.

[41] PCA, HC 116, (1976–7), paras. 14–16; concerned a decision of the DTI that an individual was unfit to act as a controller of a company.

[42] Mowbray (above, n. 14), at 579.   [43] PCA, HC 275, (1985–6), and HC 301, (1988–9).

[44] Mowbray (above, n. 14), at 579.

Put in positive terms the PCA's concern is the 'establishment of a general social right to good administration'.[45] This includes the right to have one's case dealt with accurately and promptly, the right to a reasoned decision which is communicated as quickly as possible; the right to justice, the access to which must be unimpeded; the right to a remedy; the right to accurate, adequate advice and information; the right to be treated according to known rules, together with the right to argue an exceptional case; and the right to be treated fairly and without bias. These rights are necessarily both reinforced and modified by the needs of society as a whole for equitable, consistent and coherent systems which carry public support and contribute to a 'contented society'.[46]

Efficiency and Cost-Cutting

The PCA's view of good administration includes an expectation of efficiency, although he has recognized that equity and efficiency can be 'mutually antagonistic abstractions'[47] and that any gain in efficiency may be at the expense of equity. As a result, on the one hand, the need for equitable arrangements between citizens produces a complex set of rules 'which creates enormous difficulties for the administrator and adds to the probability of error in applying the law',[48] while on the other, the requirements of efficiency suggest a simplification of the system, which would have the effect of undermining the equitable principles on which it is built. For the PCA there is 'no practical escape from the dilemma . . . One can only try to balance the opposing forces, to contain the inevitable mistakes and to have a good system for investigating allegations of error and providing a remedy when the allegations are well-founded.'[49] The PCA's concern for equity thus outweighs that for efficiency and inevitably impedes cost-cutting.

As far back as 1980 the PCA was exercised by the cuts in expenditure on public services. In his report for that year he noted that as yet no hardships caused by the 'economies' had come to light.[50] Nevertheless he recognized that 'it may be that for a time we shall need to learn to accept that standard of public service which we can afford as a nation, rather than that which we demand as individuals.'[51] The reduction in resources has had obvious implications for the administrative process and the standard at which it operates, a fact accepted by the PCA who stated that he would not criticize a department whose deficiencies were caused by under-resourcing, providing officials were doing their best. He did say, however, that it would 'still . . . be my function to test the validity of economic necessity as an excuse for lowered standards.'[52]

The apparent acceptance by the PCA of expenditure cuts as an excuse for administrative failings would seem to be limited to those requirements of good

---

[45] Ibid. at 580.
[48] Ibid.
[51] Ibid., para. 7.

[46] PCA, HC 148, (1980–1), para. 6.
[49] Ibid.
[52] Ibid., para. 8.

[47] Ibid., para. 3.
[50] Ibid., para. 6.

administration affected by a reduction in personnel. It is unlikely that unfair or unequitable treatment would pass the PCA's validity test of economic necessity. Increased waiting lists and delays caused by a backlog of correspondence may, on the other hand, be a direct consequence of a reduction of staff. Indeed, the following year the PCA found that unacceptable delay was due to budgetary restrictions not maladministration.[53]

However, in his Report for 1983 he expressed concern that Departments saw delay as an inevitable consequence of the limitation on resources and stressed the continuing importance of promptness of action, warning, 'there are areas where unreasonable delay is seen as a denial of justice'.[54] He was clearly alarmed that the situation could only deteriorate further, noting, 'if resources have to be reduced some of the functions of the public service must be correspondingly reduced either in quantity or quality. It cannot always be the case that by working harder a shrinking Civil Service can maintain both.'[55] His fear would seem to have been that if the programme of cuts continued, the only way outputs in terms of quantity could be maintained would be at the expense of the process. This would inevitably reduce the quality of the service, which, he believed, was not what the public wanted. He suggested that there was 'a discernible order of priority of services at any rate in the mind of the ordinary citizen. And although good organisation and leadership can effect great economies in the provision of a public service, there comes a point at which these services cannot be maintained or improved without the application of funds.'[56]

The PCA's concern was that the standard of administration was being affected by cost-cutting exercises and by the needs of efficiency, a concern that was heightened by the replacement of people by computers, despite the fact that '[p]eople may well prefer to deal with human beings who make mistakes than with machines who cannot be addressed.'[57] For the outgoing PCA (Sir Cecil Clothier) it is clear that good administration was about more than procedures and accuracy. It was about the relationship between those who administer public services and their client groups and was a product of the values and understandings underlying public service which, he was concerned, technology could not encapsulate. Hence his conclusion: 'So if a contented society is one aim of good administration, money may be as well spent on personal relations as on computers.'[58]

Next Steps Executive Agencies

Improving the relationship of those who administer public services with their users or customers has been an important aspect of Next Steps executive agencies. However, the main focus has been on increasing efficiency in terms of value for money. This at times results in agencies undertaking their own cost-cutting

---

[53] PCA, HC 258, (1981–2), para. 29. [54] Sel. Cttee on PCA, HC 322, (1983–4), para. 6.
[55] Ibid. [56] Ibid., para. 4. [57] Ibid., para. 5. [58] Ibid.

exercises and, whilst the PCA has made it clear that he is unlikely to find malad-ministration when a reduction in resources is responsible for a lowering of stan-dards, he is not necessarily tolerant of all cost-cutting practices. This was evident in his response to a complaint about a Benefits Office which was only answering incoming calls between 9.00 a.m. and 2.00 p.m. He considered 'such restrictions on public access is warranted in only very exceptional circumstances' and he upheld the complainant's grievance that 'limiting telephone calls to the most expensive time of the day, particularly as many claimants were hard up and there was a reduction in the counter service, was unreasonable.'[59]

The establishment of Next Steps agencies did not require an extension to the jurisdiction of the PCA. Their position within departments meant that they remained within his investigative remit. The PCA has broadly welcomed their introduction, considering 'the general thesis of setting up these agencies [to be] . . . right; that the responsibility for getting things effectively administered lies with those who are nearer the customers.'[60] The Select Committee on the PCA sug-gested that the level of the complaints referred to the PCA would be a good indi-cator of how effectively the agencies were performing.[61] The aim from the agency point of view is to 'try to avoid complaints going to [the PCA] by giving a better service in the first place and getting Members and members of the public to deal with local office managers and district office managers.'[62] If a complaint does reach the PCA, then agency officials should 'learn from it and respond positively to it',[63] thereby increasing customer satisfaction and efficiency.

The most controversial Next Steps agency in terms of complaints has been the CSA. The Agency was set up in April 1993 under the Child Support Act 1991. By the end of 1994 the PCA had received complaints from ninety-five Members of Parliament.[64] Indeed, so many referrals were made to the PCA that it was neces-sary for him to come to a policy decision not to pursue them all. He decided: '[I]t was not the best use of my resources to investigate additional individual com-plaints unless either they involved aspects of CSA's work which had not previ-ously been drawn to my attention, or the complainant had been caused actual financial loss.'[65] He stated he had taken 'the view that investigation of a number of representative cases should identify any administrative shortcomings that needed to be remedied and that any resulting improvements to the system should bring general benefits in which others should share.'[66]

This explanation by the PCA of his policy decision clearly indicated an accep-tance of a dual role which was concerned with mistake avoidance, through the cor-rection of individual grievances, and with the improvement of administrative practice in accordance with his view of good administration. This latter role would

[59] PCA, HC 569, (1992–3), para. 30.   [60] Sel. Cttee on PCA, HC 368, (1990–1), para. 24.
[61] Ibid.
[62] Sir Michael Partridge, Perm. Sec., DSS, in evidence to Sel. Cttee on PCA, HC 368, (1990–1), Q74.
[63] M. Bichard, CE Benefits Agency, in evidence to Sel. Cttee on PCA, HC 368, (1990–1), Q72.
[64] PCA, HC 307, (1994–5).   [65] Ibid., para. 29.   [66] Ibid.

seem to have become more prominent in recent years, either because the PCA has become more confident in the exercise of his office, or because he has become increasingly concerned that standards in administration are being compromised by the need to cut costs.

The failures within the Agency, which came within the remit of the PCA, included, 'mistaken identity, inadequate procedures, failure to answer correspondence, incorrect or misleading advice, delay in the assessment and review of child support maintenance and in its payment to the parent with care.'[67] The PCA was particularly critical of the failure of the Department of Social Security (DSS) to undertake a pilot scheme and of the 'heinous' delays which had resulted in a unmanageable backlog of cases. He subsequently concluded, 'The lesson which I drew from this episode was that maladministration leading to an injustice is likely to arise when a new administrative task is not tested first by a pilot project; when new staff, perhaps inadequately trained, form a substantial fraction of the workforce; where procedures and technology supporting them are untried and where quality of service is subordinated to sheer throughput.'[68]

This condemnation of the administration of the CSA indicated that whilst sensitive to the needs of efficiency and the reduction of costs, the PCA will not allow their consideration to outweigh the traditional principles upon which his view of good administration is based. His criticisms were reinforced by the Select Committee on the PCA which took the unusual step of questioning a minister on the contents of the PCA's Report. The Committee was concerned by the degree of maladministration and by the fact that targets for benefit savings were given priority over quality of service; indeed, that there were no effective quality targets in place. It therefore recommended that 'the Government review its policy on the setting of targets in the light of the failures of the CSA. Targets should place efficient service to the public before savings to the Treasury.'[69] It concluded, 'We are in no doubt that maladministration in the CSA cannot be divorced from the responsibility of Ministers for the framework within which it operated.'[70] In other words, the policy was such that failings in administration were inevitable. The benefit-saving target was too high and this had a 'direct effect on the lack of quality in the system so the majority of assessments turned out wrong because staff were under pressure to get throughput through the system.'[71]

By the time the Reports were published, the Government had already made significant changes in the Agency. These included replacing its Chief Executive, modifying the formula used for making assessments, and reducing the benefit-saving target. However, it refused to give quality targets a higher priority than saving money, arguing that '[i]t would not be sensible to ignore value for money for the taxpayer and the level of service to the public generally must rank with service to the Agency's customers.'[72] Such a response suggests that when conflicts arise

[67] Ibid., para. 30. [68] Ibid., para. 31. [69] PCA, HC 135, (1994–5), para. 15.
[70] Ibid., para. 27. [71] Dr Tony Wright MP, Ibid., Q108.
[72] Cm. 2865, (1994–5) para. 13.

between cost-cutting and good administration, the latter is likely to be the casualty. This reflects a fundamental difference between the Government, attuned to a new public management model of administration, and the PCA, whose view owes more to the public service model. It also confirms that the recommendation of the PCA in 1978 that Departments 'might . . . consider putting more of their resources into achieving fair and humane administration' belongs to another age.[73]

Contracting Out

The PCA not only has jurisdiction over administrative functions being carried out by departments and specified public bodies, but also over those functions carried out on their behalf. As a result, the work of the PCA 'sometimes involves looking into the actions of bodies which, though themselves outside [his] jurisdiction, are effectively brought within it because of arrangements under which they act as agents for a government department.'[74] So, for instance, the PCA has jurisdiction over British Telecom's responsibility for monitoring amateur radio. Interestingly and disturbingly, in an investigation into the administration of this responsibility the PCA found '[T]heir performance had not been of the standard to be expected of officers acting as agents of the Home Office and dealing with the public.'[75] Such a finding gives grounds for the suggestion that the standards to which the private sector operates are different from those of the public sector. This is to be expected but causes concern when the private sector is employed to carry out public functions and when managers from the private sector, together with private sector methods, are imported into the public service.

The jurisdiction of the PCA, with regard to administrative functions which are contracted-out, had generally been presumed unaffected because these functions are being carried out on behalf of departments. This was explicitly confirmed by the Deregulation and Contracting Out Act 1994. Nevertheless, the PCA sees contracting-out as having considerable practical implications for his investigations,[76] particularly because he has no jurisdiction to investigate the actual contracts themselves, the PCA Act specifically excluding 'contractual and other commercial transactions'.[77] As a result problems may arise if the substance of a complaint or grievance is related to the terms of the contract.

The PCA and the Select Committee on the PCA have regularly recommended that 'contractual and other commercial transactions' should be within the remit of the PCA. In 1988 the outgoing Ombudsman[78] noted that the wording of the exclusion had been 'the cause of some concern and difficulty'.[79] This was because 'the dealings of departments and public bodies with citizens qua citizens, can in some

---

[73] PCA, HC 205, (1978–9).
[75] Ibid.
[77] PCA Act 1967, Sched. 3, para. 9.
[79] PCA, HC 301, (1988–9), para. 3.

[74] PCA, HC 257, (1982–3), para. 41.
[76] PCA, HC 290, (1993–4).
[78] A. R. Barrowclough.

instances take on the appearance—and perhaps the reality—of "contractual . . . transactions".' The PCA saw this as being the position with many of the non-departmental public bodies brought within his jurisdiction by the Parliamentary and Health Service Commissioners Act, 'whose functions will often include the giving of aid or assistance on terms which may have a contractual flavour'.[80] He considered that the position needed clarification, a point which has also been made by others critical of the limitation.[81] Such clarification seems even more important with the steady move towards government by contract.

However, the Government has neither clarified the position nor accepted that such matters should be within the jurisdiction of the PCA. In 1993 it gave one of its reasons as being that 'those in a contractual relationship with Government have recourse to a court of law if they have a grievance, under the laws of contract'.[82] It is interesting to compare the Government's enthusiasm for the courts as arbiter when the matter is one of private law with its resistance to judicial review. This suggests that it sees an advantage in grievances being contractual rather than related to public law rights or even to maladministration. The other reasons given by the Government for the exclusion of contractual and commercial transactions from the jurisdiction of the PCA were that 'it would be inappropriate for the PCA to review the commercial judgment of departments and other bodies within his jurisdiction', and that '[i]n the commercial and contractual field departments are not performing a function peculiar to Government. Singling out the Government's commercial operations for scrutiny could place departments at a unique disadvantage in their commercial activities.'[83]

Some would argue that such scrutiny would act as a minor counterbalance to the advantage the government has as a contracting party and that, in any case, because of its power and responsibilities, government should not be treated as just another contractor. As Patrick Birkenshaw states, 'The point is that it *is* exercise of power of government that is in question, but a power that is exercised through the medium of contract.'[84] As a result of the exclusion of the PCA, this power is 'inadequately supervised',[85] for whilst the C & AG has jurisdiction to conduct value for money audits, there can be no investigation to determine whether a contract has been allocated fairly, equitably and with propriety.

Moreover the possibility exists that as long as contractual arrangements remain outside the jurisdiction of the PCA, departments will seek to blame the contractor for shortcomings. This, according to the PCA (Sir William Reid) 'would be wholly unacceptable'.[86] In 1992 the PCA reported that so far he had 'not experienced any difficulty' from market-testing and contracting-out policies. However, he had noticed that 'some things' had been removed from his jurisdiction and he

---

[80] Ibid.
[81] E.g. Sel. Cttee on PCA, HC 615, (1977–8); HC 544, (1977–8); HC 593 (1979–80) and HC 322, (1983–4).
[82] Cabinet Office, Memorandum to Sel. Cttee on PCA, HC 33–II, (1993–4), 201. [83] Ibid.
[84] P. Birkenshaw, *Grievances, Remedies and the State* 200. [85] Ibid.
[86] Sel. Cttee on PCA, HC 64, (1993–4), para. 18.

warned that if contracting-out 'led to certain matters going outside my jurisdiction, and thereby depriving citizens of the right to complain and have their complaints investigated, I should be very disturbed indeed.'[87]

The task of the PCA has clearly become more complex as government has become fragmented. Moreover, according to him, 'practical difficulties' may arise as a result of this fragmentation and 'the resulting lack of familiarity with [his] ... role' regarding contracting-out.[88] Thus whilst the PCA has become more important as a mechanism for ensuring standards of good administration across the breadth of government and quasi-government, there are significant gaps in his jurisdiction. These the Government refuse to fill. This would seem to confirm a less than wholehearted commitment to good administration. It would seem that good administration, as supported by the PCA, becomes a secondary consideration when it is inconvenient because it interferes with the Government's freedom to contract, or costs money.

The Citizen's Charter

The apparent carelessness of the Government with regard to good administration in some ways conflicts with the development of the Citizen's Charter which has focused attention on the meeting of specified standards and upon the need for an adequate complaints system if these standards are not fulfilled. The PCA has viewed the Citizen's Charter and its offspring charters positively, 'The Charters will help to provide me with some useful yardsticks against which I can measure whether the actions of the department or the agency concerned amount to maladministration.'[89] However, he was clear that Charter standards did not fetter him in any way: 'They will not be the determinant of maladministration'.[90] This is an important assertion by the PCA. There is otherwise a danger that maladministration might be confined to the failure of Charter standards with the consequence that good administration would correspondingly be defined in terms of Charter requirements.

In 1993 the PCA clarified his view of the relationship between maladministration and published Charter standards. He made a distinction between those targets which are expressed as mandatory and those which are 'persuasive indicators' and considered that where mandatory targets were concerned, the case for compensatory redress was strong. Otherwise, cases would be judged on their merits with targets being 'taken as indicators of a satisfactory or unsatisfactory performance'.[91] The division made by the PCA is a useful one distinguishing those targets which provide the individual with a substantive right, for example, the right of appeal to an internal review body, the right to a decision, the right to reasons,

---

[87] Sel. Cttee on PCA, HC 64, (1993–4), para. 18, Q38.
[88] Sel. Cttee on PCA, HC 345, (1993–4).   [89] PCA, HC 347, (1991–2), para. 8.
[90] Ibid.   [91] Sel. Cttee on PCA, HC 345, (1993–4), para. 12.

from those concerned with responsiveness and politeness. It could provide a possible blueprint for justiciability in the future. The approach by the PCA was approved by the Select Committee. The Committee also wanted to see departments involved in making their own investigations into maladministration, suggesting that 'if a complaint to a department reveals the failure to meet a Charter target that department should as a matter of course examine whether maladministration has contributed to that failure. If it has, the complainant should be offered suitable redress.'[92] Such a process and the linking of Charter standards directly to maladministration would provide Charters with greater importance, removing the criticism that they are simply a public relations exercise.

Between 1989 and 1994 complaints to the PCA rose by 46 per cent.[93] The PCA considered the increase was due to the 'expectations stimulated by various Government Departmental and Agency charters which, in the complainant's eyes at least, have not been justified. It is the gap between hope and performances which is the largest single factor in evoking more complaints.'[94] He also thought 'charterism'—a greater willingness to complain—could have been a factor. For its part the Government has expressed the hope that the Charter emphasis on internal complaints procedure will actually diminish the workload of the PCA.[95] However, both the PCA and the Select Committee have reservations about this emphasis and have indicated their belief that internal procedures must be backed by access for the citizen to an independent and powerful investigator who will intervene if internal procedures prove inadequate.[96] Even where independent adjudicators are appointed, as for instance for the Inland Revenue, Customs and Excise, and the Prison Service, the PCA and the Select Committee still see it as essential that Charters indicate the role of the PCA. They were therefore critical of the Charter on the Prison Service for its lack of a reference to the PCA's powers to consider appropriate complaints[97] and of the CSA, which was criticized 'most strongly for the omission of any reference to the Ombudsman in its complaints literature'.[98]

The role of the PCA in reinforcing internal complaints structures was also acknowledged as fundamental by Mr William Waldegrave, the minister in charge of launching the Charter initiative. He said, 'Every organization should seek to have the structures to put things right itself but those things will not necessarily work unless people know that looking over their shoulder is a powerful external voice which can draw attention to ultimate failings if there still are failings.'[99] Despite this recognition of the importance of the PCA (and the apparent ability of Mr Waldegrave to combine visual and aural faculties in a unique way), the Government has refused to provide his Office with additional resources to reduce the throughput time of investigations. This is seen as too long by many MPs.[100]

[92] Ibid.
[93] Sel. Cttee on PCA, HC 112, (1993–4).
[94] PCA, HC 569, (1992–3), paras. 2–3.
[95] Sel. Cttee on PCA, HC 158, (1991–2), Q49.
[96] Sel. Cttee on PCA, HC 33–I, (1993–4).
[97] Sel. Cttee on PCA, HC 33–II, (1993–4), 47.
[98] PCA, HC 307, (1994–5), para. 29.
[99] Sel. Cttee on PCA, HC 33–II, (1993–4), Q674.
[100] R. Gregory & J. Pearson, 'The Parliamentary Ombudsman after twenty-five years' (1992) 70 *Pub. Admin.* 4 at 492.

At the end of 1990 it was on average thirteen months and ten days and the Select Committee on the PCA considered the time taken was undermining the effectiveness of the PCA.[101] It recommended that the Government should formally accept 'the target of reducing the throughput time of investigations to nine months and make the appropriate allocation of resources.'[102]

This would seem a modest target. However, the Government refused to commit more resources to the PCA and countered by suggesting that if the PCA undertook a review of the working methods of his Office, this would increase efficiency and effectiveness sufficiently to produce the required reduction in throughput time without the need for additional resources.[103] In practice, such a reduction might not in any case change the attitude of MPs towards the usefulness of the PCA for 'even nine months is a period of a quite different order from the time taken by other grievance-handling mechanisms available to MPs.'[104]

The Government also refused to implement the recommendation that the Office of Public Service, responsible for Charters, should ensure that all departments and agencies make 'proper mention of the Commissioner in their complaints literature prior to its publication', stating that such oversight 'would not be consistent with policy on the delegation of management authority'.[105] It therefore remains a matter for individual agencies as to whether, or how, the PCA is described in their literature. The failure of the Government to accept either recommendation of the Select Committee casts doubt over its commitment to provide a complaints procedure which is subject to effective external scrutiny. As a result it would seem that scrutiny by the PCA is likely to be patchy and at times merely symbolic, the PCA lacking the resources and the publicity to provide effective oversight.

The Redress of Grievances

A particular issue in relation to Charters which has been addressed by both the PCA and the Select Committee is the redress of grievances. A finding by the PCA of maladministration is usually linked to a recommendation for some form of redress. The remedy sought will depend upon the extent of personal injustice that has resulted from the maladministration and the circumstances of the case. The PCA has noted, 'Sometimes all that is required is an apology, coupled with the assurance that the department will take steps to avoid similar errors in future. In other cases some financial loss is involved and an ex gratia payment may be

---

[101] Sel. Cttee on PCA, HC 33–I, (1993–4), paras. 13 & 19.   [102] Ibid.

[103] Sel. Cttee on PCA, HC 46, (1993–4), iv. The booklet, *The Ombudsman in your Files*, produced by the Cabinet Office in 1995, states that in 1994 the average time taken for an investigation and report was 70 weeks 4 days (page 12). Thus the time taken has increased since 1990, although the stated target remains 39 weeks (9 months).

[104] Gregory & Pearson (above, n. 100), at 492.

[105] Sel. Cttee on PCA (above n. 103). Resources were increased when the PCA's jurisdiction was extended to include the Code on Access to Government Information.

needed. And on occasions a department's procedures or standing instructions are found to be deficient and I recommend their overhaul.'[106]

Recommendations regarding departmental procedures and practices are made when the PCA knows, or suspects, that a failure of administration was not confined to a single case but likely to be widespread. Such recommendations, aimed at preventing instances of maladministration in future, further the cause of good administration. They may concern an improvement in record-keeping,[107] the importance of which was demonstrated to the Home Office when the PCA held that in the absence of records, the balance of any doubt would be resolved in favour of the complainant.[108] They may suggest improving claims forms or explanatory leaflets to provide a better dissemination of information[109] or the logging of complaints.[110] Such recommendations are frequently made after discussions with the department concerned. For example, the PCA reported that, after having found a failure by the Benefits Agency to consider all the evidence when ruling on entitlement to severe disability premium, the Agency was looking at further measures to reduce the risk of relevant information not being considered. One such measure would be 'the automatic issue of a request for information whenever there was understood to be the possibility of an entitlement to severe disability premium.'[111] The PCA also obtained an agreement from the Agency that in the future it would ensure that any claimant being investigated for fraud would be told when the investigation was concluded or dropped.[112]

However, whilst the PCA may affect the way in which a particular department or agency operates, bringing it more closely in line with principles of good administration, his recommendations may have only a narrow effect. His Reports have not traditionally been disseminated in the way that those of the Health Service Ombudsman are. This has led to suggestions by the Select Committee on the PCA that his Reports be circulated to all government departments and that the attention of civil servants should be drawn to matters of concern and examples of good practice.[113] In addition, the Committee recommended that 'the Ombudsman's office itself should produce occasional publications on good administration',[114] a watered-down version of JUSTICE's recommendation that the PCA should prepare a Code on Good Administrative Practice.[115] Subsequently, the Government has started to circulate epitomes of the Ombudsman cases and the Office of Public Service and the PCA have produced a booklet for civil servants, entitled *The Ombudsman in your Files*, a companion to *The Judge over your Shoulder*.[116]

---

[106] PCA, HC 257, (1982–3).

[107] E.g. PCA, HC 275, (1985–6), para. 65; Office of Fair Trading.

[108] PCA, HC 363, (1987–8), para. 51; lack of immigration records. *Ombudsman in Your Files* also stresses the importance of keeping records (page 17).

[109] PCA HC 301, (1988–9), para. 46; recommendation to MAFF and Welsh Office that farmers should be given information to enable them to guard against the risk of claims forms being lost in the post.

[110] Sel. Cttee of PCA, HC 387, (1992–3), para. 35.   [111] PCA, HC 290, (1993–4), para. 35.

[112] Ibid., para. 37.   [113] Sel. Cttee on PCA, HC 33–I, (1993–4), paras. 33–4.

[114] Ibid., para. 40.   [115] Ibid., para. 44.   [116] See ch. 5, n. 66.

This may increase the extent to which the investigations of the PCA affect public administration. However, even then any general benefit to the administrative process is by way of 'a spin-off benefit'.[117] This is because the role of the PCA is reactive and his central concern is with the individual and his or her grievance. It is this that provides the catalyst for investigations into maladministration. As a consequence, recommendations for the reform or improvement of administrative practices are made as a basis for the redress of that grievance, even if their effect is wider and intended to prevent a recurrence. The PCA does little to reinforce the principles of good administration for their own sake. This has led to suggestions that the PCA should take a more proactive role, undertaking investigations into departmental failures of a general nature rather than just in relation to individual grievances.[118] However, this would require more resources which are clearly not forthcoming. The PCA therefore remains constrained as to what he can do.

Usually departments co-operate with the recommendations of the PCA, although the Select Committee has expressed a desire 'that the public bodies and departments reported upon should be required to publish a report to the Ombudsman describing the ways in which the maladministration and failures of service identified have been rectified.'[119] This would lay a greater obligation upon departments; not only must they agree to consider their procedures, they must actually do so. It is obviously easier to determine whether departments have complied with the recommendations of the PCA when these have involved paying compensation or making *ex gratia* payments. Such payments are intended to rectify situations where individuals have suffered financial loss as a result of maladministration and frequently provide a remedy beyond that required by law. An example of such a remedy arose out of the investigation into the DSS's handling of an underpayment of benefit. The DSS had made mistakes in its calculation of benefit with the result that there had been long-term underpayment. When the cases were reassessed, the benefit was only backdated for fifty-two weeks, all that was required by statute. The PCA considered that this had resulted in 'palpable injustice' which should be remedied by making *ex gratia* payments.[120]

Where compensation is concerned, departments are less able to fudge their compliance with the PCA's recommendations than when the recommendations concern procedural changes, and a department wishing to avoid making the monetary payments recommended by the PCA may therefore contest his Report. There have been a number of occasions when the Government has shown a reluctance to make such payments, one of the most notable instances relating to the Barlow Clowes affair.[121] Barlow Clowes was an investment company, licensed by the

---

[117] Prof. Moore, Chair, Administrative Law Committee, in evidence to Sel. Cttee on PCA, HC 33–II, (1993–4), Q298.

[118] C. Harlow, 'Ombudsman in search of a role' (1978) 41 *MLR* 446; G. Drewry & C. Harlow, 'A cutting edge?' (1990) 53 *MLR* 745.

[119] Sel. Cttee on PCA, HC 33–II, (1993–4), para. 34.

[120] PCA, HC 275, (1985–6), para. 13.

[121] For full account see R. Gregory & G. Drewry, 'The Barlow Clowes Affair' (1991) *PL* 192 at 408.

Department of Trade and Industry (DTI), which went into liquidation with the result that some 18,000 investors lost their money. An investigation by the PCA found there had been 'significant maladministration' on five counts which, he considered, made the Government liable for compensation.[122] In an effort to avoid this liability, the Government contested the PCA's view of what constituted maladministration. It took advantage of the lack of a statutory definition of 'maladministration' and held that the way in which the PCA had applied the term was inappropriate for the regulatory activities of the DTI, stating, 'In the Government's view, the department's handling of the case was within the acceptable range of standards reasonably to be expected of a regulator.'[123]

In the event the PCA persevered, 'altogether unconvinced' by the Government's argument.[124] He insisted that the failure of the DTI to adequately consider the viability of the scheme offered by Barlow Clowes and the delay in responding to the evidence available was an indication of serious shortcomings within the department which amounted to maladministration. Political pressure from Members of Parliament, whose constituents had been affected by the crash of the companies, did the rest and the Government yielded, providing £150m in *ex gratia* payments.

There was a similar attempt to avoid monetary payments when the PCA was critical of the Welsh Office's failure to give sufficient notice to local authorities of the date of a change in the housing repair grant from 75 per cent to 20 per cent. Because of the lack of notice, some potential applicants needlessly missed the higher rate of grant and the PCA considered they should be compensated. The Government contested the conclusions of the PCA on the basis that the relevant statute did not impose a duty to give such forewarning of a change in the grant. The Select Committee of the PCA noted, 'The quibbling over the term "maladministration" is at root an attempt to deny fault. This attempt we consider to have been prompted originally not by the merits of the case but by a narrow and legalistic view of the department's obligations to the public and a desire to avoid the payment of compensation.'[125]

This desire to avoid paying compensation was also evident in the Department of Transport's rejection of the PCA's report of the Channel Tunnel rail link on the grounds that he was acting outside his jurisdiction and concerning himself with matters of policy,[126] whilst the CSA refused to consider financial compensation in cases where it had incorrectly identified a parent unless there was medical evidence of damage to health attributable to the Agency's actions.[127]

The overall costs incurred by Government for maladministration are difficult to determine. As the PCA has commented, 'mistakes cost money . . . the cost may be either the payment of compensation or the administrative expenditure incurred in

[122] PCA, HC 76, (1989–90), para. 8.13.
[123] HC Debs., 19 Dec. 1989, col. 104 (N. Ridley, Sec. of State for DTI).
[124] PCA (above, n. 122) para. 8.21. [125] Sel. Cttee on PCA, HC 64, (1993–4), para. 26.
[126] PCA, HC 193, (1994–5). [127] Cm. 2865, (1994) para. 29.

giving repeated attention to a matter which was not handled properly in the first instance.'[128] The second cost may be impossible to calculate. As far as compensation payments are concerned, these are not confined just to instances where the PCA had made recommendations. Departments and agencies have compensation schemes which are activated internally when mistakes are found to have been made, although they are limited in the extent to which they can give monetary redress for maladministration without reference to the Treasury. The delegated limits of compensation varies considerably but all novel or contentious cases must be referred to the Treasury to prevent the setting of awkward precedents and to prevent extravagance in the granting of financial redress.

However, it would seem that few coherent records are kept on monetary payments which relate to maladministration, even though these would seem relatively straightforward. The Home Office told the Select Committee on the PCA that it did not have the ability to separate out complaints dealing with maladministration from other complaints. In relation to prisons it could 'give no statistical breakdown of financial redress granted because of an administrative error'.[129] Similarly with regard to the Passport Office, officials stated, 'Not all payments are due to maladministration but the information available does not show the number of cases in which compensation was awarded or categorize the circumstances.'[130] The lack of statistical information was justified on the basis that determining whether a complaint was one of maladministration would constitute too much bureaucratic effort.[131] However, it could be argued that the effort would be cost-effective if it reduced maladministration and thus complaints. In any case, good administration requires that agencies and departments pick up and correct patterns of maladministration, whether cost-effective or not. As the Select Committee on the PCA commented, 'if future individuals are not to have similar grievances, all departments and agencies must be able to monitor and learn from complaints.'[132]

The failure of departments to keep records of instances of maladministration suggests a lack of commitment by Government to the improvement of the administrative process for its own sake. This, coupled with instances where there has been a reluctance to provide redress in terms of financial compensation, reflects the preoccupation with saving money. This preoccupation is not shared by the PCA, who 'see[s] as vital the need to deal fairly with all, to keep adequate records and appropriate audit trails and to show willingness in justified cases to offer redress when matters go wrong—even if at a financial penalty to those providing the service.'[133]

The advent of the Citizen's Charter has brought to the fore the debate about what constitutes adequate redress. The Select Committee on the PCA commented, 'The Citizen's Charter in 1991 promised "better redress for the citizen when things go wrong" '.[134] However, it continued: 'in recent years reports of the

---

[128] PCA, HC 762 vol. 5, (1994–5), i.
[130] Ibid., Q170.   [131] Ibid.
[133] PCA, HC 290, (1993–4), para. 8.

[129] Sel. Cttee for PCA, HC 112, (1993–4), Q165.
[132] Ibid., para. 16.
[134] Sel. Cttee for PCA, HC 112, (1993–4), para. 1.

Ombudsman and evidence taken by this Committee have revealed the inadequacy of much of the redress offered by departments and agencies . . . The Ombudsman . . . has done much to persuade departments to improve their procedures in the consideration of redress and their compensation to those adversely affected by maladministration. It is, however, apparent that many departments have yet to adopt practices of redress which adequately reflect Charter principles.'[135]

The Select Committee was particularly critical of the Guidance to departments on redress and *ex gratia* compensation[136] in which statements of principle are expressed in negative terms. Thus departments are reminded that 'by definition the complainant has no legal right to any compensation at all'[137] and, with reference to compensation for loss of earnings, '[i]f ex gratia compensation is felt to be justified, its aim should be to provide a lump-sum payment in general recognition of the injustice suffered as a result of maladministration . . . In general a lump-sum settlement amounting to more than 50% of the loss claimed is unlikely to be justified; and a lower figure might well be appropriate.'[138] In addition, the Guidance advises departments that any financial redress should be described as 'an ex gratia payment' rather than 'compensation', 'damages' or 'interest'. This, the Guidance states, 'helps to avoid any suggestion of an entitlement to interest and to preclude argument about proper interest rates.'[139]

The Select Committee stated that it was 'amazed that guidance on compensation should so cynically admit that a principle is designed to hoodwink the public' and thus make it impossible to determine whether the compensation is fair.[140] The lack of information as to how a sum of compensation has been arrived at makes an effective challenge on the basis of equity impossible. This was noted by the PCA in his investigation into the compensation awarded to farmers whose poultry flocks had had to be slaughtered, where the Ministry of Agriculture, Fisheries, and Food (MAFF) refused to divulge how it had calculated a 40 per cent compensation figure.[141] As the Select Committee commented, 'It may be convenient from the perspective of the official to avoid challenge by withholding information. It does not, however, sit happily with any notion of fairness or with the Government's welcome policy on openness.'[142]

The Select Committee was also concerned that the Guidance did not require departments to offer compensation to those, other than the complainant, who had also been affected by maladministration but confined itself to suggesting that departments 'should consider whether, in the interests of equity, they should offer compensation to others'.[143] The Select Committee considered this to be insufficient and recommended that 'it should be a clear instruction to departments

---

[135] Ibid.
[136] Contained in the 'Dear Accounting Officer' letter DAO(GEN) 15/92 and *Government Accounting*, ch. 36.
[137] Quoted in Sel. Cttee on PCA, HC 112, (1993–4), para. 6.
[138] Ibid.
[139] Ibid.
[140] Ibid., para. 56.
[141] Ibid., Q292.
[142] Ibid., para. 56.
[143] Ibid., para. 11.

and agencies to seek out others affected where maladministration comes to light and to grant them redress.'[144]

Overall, the Select Committee wished to see a more positive approach to the redress of grievances, believing this to accord with the spirit of the Citizen's Charter. It suggested that the review of the Guidance, which at that time was being undertaken by the Government, should include the statement of general principle given by the PCA, namely, that 'the person who has suffered injustice as a result of maladministration should be back in the same position as he or she would have been had things gone right in the first place.'[145] This would mean that lump sums, which often seem to be figures plucked from the air, would be replaced by reasoned calculations that are fair and equitable. The Select Committee noted, 'It is time to end the grudging and defensive culture so evident in current Guidance to departments'.[146]

It also recommended that the Guidance should adopt the PCA's 1993 statement on what constituted maladministration. This reiterated the Crossman list of 'bias, neglect, inattention, delay, incompetence, ineptitude, perversity, turpitude, arbitrariness, and so on'[147] but in the light of the experiences of the last twenty-five years and to accord with 'the language of the 1990s', added, 'rudeness (though that is a matter of degree); unwillingness to treat the complainant as a person with rights; refusal to answer reasonable questions; neglecting to inform a complainant on request of his or her rights of entitlement; knowingly giving advice which is misleading or inadequate; ignoring valid advice or overruling considerations which would produce an uncomfortable result for the overruler; offering no redress or manifestly disproportionate redress; showing bias whether because of colour, sex or any other grounds; omission to notify those who might lose a right of appeal; faulty procedures; failure by management to monitor compliance with adequate procedures; cavalier disregard of guidance which is intended to be followed in the interest of equitable treatment of those who use the service; partiality; and failure to mitigate the effects of rigid adherence to the letter of the law where that produces manifestly inequitable treatment.'[148]

In part this can be seen as a translation of Crossman's 1960s statement.[149] Public administration has moved on since then and so has the language attached to it. However, there are important amplifications, even additions, to the original description of maladministration and a change of emphasis. This can be transposed to provide certain standards of good administration which, although still concerned with equity, reasonableness and fairness, are to an extent expressed in terms of rights and centre upon the provision of appropriate information and upon

[144] Quoted in Sel. Cttee on PCA, HC 112, (1993–4), para. 12.   [145] Ibid., para. 7.
[146] Ibid, para. 70.   [147] HC Debs., col. 51, 18 Nov. 1996.
[148] Sel. Cttee for PCA, HC 112, (1993–4), (Statement in PCA, HC 290, (1993–94). This, together with the Crossman list (above, n. 4), is the statement of maladministration given in *Ombudsman in your Files*, although it is noted that 'neither of these lists is intended to be a comprehensive definition of maladministration.'
[149] Above, n. 4.

there being an adequate, and known, mechanism for the redress of grievances. This suggests that both the Citizen's Charter and the Code of Practice on Access to Government Information have had a significant impact upon the office of the PCA.

The Select Committee also recommended the establishment of a Redress Team within the Charter Unit to monitor and advise on the granting of redress within departments and agencies. This would lessen the domination of the Treasury and thus the preoccupation with cost at the expense of fairness and equity. The Select Committee considered that the Redress Team should be 'as concerned to promote equity as to protect funds'.[150] Moreover, equity should be encouraged across, as well as within, departments, for although complete consistency is unrealistic, 'it remains an essential aspect of any system of redress'.[151] The Select Committee concluded that the system of redress should include a section in every Charter 'in which the reader will find listed those standards which, if not met, entitle the citizen to redress, financial or otherwise', and it recommended that the Redress Team should 'conduct a survey of public services in all departments and agencies to identify those which are susceptible to schemes for financial and other redress.'[152]

The Government concurred with most of the recommendations and suggestions of the Select Committee, indicating a commitment to the redress of grievances which had previously seemed missing. This commitment accords with the thinking behind the Citizen's Charter whereby redress 'can be made to stimulate rather than detract from efficiency' by preventing the re-occurrence of mistakes.[153] However, there is still a reluctance to specify the nature of redress that will be available for a failure to meet a particular Charter standard, on the basis that what is appropriate 'may depend on other factors, e.g. the extent to which there has been a failure to meet a standard; whether the complainant has suffered financial loss as a result; whether the handling of the original complaint has been maladministration, etc.'[154] Thus the Government did not see it as 'useful or cost-effective to revise every Charter in order to list standards in the manner proposed'.[155] It did, however, state that when new charters were produced or existing ones revised, it would seek to make clear that users of the service are entitled to redress when Charter standards are not met.[156]

Doubt remains over the extent to which the Government is concerned with maladministration or simply Charter standards and as to whether the concern extends beyond increasing efficiency and cost-effectiveness to principles such as fairness and equity or whether these are only relevant as a means to an end. There is a clear tension between the thinking behind the Charter initiative and the Treasury, evident in Charter support for redress and the delegation of responsibility for providing it, and the Treasury's traditional resistance to financial compensation and delegated authority. Moreover, some doubt may be cast over the apparent

---

[150] Ibid, para. 34. [151] Ibid, para. 17. [152] Ibid, para. 70.
[153] See n. 135. [154] PCA, HC 316, (1994–5), para. 23. [155] Ibid.
[156] Ibid.

importance of the PCA with regard to grievance procedures. On the one hand, the Government has recognized him as a vital check on the administrative process and as a mechanism for ensuring that Charter standards are upheld. On the other, it has refused to increase his resources or to insist that all Charters detail his role. This suggests that whilst much preferred to the courts as a mechanism for external control, the PCA is still seen in a negative rather than a positive light. This accords with the new public management model's distrust of external review. The goal is for most complaints to be resolved internally without need for a reference to the PCA. Whether this is achieved or not, it might be that the complainant's energy becomes exhausted by the internal system, and thus no complaint to the PCA is made. Either way the PCA's importance regarding the redress of grievances in relation to the Citizen's Charter is diminished. Moreover, the Citizen's Charter may detract attention from wider requirements of good administration and there is concern that achieving Charter standards will in itself be seen as a hallmark of good administration.

The PCA and Freedom of Information

On 4 April 1994 the Code of Practice on Access to Government Information came into force. The Government stated that the Code was in support of its 'policy under the Citizen's Charter of extending access to official information, and responding to reasonable requests for information, except where disclosure would not be in the public interest.'[157] The connection between the Code and the PCA is apparent not just because he acts as adjudicator for the Code but because the Code's application is limited to departments and public bodies under his jurisdiction.[158] The aims of the Code are threefold; firstly, 'to improve policy-making and the democratic process by extending access to the facts and analyses which provide the basis for the consideration of proposed policy'; secondly, 'to protect the interests of individuals and companies by ensuring that reasons are given for administrative decisions'; thirdly, 'to support and extend the principles of public service established under the Citizen's Charter.'[159]

To give effect to these aims departments are committed to publishing the facts and analysis they consider relevant to major policy proposals and to make available material (for example rules, procedures, guidance) which aids understanding of the way in which a department relates to the public. They are also required, with some exceptions, to give reasons for administrative decisions to those affected and to publish the information required by the Citizen's Charter. This includes details about 'how public services are run, how much they cost, who is in charge, and what complaints and redress procedures are available' as well as information about 'what services are being provided, what targets are set, what standards of

---

[157] Code, Pt I, para. 1.   [158] Ibid., Pt II, para. 3.   [159] Ibid., Pt I, para. 2.

service are expected and the results achieved'.[160] Departments are also committed 'to release, in response to specific requests, information relating to their policies, actions and decisions and other matters related to their areas of responsibility.'[161]

There are inevitably exceptions to the release of information. Significantly, the section dealing with these exceptions is longer than the section requiring disclosure. The exceptions include information that would harm defence, security or international relations, or 'the frankness and candour of internal discussion'.[162] This precludes divulging proceedings of Cabinet or its committees, advice given by civil servants, matters relating to policy options, and confidential communications between departments, public bodies and regulatory agencies. Also excluded is information 'whose disclosure would harm the proper and efficient conduct of the operations of a department or other public body or authority'.[163] More generally there are exclusions related to the Royal Household, law enforcement and legal proceedings, immigration and nationality, the effective management of the economy and collection of taxes, public employment, appointments and honours, the privacy of an individual, and commercial confidentiality.[164]

The Code includes a provision for departments to charge for the information they provide upon request. 'Schemes may include a standard charge for processing simple requests for information. Where a request is complex and would require extensive searches of records or processing or collation of information, an additional charge, reflecting reasonable costs, may be notified.'[165]

The Code has been criticized for the limitation of its scope to those areas of government within the jurisdiction of the PCA and for the fact that it is voluntary rather than legally enforceable. The Government's argument for introducing a non-statutory code rather than freedom of information legislation is based on the dubious constitutional grounds that a code, policed by the PCA, accords with the convention of ministerial responsibility and the requirement of accountability to Parliament, whilst legislation would interfere with these constitutional arrangements. It is also grounded in the claim that a code is cheaper for those seeking information and, being unconstrained by judicial interpretation, offers greater flexibility which, it is argued, is 'in the interests of good government . . . leaving room for judgement in the light of particular circumstances'.[166] However, the Campaign for Freedom of Information noted '[O]verseas experience with disclosure of information suggests that 'persuasion and reason are not enough—a legal remedy is also necessary.'[167] Cynics might suggest that 'not enough' is what the Government wants the Code to be. It is not concerned with giving the citizen 'information rights' in the legal or constitutional sense but with allowing him or her controlled access to certain information.

---

[160] Ibid., para. 3. [161] Ibid. [162] Ibid., Pt II, paras. 1 & 2.
[163] Ibid., para.7. [164] Ibid., paras. 3, 4, 5, 6, 8, 12 & 13. [165] Ibid., Pt I, para. 7.
[166] OPSS, Memorandum, para. 9, to Sel. Cttee on PCA, HC 290, (1994–5).
[167] M. Frankel, Campaign for Freedom of Information, Memorandum to Sel. Cttee on PCA, HC 33–II, (1993–4) 258.

The decision by the Government not to give the Code legal effect accords with the new public management model and rational choice thinking. In contrast to the courts the position of the PCA as adjudicator is containable. He has no power to enforce his decisions and the fact that complaints have to be made through a Member of Parliament limits the access of the public to him and the access of MPs who themselves wish to complain for they too have to find an MP who will refer their complaint. Ministers can also exercise a degree of control over the PCA by virtue of section 11(3) of the PCA Act. This provides ministers with the power to prevent the disclosure of information by the PCA and it could be used to prevent disclosure by him of information gleaned whilst investigating freedom of information complaints. The Government has said this power will only be used very rarely, providing the PCA uses his own power of disclosure 'responsibly'.[168] However, there is likely to be a divergence of opinion over what constitutes responsible disclosure between those seeking information and those wishing to prevent disclosure.

The preference of the Government for control by the PCA rather than the courts also arises from the fact that the PCA, whilst independent, is not an 'outsider'. He and his Office have ongoing relations with Departments, are aware of their problems, and are used to arriving at agreements rather than imposing decisions. This somewhat cosy relationship was suggested by William Waldegrave when stating his preference for control by the PCA rather than the courts. He said, 'I actually think we will get a swifter, more practical, more common-sense outcome by using [the Ombudsman] . . . and we will get case law established rather quicker, we will get a good negotiated outcome using common sense and using the Ombudsman's office with departments.'[169]

Thus the advantage for Government is that whereas the courts would be able to impose a decision for the release of information, the PCA has to tread more warily, seeking departmental agreement. Challenges to the non-release of information could therefore have a lower rate of success. They may in any case be limited because of the lack of publicity given to the work of the PCA. This has led to suggestions that 'the choice of the PCA to police the Code on Open Government is an indication of government's attempts not only to minimize successful challenges but to minimize the number of complaints.'[170]

The PCA has refused 'to take sides' between the Government and those who seek a statutory Freedom of Information Act. He commented, 'The White Paper [on the Code] argued that my powers to send for departmental papers, my independence from Government, and my ability to make reports to Parliament would all help to generate confidence in the public and in Parliament in the workings of the Code and would preserve parliamentary accountability. It maintained that that was a better way to influence departmental culture and reduce the risk of the

---

[168] In evidence to Sel. Cttee on PCA, HC 33–II, (1993–4), Q728.   [169] Ibid., Q718.
[170] Birkenshaw (above, n. 84), 209. In fact the PCA only investigated 9 complaints during the first 9 months of the Code's operation (see n. 171 below).

bodies within my jurisdiction adopting an unduly cautious legalistic approach to the requests for information. Time will tell whether this is the case.'[171] Much will depend upon the PCA having sufficient resources to handle those complaints he does receive effectively. If this proves not to be the case, then delays in dealing with complaints will inevitably occur. These 'may frustrate applicants as effectively as outright refusals to disclose'.[172]

A further criticism of the Code is that it is based upon the disclosure of information rather than actual documents. The White Paper on Open Government gave the reason for this as being the fact that '[p]eople will in general find it easier to describe the information they seek, rather than the documents they wish to see.'[173] In addition, it stated that '[e]diting policy papers against exemptions . . . can be a laborious process, and in the end produces a document that is at worst partial and at best misleading'.[174] In support of this, Mr Waldegrave suggested that disclosing documents could result in a greater suspicion that information was being withheld. He reasoned, 'you have to edit documents, both to deal with legitimate exclusions that there may be and to protect privacy of third parties . . . That can actually end up creating more suspicion.'[175]

However, the focus on information rather than documents is seen by some critics as being one of the most significant defects of the Code, giving departments the opportunity to be selective and to exclude embarrassing or inconvenient information. Indeed, '[a] body which anticipates that full disclosure may expose it to criticism is unlikely to be able to resist the temptation to produce a summary which slants or even conceals the truth.'[176] For this reason the Select Committee on the PCA has recommended an amendment to the Code to assert a right of access to documents rather than information,[177] a recommendation that has been supported by the Public Service Committee.[178]

The effectiveness of any provision on access to information depends very largely on the extent of the exclusions or exemptions. Many consider those provided by the Code to be excessive. There is criticism of the fact that access to virtually all aspects of policy information may be denied on the basis that its disclosure would harm the frankness of internal discussion. Moreover, the commitment to publish the facts and the analysis behind the facts in relation to major policy decisions as soon as possible after their announcement is tempered by the restriction that it is the Government that decides what is important and relevant. This has the potential for being a very wide exclusion.

In addition, there has been concern over the exemption given to immigration and nationality. The PCA himself 'found it slightly surprising that the part of the Home Office that deals with immigration and nationality should be given an

---

[171] PCA, HC 91, (1994–5), para. 3.   [172] M. Frankel, Memo. (above, n. 167).
[173] Cm. 2290, (1993).   [174] Ibid.
[175] In evidence to Sel. Cttee on PCA, HC 33–II, (1993–4), Q726.
[176] M. Frankel, Memorandum to Sel. Cttee on PCA, HC 290, (1994–5), 46.
[177] Sel. Cttee on PCA, HC 84, (1995–6).   [178] Pub. Ser. Cttee, HC 313–I, (1995–6).

exemption.'[179] Particularly disconcerting is the absolute nature of the exemption. This makes it different from the exemptions that apply to other subject areas, such as defence or taxation, which are subject to a harm test. It is therefore only in cases where disclosure would cause 'actual harm or prejudice' or a 'risk or reasonable expectation of harm or prejudice' that information should be refused.[180] Even then, 'it should be considered whether any harm or prejudice arising from disclosure is outweighed by the public interest in making information available.'[181]

However, where immigration and nationality are concerned, such considerations are not required; the exemption is absolute. The White Paper gave the reason for this absolute exemption as being that immigration and nationality records 'frequently contain sensitive information provided in confidence by individuals and organizations'. It also argued that there were already established procedures for the giving of reasons and explanations in immigration cases and that any right of access to further information 'would seriously weaken the maintenance of an effective immigration control to which the Government attaches great importance'.[182] It seems difficult to see how, as long as third party information is protected, greater openness could weaken the system. It might, however, expose instances of poor decision-making or maladministration.

Other criticisms relate to the stipulation that 'the Code should not be regarded as a means of access to original documents or personal files'.[183] This is seen as being inhibitory to requests for personal information. Also of concern are the 400 or so existing restrictions on disclosure contained in legislation which cannot be overridden by the Code because of its lack of a statutory basis.[184] Maurice Frankel, Director of the Campaign for Freedom of Information, commented of these restrictions that 'many are unobjectionable and protect the privacy of individuals. Others prohibit the disclosure of all information obtained under particular powers . . . One instance is section 118 of the Medicines Act 1968, which prevents the medicines licensing authority from revealing information about the safety of pharmaceuticals which it has received from manufacturers.'[185] Such information, it would seem, should, under any move towards open government, be in the public domain and not protected from disclosure. There are also reservations about the charging arrangements for requests for information. These arise because there is no coherent charging scheme and thus departments are left to determine their own charges, and because of fears that providing information in the form of summaries may be expensive. Departments are allowed to make a charge which constitutes a reflection of 'reasonable costs'. However, such costs may be prohibitive for the private individual or group.

The Code of Practice on Access to Government Information provides for the investigation by the PCA of complaints that 'information which should have been

---

[179] Sel. Cttee on PCA, HC 290, (1994–5), Q34.   [180] Code, Pt II.   [181] Ibid.
[182] Cm. 2290, (1993).   [183] Code, Pt II, para. 8.
[184] Figure taken from Cm. 2290, (1993).
[185] Memorandum to Sel. Cttee on PCA, HC 290, (1994–5), 37.

provided under the Code has not been provided, or that unreasonable charges have been demanded'.[186] This suggests an investigation which is 'primarily . . . a matter of judgement'.[187] It is therefore very different from investigations into maladministration where evidence is taken from both sides in order to determine the facts and reconcile discrepancies.[188] Moreover, it is not a question, as with a conventional complaint, of the complainant providing some evidence of a personal injustice. The PCA has stated that 'when considering complaints about breaches of the Code . . . [he would be] prepared to accept that a refusal to release information which should have been released is itself enough to found a complaint.'[189]

Prior to undertaking any investigation, the PCA made known that the key principles or 'watchwords' of his investigations would be 'fairness and speed' and that he would 'need to be persuaded that no breach of the Code had occurred' if he were not to uphold a complaint.[190] Once he had accepted a complaint for investigation, 'the onus would be on the Department or other public body concerned to show that the Code has not been breached, not the other way round.'[191] Thus the PCA uses the onus of proof traditional to Freedom of Information Acts; it is for the non-discloser to prove that the refusal to release information accords with an allowed exclusion, not for the claimant to prove his or her entitlement. The difference with the Code is, of course, that individuals have no right to a legal remedy. Even if the PCA finds in their favour, they cannot assume they will have access to the withheld information. This remains within the gift of Government.

The operation of the Code

In 1994 the PCA reported on the eight months since the Code came into operation. He expressed his surprise at the small number of complaints referred to him. On the basis of the initial experience in Australia, New Zealand and Canada, when they had introduced Freedom of Information legislation, he had expected some 200 complaints but in fact only received twenty-four.[192] He noted, 'So far the individual citizen's attitude to *finding out* information seems apathetic'.[193] Maurice Frankel subsequently suggested a number of reasons for this apathy. Firstly, he considered that the focus on information rather than documents may not encourage requests under the Code as it has always been possible to seek information from Departments.[194] Secondly, he noted, '[T]hose seeking access to their own personal files—perhaps the largest group of potential users—will have been specifically deterred by the explicit statement that "the Code should not be regarded as a means of access to original documents or personal files".'[195]

---

186 Code Pt I, para. 11.
187 Parl. Commissioner, Memorandum to Sel. Cttee on PCA, HC 33–II, (1993–4).
188 Ibid.   189 PCA, HC 91, (1994–5), para. 14.
190 Memorandum to Sel. Cttee on PCA, HC 33–II, (1993–4).
191 Ibid.   192 PCA, HC 91, (1994–5), para. 12.   193 Ibid.
194 Memorandum to Sel. Cttee on PCA, HC 290, (1994–5), 37.
195 Ibid., referring to Code, Pt I, para. 8.

Thirdly, he believed the lack of publicity given to the launch of the Code to be a factor, commenting, 'The fact that the Code was brought into force on a bank holiday during the parliamentary recess, guaranteed an inconspicuous start.'[196] This was exacerbated by the lateness in publication of the final Code, only three working days before its implementation. As a result, '[j]ournalists who might otherwise have written stories anticipating the code's introduction had no final text until the last moment, and little opportunity to publicise the event.'[197]

The lack of publicity given to the Code was also a point raised by the Select Committee on the PCA who contrasted the amount of money spent on advertising the Charter initiative and that spent on the Code. The Committee drew attention to the 20m Parent's Charter leaflets which were sent out to households, despite only 5m households having children, and the 50,000 leaflets printed about the Open Government Code.[198] As far as the PCA is concerned, an important factor in the low use of the Code could be the costs incurred, which may be prohibitive.[199]

The concern of the PCA about the low use of the Code would seem to be a reflection of his commitment to it. Moreover, the line taken by the PCA in his initial reports seemed strongly to support the presumption of the Code for disclosure and his role as being a facilitator of that disclosure. To this effect he had accepted complaints which had not been through the internal review procedure, despite the requirements of the Code that complaints 'should be made first to the department or body concerned'.[200] He reasoned that it was 'not good administration to send complainants from pillar to post in their search for information'.[201] Thus, if the complainant had not been made aware of the internal review procedure by the department concerned, the PCA would not refuse an investigation. He also emphasised the importance of departments conducting a balancing exercise when deciding whether to disclose information. They should consider 'whether any harm or prejudice arising or likely to arise from the disclosure would be outweighed by the public interest in making information available'[202] rather than rely upon a straight 'harm' test.

He addressed the criticism that the Code places no obligation on a department to give the public access to documents as opposed to information, commenting 'My remit is to investigate and report whether bodies within my jurisdiction have complied with the requirements of the Code. I would not therefore criticize a body

---

[196] Above, n. 194.

[197] Ibid. In a personal survey, undertaken in Nov. 1996 amongst 110 2nd and 3rd year law undergraduates, only 5 students knew of the Code's existence. None had seen a copy or knew what it contained.

[198] Office of Pub. Ser. in evidence to Sel. Cttee of PCA, HC 112, (1993–4), Q392.

[199] He reported that the National Rivers Authority charged £100 for photocopying information on A3 paper and £50 for A4; the Public Health Laboratory Service charged between £2,000 and £3,000 for naming any local authority in any reported incident; the Health and Safety Executive charged £45 an hour; and the Inspectorate of Pollution charged £993 per day per person (in evidence to Sel. Cttee on PCA, HC 290, (1993–4), Q45).

[200] Code, Pt I, para. 11.   [201] PCA, HC 91, (1994–5), para. 14.   [202] Ibid., para. 16.

if it had fulfilled its obligations under the Code without releasing copies of the documents involved. However, I normally construe a request for documents as meaning that a complainant is seeking *all* the information contained in the document specified and, save when all or part of that information can legitimately be withheld under the exemptions contained in part II of the Code, I normally expect all that information to be released.'[203] He continued, 'Thus . . . there are likely to be a number of occasions when . . . I conclude that the most practical way to release the information sought is to provide a copy of the actual document in which the information is contained.'[204]

This approach to disclosure was demonstrated in one of the first cases brought to the PCA.[205] It concerned the failure of the Department of Transport to release the Report of an Inspector into a proposed road scheme. The publication of such Reports is normally a statutory requirement but, in this case, the scheme in question was overtaken by new plans before the required publication date. The new plans themselves became the object of a subsequent public inquiry and the Department refused the request for the release of the original Inspector's Report, relying on Code Exemptions 2 (non-disclosure of internal discussion and advice) and 4 (non-disclosure of information relating to law enforcement and legal proceedings).

The PCA upheld the complaint that the Report should be released. He rejected the use of Exemption 2 on the grounds that the Inspector's Report had been written in the expectation that it would be published. It should not therefore contain material that might need protection. He also rejected the application of clauses (b) and (c) of Exemption 4, as, once again, the Inspector had written it for publication, and, on the facts, it was evident that the disclosure of the original report would not prejudice the second public inquiry. The PCA held that although the Code did not require the provision of documents but of information, the easiest way to provide the information requested was to release the actual Inspector's Report. This the department agreed to do, also making a commitment to release such Reports if similar circumstances arose in the future.

The Department of Transport case demonstrated the PCA's approach to the release of documents. It also showed his determination that the exemptions within the Code should be interpreted narrowly rather than given wide effect.[206] This was further illustrated in his investigation of a complaint against the DSS for refusing to disclose a report on the complainants.[207] The Report had been undertaken by an Inquirer, nominated by the DSS, and concerned a National Insurance question. The DSS claimed Exemption 4(d)—legal professional privilege. However, the PCA found this did not apply, firstly, because the Report was not of a legal nature and, secondly, because the Inquirer, although in this case a barrister, was not acting as lawyer to the DSS. Once again, although recognizing that the Code required the release of the information required in the document and not the document

---

[203] Ibid., para. 15.   [204] Ibid.   [205] Case No. A. 4/94 PCA, HC 14 vol. 4, (1994–5), 1.
[206] PCA, HC 91, (1994–5), para. 16.   [207] PCA, HC 606 vol. 3, (1994–5).

itself, he concluded that the common-sense approach would be to release the actual Report.

The PCA has also indicated that he will interpret the Exemptions in accordance with the wording of the Code and not with regard to the Guidance on interpretation given by the Government. The matter arose in connection with the refusal by the Home Office to disclose information about records held by the Security Service.[208] The Home Office claimed that the request lay outside the scope of the Code and maintained this refusal on review. The PCA began an investigation whereupon the Permanent Secretary drew his attention to Guidance produced by the Office of Public Service. This states, 'The Security and Intelligence Services are not within the scope of the Code nor is information originating from them'.[209] The status of the Guidance, according to the document itself, is 'advisory only' and it 'cannot cover all possible circumstances'. However, the Permanent Secretary assured the PCA that the part of the Guidance with which they were concerned was a 'firm and authoritative'[210] statement of the Government's intentions. The PCA took the view that as the Code did not use the words quoted in the Guidance, he would not interpret the Code to include such exemptions.

In the event he discontinued the investigation because the Home Office stated its refusal to release the information was to protect the security of the state. Exemption 1(a)—national security and defence—therefore applied and because of limitations placed on the PCA by the PCA Act,[211] he was in no position to make a ' "harm" test' decision on national security. That was for the Government alone. Nevertheless he secured a promise from the Home Office that it would write to the complainant to correct an earlier statement that they did not hold the information of the kind requested.

The investigations undertaken to date by the PCA suggest that he sees his role with regard to the Code as different from his role in relation to the administrative process. The Code not only lays down his jurisdiction and powers, it also provides an adjudicatory framework which is subject to his interpretation. He has already made clear that this framework will be interpreted reasonably and fairly and that the presumption will be in favour of disclosure. Such a presumption should increase the openness of government, a process that began modestly with the establishment of Next Steps agencies, and should be in the interests of good administration.

Conclusion

The investigations of the PCA into instances of maladministration and, more recently, into the non-disclosure of information, provide a useful indicator of his

---

[208] Case No. A. 11/95 in PCA, HC 758 vol. 4, (1994–5), 13.

[209] Guidance on Interpretation of the Code of Practice on Access to Government Information.

[210] Above. n. 208.   [211] PCA Act, s. 5(3) & Sch. 3, para. 5.

view of what constitutes good administration. This view accords to a large extent with the public service model. The PCA has consistently upheld the principles associated with this model, wherever possible giving them greater weight than considerations of efficiency. He has sought to maintain standards of fairness and reasonableness against cost-cutting, and has expressed his concern that efficiency is frequently achieved only at the expense of equity, a fundamental requirement of good administration. His perspective of good administration therefore contrasts with that of the new public management model, where efficiency, in terms of value for money and cost savings, dominates.

As a consequence, it is somewhat ironic that the role of the PCA should have become more extensive at a time when the new public management model is in the ascendancy, and that the Government reforms should have improved the ability of the PCA to uphold two important requirements of good administration: openness, through the disclosure of information, and the redress of grievances, through the Citizen's Charter. The Charter and Access to Information initiatives have provided the PCA with a platform for stressing the importance of coherent complaints procedures which ensure that grievances are redressed, even if this imposes a financial penalty upon the agency concerned. They have also given him the opportunity to encourage the greater openness of government and to talk in the language of 'rights' in relation to good administration.

However, neither the Citizen's Charter nor the Code of Practice on Access to Government Information were introduced in the interests of good administration, at least as it is upheld by the PCA. They were motivated by efficiency objectives. Greater openness is intended to make inefficiency more difficult to hide and to make those responsible for administrative processes visible and accountable. Charter standards are intended to improve performance without the injection of further funds and to guide the expectations of customers, providing them with ready-made complaints when these expectations are not met. These complaints, handled internally, provide a further impetus to improved efficiency. The Government and the PCA therefore have different perspectives on what the reforms provide in relation to the administrative process. This suggests that from time to time there will be disagreement over what constitutes maladministration and the importance of good administration.

To a large extent the basic principles that guide the PCA are similar to those that guide the courts. This means there is 'a great potential for the cross-fertilization of ideas' between the two institutions, particularly 'in their respective assessments of the limits placed upon the departmental creation and utilisation of . . . procedural guidance when assessed against the criteria of "good administrative practice" and procedural fairness/impropriety.'[212] However, whilst the PCA upholds similar principles to the courts in relation to good administration, his response is shaped entirely by the concept of maladministration. This enables him to make

[212] Mowbray (above, n. 14) at 585.

recommendations that both redress the individual grievance and improve the administrative process to the benefit of the wider public. He is not 'forced to choose between conflicting demands of justice for the public, and justice for the individual' as the courts sometimes are, as, for instance, when there has been reliance upon misinformation.[213]

There have been a number of calls for the PCA to be given the power to conduct audits of the operation of administrative procedures within departments and other public bodies.[214] There have also been repeated suggestions that he should be given an explicit role in developing guidance on best administrative practice, perhaps culminating in a Code. Both of these developments would provide the PCA with 'a substantial and recognized input into improving the quality of administration as well as providing redress after the event'.[215] The Select Committee for the PCA has also recommended on several occasions that the PCA should be given jurisdiction over contractual and commercial transactions, an increasingly important aspect of public administration.

Any further extension of the role of the PCA has been resisted by the Government, not least because of the resource implications. However, it would seem essential that the importance of good administration should be underpinned and that the principles that attach to it are made explicit. This would seem a necessary protection against their possible erosion by over-zealous efficiency objectives and the use of private sector methods. Moreover, any 'best practice guidance' or code could aid judicial interpretation and thus the cross-fertilization between the PCA and the courts. At a time when government is becoming increasingly fragmented, the role of the PCA and the courts in upholding standards of good administration across the range of administrative activities becomes even more important. The remit of the PCA to investigate maladministration and the powers that he is given to do this suggests he should take the lead role.

---

[213] P. Brown, 'Ombudsman' in Richardson & Genn (eds.), *Administrative Law and Government Action* at 335.

[214] See, e.g., Sel. Cttee on PCA, HC 33–I, (1993–4).

[215] G. Drewry & D. Oliver, Memorandum to Pub. Serv. Cttee, HC 313–II, (1995–6), 21.

Part II

JUDICIAL PERSPECTIVES ON GOOD ADMINISTRATION

In a system where the constitutional arrangements have tended to marginalize the role of the courts in relation to central public administration, judicial involvement and concern with the principles of good administration may not always be apparent. Nevertheless, the courts play an important part in determining and reinforcing principles they consider appropriate. These principles, or the weight attached to them in particular situations, may not always accord with the views of officials. There is therefore an inevitable, although usually hidden, tension between judges and those engaged in public administration. However, since the 1980s this tension has become increasingly apparent as Civil Service reform and the resulting change in administrative culture has coincided with a judiciary whose approach is more interventionist than at any time this century.

This Part examines the traditional role of the courts within the administrative process. It then moves on to consider the reasons for, and effects of, the heightened tension between the executive and judicial branches of government and, against this background, assesses judicial perspectives of good administration and how these accord with the public service and new public management models, both with regard to the principles upheld and the interest, individual or public, that these principles are seen as serving.

5

THE COURTS AND PUBLIC ADMINISTRATION

Law and Lawyers in the Civil Service

Unlike some continental counterparts, the British Civil Service is not dominated by those with legal training. Lawyers are employed as specialist legal advisers but seldom as administrators and there is generally a lack of 'interaction in ordinary business between civil servants and lawyers'.[1] As a result 'neither wholly understands the other's point of view and the civil servant is not as responsive to problems about law as he is to problems about politics.'[2] This accords with the domination of political rather than legal accountability in the British system of government, and with the constitutional position of civil servants as publicly accountable through the minister to Parliament, a position that became established during the nineteenth century and owed much to the apparent success of the mid-nineteenth century Parliament in its role as scrutineer and controller of government. This success fostered the belief that accountability through ministers to Parliament was practically and constitutionally superior to other forms of accountability, including accountability to the courts. Dicey, writing in 1885, reflected this belief, although his motive was at least in part to prevent the French *droit administratif* from being adopted.[3]

Thus while on the continent administrative courts were being established to police the expanding administrative functions of the State, and in the United States the foundation of a regulatory system centring on agencies was being laid, in Britain ministerial departments were established and began to absorb the responsibility for most regulatory functions. Individual ministerial responsibility therefore became the political rationale around which an expanding system of government was structured. Such an arrangement confirmed the centrality of Parliament within the constitution, recognizing not just the legal supremacy of the Crown-in-Parliament but the political sovereignty of the House of Commons. It was the Members of this House, rather than the courts, who were entrusted with holding Government accountable and the courts' role was limited to ensuring that ministerial actions were *intra vires* and in accordance with the legal authority granted by Parliament.

The constitutional primacy of political accountability together with the dominance of the generalist-administrator over the lawyer has resulted in the culture of the Civil Service being non-legal. This is demonstrated by the paucity of

---

[1] W. J. M. MacKenzie & J. W. Grove, *Central Administration in Britain*, 388.
[2] Ibid.   [3] A. V. Dicey, *Introduction to Study of Law of the Constitution*.

references to the law in the public administration literature.[4] This is not to say that civil servants are detached from, or unaware of the law. They have a part in shaping and defining it and the powers that they exercise are provided by it. They need the law, at the very least as a 'set of pegs on which to hang policies',[5] and they adhere strictly to the *intra vires* principle. However, the lack of a legal culture means that administrative behaviour is governed by conventions and understandings rather than by legalistic-type rules, and discretion is advised by circulars and guidelines rather than legislation. It also means that whilst officials develop political antennae to alert them to the political implications of their actions, they do not always develop corresponding legal ones. Moreover, whilst the system is shaped to respond to political control, it 'is sometimes shaped to evade . . . formal [legal] controls'.[6] Indeed, legal control may be resented and seen as an irritant that interferes with the job in hand.

Part of the problem lies in the fact that just as civil servants lack an understanding of legal principles, so judges who exercise authority over public administration 'are by training exclusively lawyers; they do not, for example, enjoy the mixture of legal and administrative training that members of the French Conseil d'Etat possess.'[7] As a consequence, they do not understand the competing pressures upon administrators or 'the dynamics of the processes they seek to control'.[8] There is therefore an inevitable gap in communication between administrators with no legal training and judges with no experience of public administration.

The Traditional Role of the Courts

It is partly in recognition of their lack of knowledge of the workings of public administration that the courts themselves have traditionally adopted a limited role in relation to it. They have also been constrained by the constitutional relationship between civil servants and ministers and by the position of civil servants as servants of the Crown. This has resulted in a judicial reluctance to become involved in employment questions between the Crown and civil servants with the result that the law in this area is in many respects uncertain. Moreover, where judicial review is concerned, the internal discipline imposed by departments upon their staff has resulted in legal control being seen as unnecessary in all but extreme cases.[9] The

---

[4] Noted *inter alia* by H. W. R. Wade & C. F. Forsyth, *Administrative Law*, 62 n. 39; they comment on the fact that judicial review receives no mention in 'Hennessy's influential description of the civil service (*Whitehall*, 1990) . . . and the law and lawyers are referred to only *en passant*'.

[5] R. Cranston, 'Reviewing judicial review', in Richardson & Genn (eds.), *Administrative Law and Government Action* at 64. See also C. Harlow & R. Rawlings, *Pressure through the Law*.

[6] MacKenzie & Grove (above, n. 1), 400.

[7] A. E. Boyle, 'Sovereignty, accountability and the reform of administrative law' in Richardson & Genn (above, n. 5) at 101.

[8] I. Loveland, 'Housing Benefit; administrative law and administrative practice' (1986) 66 *Pub. Admin*. 57 at 72.

[9] MacKenzie & Grove (above, n. 1), 389.

assumption has been that civil servants, imbued with the principles of objectivity and impartiality, will conduct themselves appropriately and will recognize, without the need for judicial intervention, that administration 'aims at justice as well as efficiency'.[10]

The limited role of the courts in relation to government also stems from their marginalized constitutional position and from judicial concern to act in accordance with the separation of powers and to guard the independence of the judiciary from the other arms of government. Thus judges have been reluctant to entertain legal challenges of policy decisions for which the minister is accountable to Parliament. To do so would be to enter the realms of policy-making, the responsibility of the executive, and to usurp one of the functions of Parliament. Ministerial responsibility has therefore acted to limit the jurisdiction of the courts, providing a demarcation line for the judges over which they are concerned not to cross.

Lord Greene demonstrated the division made by the courts in *Carltona*, when he held that whilst the court could rule on the legality of the principle of delegation by the minister to his officials, the appropriateness of delegating a particular function to a particular official was not for the court to judge.[11] This concerned the minister's management of his department and, as a consequence, 'if for an important matter he selected an official of such junior standing that he could not be expected competently to perform the work, the minister could have to answer . . . to Parliament.'[12]

The division was subsequently succinctly enunciated by Lord Diplock who said that departments 'are accountable to Parliament for what they do as far as efficiency and policy, and of that Parliament is the only judge; they are responsible to a court of justice for the lawfulness of what they do, and of that the court is the only judge.'[13] Of course what constitutes policy and efficiency rather than lawfulness is open to interpretation but the political accountability of ministers to Parliament provides a useful justification for judicial inaction, when such action might be seen as controversial or offending the body politic.

However, the most significant effect of political accountability being given the 'primary position' in the constitution is that it 'nipped in the bud the development of any wider ranging and specific public law accountability'.[14] This has resulted in an under-developed system of administrative law which, until recently, has had few established principles to govern its operation. It has also had an effect on the public's perception of lawyers and judges who have not traditionally been seen as operating in the public law sphere and thus have not been associated with controlling the exercise of government or State power, a position exacerbated by the lack of a constitutional document which is subject to judicial interpretation and protection. Judges have therefore been denied an opportunity to secure popular

---

[10] Ibid., 100.   [11] *Carltona Ltd v. Commissioner of Works* [1943] 2 All ER 560.
[12] At 563, but see *R. v. Sec. of State for Home Dept, ex p. Oladehinde* [1991] 1 AC 254.
[13] *R. v. IRC, ex p. National Federation of Self-Employed and Small Businesses* [1982] AC 617.
[14] P. Birkenshaw, *Grievances, Remedies and the State*, 37.

acceptance as players within the political arena. In particular, the absence of a Bill of Rights has meant that upholding citizens' rights against an encroachment of State power has been at the sidelines of judicial activity. Judges have in the main confined themselves to dealing with private law rights, such as those arising from property and contract, rather than addressing issues concerned with fundamental human rights familiar to their American and, latterly, their continental counter-parts. This has had an effect on the development of English jurisprudence and encouraged the notion that judges are not in the business of protecting the ordin-ary person (who has few property and contractual rights) against the State but of protecting the interests of big business and the Establishment, of which the gov-ernment and the judiciary are a part. Thus political culture has supported judicial marginalization.

It is perhaps not surprising therefore that citizens with grievances against the Government have tended to use political rather than legal channels through which to seek redress, particularly when the cumbersome nature of the old judicial review procedures are taken into account and the costs incurred are considered. Writing about judicial review in 1957, Mackenzie and Grove noted that 'the ordin-ary litigant has little power to compel the production of documents which the department does not wish to make public: a civil servant in the witness box can safely limit himself to matters of fact, and refuse to answer questions on matters of departmental policy. The trend of judicial decision is still against allowing inquiry into the manner in which decisions are actually taken in the Minister's name.'[15] Such an account illustrates some of the inadequacies of judicial review at this time. These inevitably contributed to a lack of public confidence in the legal system as a mechanism for dealing with citizen/State conflicts.

In addition, the professional status accorded civil servants has resulted in the courts tending to assume that 'this professional elite . . . is acting paternalistically, in good faith, for the good of its "clients".'[16] This trust in the public service was engendered by the Northcote–Trevelyn reforms which produced a skilled and com-petent public administration, rooted in Oxbridge. The result was that 'all the upper echelons of the civil service were populated by men . . . who had shared their schools, universities and clubs with the barristers who became the judiciary of the inter-war years'.[17] With such a background, it was not surprising that there was judicial confidence that 'public administration at the highest level was . . . in trust-worthy hands and that ministers would be competently advised on the implemen-tation of policy'.[18] This confidence had the effect of discouraging judicial review of public administration and encouraged the courts 'to facilitate rather than restrict social programmes and administrative processes'.[19] Thus judicial intervention has tended to be restricted to the 'enforcement of minimum standards of procedure'.[20]

---

[15] Mackenzie & Grove (above, n. 1), 298.
[16] D. Feldman, 'Public law values in the House of Lords' (1990) *LQR* 246.
[17] S. Sedley, 'The sound of silence' (1994) 110 *LQR* 280
[18] Ibid.   [19] Feldman, (above, n. 16).   [20] Ibid.

In any case, 'the courts only have a limited capacity to implement policies (for example of good administration) even if they were inclined to do so; and their moral authority may not be strong in the area of judicial review, which flows against the tide of political legitimacy.'[21] Thus in a system in which public accountability is dominated by politics rather than law and in which there is suspicion of lawyers playing more than an auxiliary part in the administrative process, judges have traditionally been wary of making too many incursions into the administrative territory. They have worked on the assumption that the Civil Service operates more or less in accordance with publicly accepted principles and with the values supported by the legal system. As a consequence, they have felt little need to intervene or to assert their view of good administration.

Judicial Review and Public Administration

Not surprisingly the effect of judicial review upon the administrative process would seem to have been very limited. Thus not only has legal action traditionally been seen as ineffectual for the individual with a grievance against the State, it has appeared to be an inadequate mechanism through which to introduce standards of administrative practice. Moreover, there is uncertainty as to whether any effect it does have is beneficial or detrimental to decision-making.

There is little evidence from empirical research upon which to determine the practical effect of judicial review. Sunkin suggests that it has played 'a strategically important role in the way prisons are run', hence the decline in applications in the period 1987–9.[22] Loveland, on the other hand, found that in relation to housing issues, judicial review had only a short term effect and that the concern was to avoid the cost of judicial review rather than to use judicial decisions to improve decision-making.[23] At best it may be that judicial control 'encourages greater respect for the limits of decision-making power, and better (in the sense of more acceptable) decision-making procedures',[24] and that the general principles of procedure and the rules relating to the exercise of discretion, as laid down by the courts, provide helpful guides, supplementing policy guidelines devised by the department itself. If this is so, then administrators may accept administrative law as providing 'an essential framework for most routine governmental activities'[25] and thus as helping to foster principles of good administration.[26]

However, suggested effects on the quality of decision-making are difficult to measure and in any case are likely to be patchy. Moreover, claims that judicial control is beneficial to the administrative process are countered by suggestions to

[21] Cranston (above, n. 5) at 74.
[22] M. Sunkin, 'The judicial review case-load 1987–89' (1991) *PL* 490 at 491.
[23] Loveland (above, n. 8), at 70.   [24] P. Cane, *Introduction to Administrative Law*, 283.
[25] R. Cotterall, 'Judicial review and legal theory', in Richardson & Genn (above, n. 5) at 13.
[26] The Govt. publication *Judge over Your Shoulder* (2nd edn.) states that judicial review is 'part of the whole process of good administration' (para. 3).

the contrary and the accusation that administrators at times adopt 'time-consuming "defensive" administrative practices designed to minimize the risk that decisions will be successfully challenged'.[27] Ideas relating to the benefits of legal control are not part of Civil Service culture and more frequently judicial review is portrayed as 'a series of hurdles to be jumped before policy can be implemented'.[28] From this perspective legal control undermines the administrative process, imposing procedures that conflict with requirements, such as speed, efficiency, workload, departmental ethos, and performance targets. Moreover, the support of the law for openness, seen as necessary in the interests of fairness, is contrary to a culture founded on confidentiality and which, in the absence of legal involvement, has engendered one of the most secretive administrative systems in the world.[29]

Whether judicial control is seen as beneficial or detrimental its effect has been minimal for a number of reasons which relate to, or arise from, judicial restraint. Firstly, much of central government has, until recently, been untouched by judicial review. This was partly because of the small number of applicants granted leave,[30] and partly because the Home Office has borne the brunt of applications.[31] Secondly, administrators have often been unaware of particular decisions which might affect them. Traditionally, they have not worked with the possibility of a legal challenge at the forefront of their minds. Indeed, Louis Blom-Cooper commented in 1984 that it was tempting 'to observe that there are some administrators who appear to operate oblivious of even the existence of public law'.[32] Certainly 'less grandiose concerns' such as speed, efficiency, performance targets and the pressure of work were, and remain, as important, if not more so, than how a judge will view the legality of the decision. Thus 'heavy workloads are likely to lead administrators to "cut corners" when applying discretionary powers . . . [and] promotion opportunities may also be related to an officer's willingness to pursue organizational goals which conflict with legal requirements'.[33]

In addition, whilst public administration shares with the law concern for the principles of fairness and equity, 'other determinants may impinge; political and economic considerations—and of course fairness to the public at large—are sometimes more real concerns than may be the case in the courts'.[34] Thus the concern

---

[27] Cane (above, n. 24), 382.   [28] Cranston (above, n. 5) at 64.

[29] This view remains despite the Code of Practice on Access to Government Information which has had a minimal effect on departmental openness. In his Report, Sir Richard Scott noted the secretive nature of British Govt., commenting, in relation to public interest immunity certificates, 'I do not believe that the instinctive Whitehall reaction to seek to withhold Government documents from public inspection is likely to change' (HC 115–IV, 1996), K6.16).

[30] In 1983, 1984, and 1985 there were only approximately 100 applications a year (Sir Michael Kerry, Treasury Solicitor 1980–4, 'Administrative law and judicial review' (1986) 64 *Pub. Admin.* 2 at 164).

[31] In the first 6 months of 1985, 94% of challenges were against the Home Secretary, although since then there has been a greater spread to include Depts of Environment, Trade and Industry, Health & Social Security, Education, and the Inland Revenue (Sunkin (above, n. 22) at 490).

[32] L. Blom-Cooper, 'Lawyers and public administration' (1984) *PL* 215.

[33] Loveland (above, n. 8) at 72.   [34] Kerry (above, n. 30) at 164.

of administrators for the law has to be seen in the context of the dynamics of public administration and other considerations may limit the attention that is given to the law, thereby limiting the impact of judicial decisions upon day-to-day work.

Thirdly, the principles which guide administrative law in general, and judicial review in particular, 'are not sufficiently precise to offer any meaningful guidance to administrators in their day-to-day decision making.'[35] '[W]ords like "fairness", "reasonableness", "legitimate expectations", and "abuse of power" allow the courts a considerable degree of flexibility in deciding how the legal principles are to be applied in different cases. This makes it difficult to be certain in advance how the courts will decide a particular case.'[36] The consequence is that 'results . . . may seem surprising'.[37] Decisions thought to be reasonable when they were made, may, in hindsight, be struck down by the courts as *Wednesbury* unreasonable, and broad discretions, which administrators had thought were intended to be used to deal with diverse circumstances, may be held to be exercised for improper purposes.[38] Thus it is arguable that judicial review has not improved the quality of decision-making or the effectiveness of public administration. It has not provided administrators, who lack a legal background or the support of a legal culture, with a workable check-list against which they can measure their decisions with some degree of accuracy. Thus the tendency is to carry on regardless unless or until a decision is challenged.

This leads on to the fourth and final point. The impact of judicial review upon public administration and its suitability for ensuring good administration is limited by its retrospective and haphazard nature. It is complaint-driven and thus reactive rather than proactive and, in practice, there may be 'little that a judge can do to influence future administrative decisions'.[39] Administrators can often safely ignore judicial decisions, or adopt techniques which enable the 'circumvention of court orders'.[40] These include delaying tactics and remaking the decision in accordance with the order but with the same effect. In addition the effect of judicial decisions can be nullified either by primary or delegated legislation, which may be retrospective, or the effect can be significantly reduced by departmental guidelines which give it a narrow application.

It is therefore apparent that judicial review has not held a centre-stage position in public administration. It has operated mainly in the wings and has had little effect on the administrative process. Its marginal position arises from Britain's constitutional arrangements, the non-legal culture within the Civil Service, and the judicial belief that administrators and the courts have traditionally operated according to the same standards and values. As a consequence, the relationship between public administration and the courts has been largely free from conflict.

[35] H. Rawlings, 'Judicial review and the control of Government' (1986) 64 *Pub. Admin.* 2 at 140.
[36] *Judge over your Shoulder*, (1st edn.) para. 44.
[37] Ibid., (2nd edn.), para. 14.   [38] Cranston (above, n. 5) at 64.
[39] Brennan, G., 'Judicial review and good administration' in Taggart (ed.) *Judicial Review of Administrative Action* at 18.
[40] C. Harlow, 'Administrative reaction to judicial review' (1976) *PL* 116 at 117.

There have been tensions but these have mainly been confined to differences regarding the balance between the interests of the individual and the public interest in administrative efficiency. They have not concerned underlying principles. Tensions have been averted or kept at bay by judicial reticence and a commonly-held basis for administrative action.

A Changing Relationship

This position of relative compatibility between the Civil Service and the courts seems during the 1990s to be changing. Two apparently unrelated developments have coincided and may be disturbing the relationship between the judicial and executive branches of government. Firstly, senior judges have become more interventionist in the 1990s than at any time this century. Second, the Civil Service has undergone a fundamental reform of its structure with an inevitable effect upon its culture. The consequence of these developments would seem to be a changing relationship between the courts and the executive and a developing tension.

From non-intervention to judicial activism

In 1987 the Treasury Solicitor produced a booklet for civil servants entitled *Judge over your Shoulder*. A second edition followed in 1995. Its production was a recognition of the growing importance of the law and the courts in public administration. This stems from an increase in legal challenges and from a more interventionist stance taken by the judiciary in relation to government. There are a number of inter-related reasons for these developments.

Firstly, whilst politics over the last decade have been more confrontational, the 'alternative methods for ventilating opposition' have decreased. 'Government has become increasingly centralized, local government marginalized, the "penumbra" state rendered largely unaccountable and no alternative system of checks and balances has been put in place.'[41] Judicial review has thus become increasingly important as a mechanism for airing public law complaints.

Secondly, in 1981 the procedural problems associated with judicial review were considerably reduced by the Supreme Court Act, which incorporated a reformed Order 53, rule 1(2) into section 31(2). This provides for a system less heavily weighted against the applicant seeking a prerogative order. It provides for discovery, allows damages to be claimed and makes provision for cross-examination, all of which had previously been denied. The reform was not all one-sided. The administrative process is protected by the requirement that leave be obtained prior to making an application, by the need for standing, by restrictive time limits for

---

[41] N. Lewis, Memorandum to TCSC, 27–II, (1993–4) and see N. Lewis & P. Birkenshaw, *When Citizens Complain*.

bringing a case, and by the discretion retained by the court to refuse a remedy in the interests of good administration. However, as far as the individual and his lawyer are concerned the process has become more understandable and thus judicial review is more accessible.

In addition, 'by 1983 the judges confident in their new system of public law had reached the point at which the law lords felt able to reject the use of any alternative form of litigation to secure redress against the state; judicial review was the only way.'[42] Thus the 'exclusivity principle' was born[43] and with it what some have seen as a system of administrative law courts, presided over by specialist administrative law judges. This system and specialism is likely to remain despite the less exclusive approach to Order 53 subsequently taken by the House of Lords.[44]

The reform of the procedure by which judicial review was sought played a considerable part in the dramatic increase in the number of applicants for judicial review during the 1980s and 1990s.[45] It is now easier to make an application. Moreover, the resultant publicity that has been generated by a few notable cases which sought to challenge the way in which government policy had been decided or was being administered, has made the process more familiar and hence even more popular. The phrase 'seeking a judicial review' now features in press headlines and in television and radio news broadcasts (although news announcers still seem less than comfortable with the term).

Thirdly, the increased involvement of the judiciary with administrative law cases has coincided in the 1990s with a judiciary which is more interventionist than in previous decades. This reflects a domination of 'liberal' judges in the superior courts who are of a mind-set which reflects the post-war consensus and its emphasis on the liberal values associated with welfarism and the fostering of community and public rights, rather than just individual private rights. Thus whilst judges accept that wide discretionary powers are necessary for the delivery of welfare provisions, they are nevertheless concerned to intervene to protect public law rights, and there has undoubtedly been a 'move towards liberal interpretation of statutes'.[46] Such an interpretation incorporates the need for fairness and reasonableness and seeks, wherever possible, to protect not just the legal rights and interests of individuals but their legitimate expectations and, increasingly although indirectly, fundamental human rights.

---

[42] S. Sedley, 'Governments, constitutions, and judges', in Richardson & Genn (above, n. 5) at 41.

[43] See *O'Reilly* v. *Mackman* [1983] 2 AC 237.

[44] See *Mercury Communications* v. *Director General of Telecommunications* [1996] 1 WLR 48, at 57, where Lord Slynn states that there should be greater flexibility, with actions under writ acceptable when there is a fusion of public/private law issues, rather than just when the public law issue is collateral and subsequently *Credit Suisse* v. *Allerdale B.C.* [1996] 3 WLR 894.

[45] From 160 in 1974, 1,529 in 1987, 2,886 in 1993 to 3,209 in 1994, of which 1,260 applications were allowed (for full breakdown of figures see L. Bridges, G. Meszaros & M. Sunkin, *Judicial Review in Perspective*. The 1996 figure was 2,805 to 30 Sept., suggesting approx. 3,800 applications for the year.

[46] *Judge over your Shoulder* (2nd edn.), para. 1.

Coupled with the predisposition of individual judges is their increased confidence as administrative law judges. The dramatic rise in applications for judicial review has resulted in High Court judges on the administrative law list becoming more attuned to the intricacies and tensions of public administration and thus more confident in their ability to determine disputes and to affect the administrative process. Moreover, the undeveloped nature of administrative law has acted to challenge some judges to engage in debate about its development.[47] There has therefore been a 'snowball' effect. The number of applications for review and the range of interests they represent and decisions they challenge act to stimulate judicial thinking and the development of the law. The more the law is developed and extended to take account of the diversity of applications, the more individuals and pressure groups are encouraged to apply.

Along with these factors is also an apparent willingness of judges to accept a more obvious constitutional role than previously. This willingness, even desire, would seem to be a response, firstly, to perceived failings within the British system, such as that exposed by Crichel Down in 1954, noted by Sir Stephen Sedley as the catalyst for the loss of judicial confidence in public administration,[48] and, secondly, to 'the increase of the powers claimed by Government'.[49] The concern is that these powers, which are frequently widely drafted, are neither subject to adequate legislative scrutiny before becoming law nor to the processes of political accountability for the way in which they are exercised. This first concern was expressed in 1990 by Mr Justice Purchas in *ex parte Stitt* over 'the wholesale, unregulated and unsupervised powers' given to the Secretary of State to pass subordinate legislation under the Social Security Act 1986.[50] His Lordship was surprised and concerned at such a delegation by Parliament, noting, 'It might be that in this case in the execution of the legislative process that "Homer nodded" . . . On the other hand it might be an unwelcome feature of a dominating executive in a basically two-party democracy.'[51]

Dissatisfaction with Parliament's ability, or desire, to hold government accountable has not been confined to judicial circles. There has been increasing public disillusionment with Parliament and its Members. As a consequence, the judiciary believes that it has public support for its control of an otherwise unaccountable Government.[52] Such support is clearly essential in a system where the courts have traditionally been on the margins of the political process and it acts to legitimate the 'refashioning of the constitution' in which the balance between public administrators and the judges is changed and '[t]he barely fictional Sir Humphrey Appleby, servant and scourge of ministers . . . [finds] his power trumped by a more potent constitutional actor, the judiciary.'[53]

[47] See, e.g., Lord Woolf, 'Droit Public—English style' (1995) *PL* 57; J. Laws, 'Law and democracy' (1995) *PL* 72; and writings by Sir Stephen Sedley.

[48] Above, n. 17 at 283.

[49] Sir Thomas Bingham MR, quoted in *The Observer*, 9 May 1993.

[50] *R. v. Sec. of State for Social Services, ex p. Stitt*, [1991] 3 Admin. LR 169.   [51] Ibid.

[52] Sedley (above, n. 42) at 41.   [53] Ibid.

Judicial activism has also, according to Lord Woolf, been a response to the more confrontational style of politics practised by the Thatcher Governments.[54] The break with consensus politics in the 1980s, together with the continuation of one political party in office for some seventeen years, has encouraged judges to move away from theories of 'democratic élitism'. These have restricted judicial review on the basis that in a democracy accountability is to the electorate. Thus once elected, a government should be free to do what it likes with minimum interference from the courts.[55]. Such theories have been contested with suggestions that they result in 'elective dictatorship'[56] or a 'democratic deficit'[57] and the House of Lords and the lower courts would now no longer seem to feel constrained by them or by a 'sympathy for and deference to democratic paternalism'.[58] The self-imposed fetters have, as a consequence, been removed.

Judges have also been encouraged to assume a more constitutional role by European influences, namely by Britain's membership of the European Union (EU) and the status of the European Convention on Human Rights within the Union. The passing of the European Communities Act in 1972 gave effect to Britain's membership of the EU (the European Economic Community as it was then), and, as a consequence, provided for the primacy of Community law over national law. This has given the judges a role not previously afforded them with regard to legislation. It has also required them to uphold the rights of individuals which arise from European Community (EC) law through the principle of direct effect.

The effect of Britain's membership of the EU upon the judges has been profound. Firstly, it has informed the method of statutory interpretation, and has encouraged a more liberal approach. This accords with the practice of the European Court of Justice (ECJ) which adopts a purposive approach, frequently resorting to implication and creativity to reach the required conclusion. Secondly, it has given the courts a constitutional role, previously denied to them under the doctrine of Parliamentary sovereignty. They have the ability, indeed duty, to determine the compatibility of national legislation with Community law and to declare instances of incompatibility. On the first occasion when such incompatibility arose in *ex parte Factortame* (No. 2), the House of Lords only took action, granting an interim injunction, after a referral to the ECJ.[59] However on the second occasion, *ex parte Commission for Equal Opportunities*, the House of Lords made a declaration without any such reference, demonstrating its increasing confidence to deal with matters of great constitutional significance.[60]

Thirdly, the doctrine of direct effect requires the courts to uphold the rights that individuals can claim from EC law against public bodies. These rights range from

[54] Quoted in *The Observer*, 9 May 1993.   [55] Feldman (above, n. 16) at 246.
[56] Lord Hailsham, *Elective Dictatorship* and *Dilemma of Democracy*.
[57] Sedley (above, n. 17) at 283.   [58] Feldman (above, n. 16) at 246.
[59] *R. v. Sec. of State for Transport, ex p. Factortame* (No. 2) [1991] 1 AC 603.
[60] *R. v. Secretary of State for Employment, ex p. Equal Opportunities Commission* [1994] 2 WLR 409.

those based in private law, such as contract, to rights such as non-discrimination or equality, as determined by Community law. Thus the courts are concerned with rights in a broader context and with according them with something akin to protected status. This may have contributed towards judicial calls for the statutory recognition of fundamental human rights in Britain, a call which is given greater resonance by the jurisprudence of the EC which supports fundamental human rights in the form of the European Convention on Human Rights (ECHR) as a general principle of law.[61] Indeed, it seems that the ECJ may require the courts of Member States to uphold this principle, along with other general principles of law, when acting within the jurisdiction of Community law. If so, given the legal position of the ECHR within Britain, the courts may find themselves operating a dual system: upholding such rights when concerned with the implementation or operation of Community law and unable to do so in the national context.[62]

This would obviously increase judicial frustration which is already evident with regard to the ECHR. Senior judges have expressed their dissatisfaction at their inability to give effect to the ECHR and at the consequence for the individual; he or she has to seek redress in Strasburg. They are also aware of international judicial opinions and are undoubtedly influenced by reports such as that produced by the United Nations Human Rights Committee which noted that the legal system of the United Kingdom 'does not ensure fully that an effective remedy is provided for all victims of violations of the rights contained in the Covenant'.[63] The report also said that the Committee was 'concerned by the extent to which the implementation of the Covenant is impeded by the combined effect of the non-incorporation into domestic law, the failure to accede to the Optional Protocol and the absence of a constitutional Bill of Rights'.[64] It is not surprising that judicial creativity is engaged in giving effect to the ECHR wherever possible.

Fourthly, membership of the EU has had an influence on the development of principles underlying administrative law. In particular, the possible introduction of proportionality as a head for the review of administrative action owes much to an awareness of European jurisprudence, whilst judicial attitudes towards granting injunctions against the Crown have been influenced by developments in relation to Community law and the absurdity and injustice that arises if a dual system operates.[65]

---

[61] See, e.g., *Nold KG* v. *Commission*, Case 4/73; *R.* v. *Kent Kirk*, Case 63/83; *Johnson* v. *Chief Constable of the RUC*, Case 223/84; and Art. F(2) of the Treaty on European Union which states that the Union 'shall respect fundamental rights, as guaranteed by the European Convention . . . as general principles of Community law'.

[62] But see also Op. 2/94 *Re Accession of the Community to the European Human Rights Convention*, given in Mar. 1996, in which the ECJ held the Community had no power under the Treaties to accede to the Convention. This would require a Treaty amendment.

[63] Britain is a signatory to the International Covenant on Civil and Political Rights as well as the ECHR.

[64] CCPR/C/79/Add. 55, 27 July 1995.

[65] See *ex p. Factortame* (No. 2) (above, n. 59) and *M.* v. *Home Office* [1992] QB 270.

Finally, membership of the EC has resulted in judges increasingly looking outwards to what is happening in other jurisdictions, both continental and Commonwealth, rather than being only concerned with their own previous decisions and past practices. All these factors are influential in shaping the character of the body of judges concerned with administrative law and thus with determining the boundaries of review of administrative decisions and the extent to which the courts should interfere in public administration.

Thus an increase in applications for leave to apply for judicial review has coincided with a judicial move towards greater activism. The inevitable effect upon public administration is greater judicial intervention in the processes of government. It can no longer be assumed that decisions will not be challenged, or, if they are, that any judicial intervention will have minimal effect. Rather it is now necessary to guard against possible challenge, as recognized by *Judge over your Shoulder*, which states, 'Judicial Review is reaching new areas all the time, and Departments which have not been the subject of legal challenge before have had to defend their decisions in the court.'[66] Such challenges can be inconvenient, costly, and at times embarrassing for the Government, and are viewed as something to be avoided. As a consequence, '[t]he existence of judicial review has clearly and substantially increased the work of both lawyers and administrators, in effect to "judicial-review" proof departmental decisions.'[67]

It has been necessary to raise the legal awareness of administrators and to an extent change administrative culture which traditionally has not been guided by legal rules and practices. It has also become necessary to afford lawyers a greater input into the administrative process. Indeed, administrators are told that '[t]he best way of avoiding Judicial Review is to follow the principles of good administration. This involves administrators working closely with lawyers.'[68] Seeking legal advice on a regular basis would therefore now seem to be recognized as a feature of good administration. If this is the case, it suggests a change from the traditional position in which lawyers have had a very low profile.

The need to consult legal advisers is supported by the courts who may see legal advice on a particular issue as a relevant and necessary consideration to be taken into account. Ministers may also find the courts more sympathetic if they and their officials have acted after consultation with their lawyers.[69] The need to take legal advice also arises with regard to the European element, which has an impact on most departments. Of particular importance, because of their widespread application, are the Community laws which prohibit discrimination on grounds of sex or, in the case of citizens from other Member States, nationality. Civil servants are advised that in 'any case which raises such questions, you should seek immediate legal advice'.[70]

---

[66] (2nd edn.) para. 1.   [67] Treasury Solicitor, Memorandum to TCSC, HC 27–II, (1993–4).
[68] *Judge over your Shoulder* (2nd edn.), para. 39.
[69] See, e.g., *M*. v. *Home Office* (above, n. 65).
[70] *Judge over your Shoulder* (2nd edn.), para. 24.

Nor are legal concerns confined to official level. In Questions of Procedure Ministers are informed that any proposals they table at Cabinet or Ministerial Committees must be accompanied by memoranda covering 'any issues on which departments have been advised that there may be a risk of challenge in the courts by means of application for judicial review'.[71] This is a clear indication of the political impact that the increase in judicial review has had and a recognition that there may be a political risk attached to accepting a proposal that is likely to be challenged. It also demonstrates the need for administrators and ministers to be 'much closer—both physically and intellectually'[72] to their legal advisers than they have hitherto been.

The 'absorption of the prospect of legal challenge into a department's political and administrative bloodstream'[73] may not necessarily have a positive effect. 'Legal advisers may be treated by ministers (and therefore also their administrative colleagues) more like administrators and lawyers at large and be asked how the department could win rather than what would be the lawful course of action'.[74] The extent to which a 'match-winning departmental mentality' has developed is unknown,[75] but, according to Barker, 'the days are gone when significant legal doubts on a proposed decision of the departmental legal adviser or Treasury counsel were enough to render that decision stillborn without further question'.[76] Whitehall no longer has the same deference to the courts and ministers are more frequently prepared to contest legal challenges to their decisions. In some instances this may be through a genuine desire to resolve an uncertain legal position. In others, however, it may be in the hope that an applicant, faced with rising legal costs, will withdraw or that the application, whatever its merits, will fail for want of the relevant documentation. There may also be the undesirable side-effect of ministers abdicating political responsibility for contested decisions on the basis that these were made on legal advice.[77]

More generally, the effect on decision-making of the increase in judicial review is, as ever, difficult to determine,[78] part of the problem being that administrators are unlikely to admit to following negative rather than positive practices. The Government states that judicial review has 'improved the quality of decision-making by making it more structured and consistent. Accordingly, judicial review is not to be seen as an irritant, but as a contribution to upholding the values of

---

[71] Para. 8.   [72] A. Barker 'The Impact of Judicial Review (1996) *PL* at 614.
[73] Ibid. at 613.   [74] Ibid. at 614.
[75] Although according to Government lawyers attending the Bristol Law and Politics Colloquium in May 1996, it is 'not yet normal' (ibid.).
[76] Ibid. at 613.
[77] E.g. Home Sec. Kenneth Baker denied responsibility for failing to follow the order of the court in *M.* v. *Home Office* (above, n. 65) on the basis that he had taken legal advice.
[78] Lawyers and administrators at the Colloquium (above, n. 77) commented that departmental reaction would depend on the 'perceived frequency and significance of this type of challenge' (A. Baker (above, n. 72) at 613).

fairness, reasonableness and objectivity in public business . . . The contribution by judges in supporting or upholding these values is therefore to be welcomed.'[79]

A reaction to these comments might be— 'They would say that, wouldn't they?' This may be too cynical. However, the view that the threat of judicial review has improved decision-making is contested. Cranston suggests that its effect has been 'to encourage officials to become more cautious in their work and more aware of the need to explain and justify action',[80] but he does not believe that this necessarily results in improved decision-making. In this he is supported by Sir Stephen Sedley who notes that public law is a 'source of anxiety to administrators'[81] but does not necessarily have an improving effect. On the positive or upside, 'well-led administrators take more careful decisions than before, paying regard to legal principles and reviewing their own decisions when legal challenge is made'.[82] On the downside, 'in some places . . . the true reasons for decisions [are] not . . . recorded and forms of defensive public administration have developed, in which fireproofing decisions against judicial review takes priority over conscientious decision-making.'[83] This suggests that at times the threat of judicial review undermines the principles of good administration rather than encouraging them.

The reform of the Civil Service and the courts

The increased involvement of the law and the courts in public administration has coincided with the reform of the Civil Service, through the creation of Next Steps executive agencies, and with the Charter and Open Government initiatives. None of these has been given legal form. 'In fact law is seen as antipathetic to the Government's broad objectives.'[84] The Government's attitude to the law and lawyers was illustrated by the response of Mr William Waldegrave, when Minister for the Public Service and Open Government, to the suggestion that redress under the Citizen's Charter might be through the Small Claims Court. He responded, 'I do not want to be rude about lawyers but if one can avoid getting too many lawyers involved in these redress systems . . . so much the better.'[85]

As a consequence of the Government's 'contempt for law', 'lawyers have not been able to apply the ideals of legality and constitutionality in a manner that would be familiar to North American and continental lawyers.'[86] Thus the reforms of the 1980s and 1990s have largely escaped constitutional scrutiny, and any critique that has been undertaken has been more or less disregarded. This is a concern for constitutionalists and public lawyers who perceive a change in Government attitudes that extends to the courts and judicial review. The position of mutual respect and non-interference seems to have given way to one of distrust and even hostility, and to an impatience with any form of legal control.

[79] Treasury Solicitor, Memorandum to TCSC, HC 27–II, (1993–4).
[80] Cranston (above, n. 5) at 73.   [81] Sedley (above, n. 42) at 42.
[82] Ibid.   [83] Ibid.   [84] Birkenshaw (above, n. 14), 3.
[85] In evidence to TCSC, 27–II, (1993–4), Q27.   [86] Birkenshaw (above, n. 14), 3.

The hostility to the law shown by proponents of the Government reforms accords with theories of anti-Statism and the desire to decrease the intervention of Government and its agencies, that is, to roll back the frontiers of the State. It also accords with the dislike of public choice supporters for legal concepts, such as reasonableness, fairness, impartiality, and justice. These concepts, which have traditionally been accepted by public administrators as underlying the exercise of their discretion, are seen by reformists as vague and 'woolly', and thus as having a minimal role in a model of government which is concerned with public management rather than public administration. In addition, the application of such concepts by the courts is seen as inevitably subjective[87] and not in accordance with objective measurements of performance, such as those provided by value-for-money audits.

Not surprisingly, therefore, the new public management model favours a move from external appeal or review by the courts or tribunals to internal review by inspectorates or review procedures. Such a move has the advantage of providing cheaper appeal mechanisms. It also ensures that appeals are subject to the same efficiency regime as the department or agency and thus removes the element of unpredictable independence which is a feature of outside control. Internal reviews are not a new feature of public administration. They have commonly been used as a first tier appeal, particularly in matters concerning social security, the rationale for providing such administrative reviews being 'to allow officials a simple and quick means of changing decisions without claimants needing to make a further claim or lodge a request for a formal appeal'.[88] Reviews are therefore used to correct errors or deal with changed circumstances whilst appeals are reserved for those instances where the claimant is challenging the outcome. The right of appeal is therefore the main mechanism for dealing with substantive challenges and resolving grievances.

However, since 1984, there has been a shift away from providing a right of appeal to an external body. This is demonstrated with regard to prison discipline, where the right has been removed, and the Social Fund, where the establishing legislation[89] provided no such right. Instead appeal operates through a 'hierarchy of reviews' with no appeal to an external tribunal.[90] In 1993 the Asylum and Immigration Act removed rights of appeal, despite the fact that as many as 20 per cent of the 10,000 cases heard under the old appeal system were found to have been wrongly decided. The justification for the removal of appeal rights was efficiency and cost-saving. However, as Birkenshaw comments, '[I]t is a poor form of efficiency that is allowed to defeat justice, or rather it is no form of efficiency at all but expediency.'[91] The action by Government would seem to

---

[87] P. McAustlan, 'Public law and public choice' (1988) 51 *MLR* 699.

[88] R. Sainsbury, 'Internal reviews and the weakening of Social Security claimants' right of appeal', in Richardson & Genn (above, n. 5) at 289 .

[89] Social Security Act 1986.   [90] Sainsbury (above, n. 88) at 293.

[91] Birkenshaw (above, n. 14), 18.

demonstrate a disregard for tribunals and the courts and their place in the administrative system. Even in areas where the right of appeal to an external tribunal remains, it may be necessary for an individual first to pursue his or her grievance through an internal review procedure (for example, disability benefits), and failure here may act as a deterrent to further action.

The assumption would seem to be that internal review procedures are not only cheaper and more efficient, in that they operate under the same restraints and with the same objectives as those they are reviewing, but, in addition, that they will sustain public confidence in the system's ability to deliver justice. This may not be the case. The independence of the appellant body and the opportunity for someone with a grievance to state his or her case in person are fundamental in securing public confidence that justice will be done. Neither of these requirements is fully met by internal review which confuses adjudication with administration and does not demand the same standards of independence or allow the same level of participation as external appeal. Public confidence may thus be undermined. It may be further weakened by the fact that the 'transition to internal reviews has seemingly taken place unnoticed and without the necessary debate about their proper place in the decision-making process'.[92]

As McAustlan asks, where is the place for the fundamental principles of public law—'openness, fairness and impartiality—and their institutional manifestations—public inquiries, appeals and other formalized systems for the redress of grievances?'[93] The likely attitude of the courts towards internal review also stands consideration. It seems possible, even probable, that where internal review procedures are challenged, the courts will be less restrained in hearing such challenges as has traditionally been the case with tribunals. In addition, the removal of external appeal means that challenge can only be by way of judicial review and thus the number of applications seems likely to rise even further.

Changes from external appeal to internal review have been accompanied by another change; the increased use of secondary legislation, particularly tertiary rules. The use of sources other than primary legislation has long been noted[94] and a Special Report from the Joint Committee on Statutory Instruments in 1978 expressed its concern at the practice of using departmental circulars, despite the fact that the primary legislation required a statutory instrument.[95] Tertiary or administrative rules are used for a number of purposes. For instance, they may give officials instructions on substantive matters, such as the criteria to be used in making certain decisions; they may be concerned with procedures to be followed by either, or both, officials and the public; they may be in the form of policy statements. Whatever their particular purpose, such rules are seen as having a number of advantages as far as administrators are concerned. Foremost of these is that 'rules allow accumulated experience and wisdom to be distilled and used

---

[92] Sainsbury (above, n. 88) at 306.
[93] McAustlan (above, n. 87) at 699.
[94] See Mackenzie & Grove (above, n. 1).
[95] HC 51, (1977–8), para. 12.

efficiently'[96] to the benefit of the decision-making process and those concerned with it. In addition, they 'supposedly encourage consistency, fairness and equality of treatment across not simply persons, groups, organizations, or regions but also across time',[97] and those that provide criteria or detail departmental policy help to prevent irrelevant factors being considered and thus are instrumental in reducing mistakes in decision-making. Rules are also seen as 'contributing to the perceived legitimacy of decisions by allowing those involved to cite the rule as a justification for action', whilst at the same time, they 'reduc[e] . . . the danger that corruption or bias will enter into the decision-making process.'[98]

Such a list suggests that administrative rules are concerned with good practice and with ensuring that decision-making benefits from accumulated knowledge and wisdom to the benefit of both the public and administrators. They are there-fore vital to the administrative process and allow quick and flexible responses in a way that primary, and even secondary, legislation, cannot. The list also suggests that rules are concerned with ensuring efficient decision-making, in the sense of using public money in the best possible way. Indeed, an advantage for the Government is that by giving detailed guidance or instructions through adminis-trative rules, 'staff of relatively low training-levels . . . [can] process highly com-plex issues.'[99] Rules therefore save money. As a consequence it is perhaps not surprising that at a time when the driving force is efficiency, in terms of value for money, the use of such rules has increased. However, as Baldwin points out, 'rules . . . cannot be assumed to be either efficient or benign'.[100] It is the type of rule and the way in which it has been devised that is important. Providing criteria for deal-ing with a particular issue will produce consistency, but not fairness if the criteria themselves are unfair. Similarly, breaking down a complex issue into easily-understood processes will reduce costs by reducing the amount of staff training that is necessary. However, if the processes over-simplify the issue, then decision-making will be distorted.

The use of tertiary rules rather than primary, or even secondary, legislation has the effect of reducing accountability, both to Parliament and to the courts. They do not undergo Parliamentary scrutiny and the courts have done little to address the problem presented by their use. Judges have so far failed 'to develop guiding prin-ciples of real utility'.[101] For example, principles which prohibit the 'unfair non-disclosure of rules' and which 'demand reasonable consultation' in their drafting.[102] At present they escape the application of these vague and subjective concepts by the courts, which might explain why there has been an increase in their use. It accords with the new public management model's distrust of legal concepts and with the move away from 'a ritualistic adherence'[103] to legal rules.

However, the making and use of tertiary rules may not remain outside main-stream judicial activity, particularly if legislation increasingly provides wide dis-

---

[96] R. Baldwin, *Rules and Government*, 13.   [97] Ibid.   [98] Ibid.   [99] Ibid.
[100] Ibid., 14.   [101] Ibid., 168.   [102] Ibid., 187.
[103] A. Yeatman, quoted in P. Bayne, 'Administrative Law' (1988) 62 *Aust. Law Journal* 1043.

cretionary powers, the exercise of which is not subject to any Parliamentary scrutiny and can be determined by departmental or ministerial guidance or rules. The concern is that discretion can then be exercised arbitrarily. This is something Sir Stephen Sedley has already noted with regard to 'the sublegal regions of constitutional convention', which he sees as providing 'opportunities for arbitrary government' and for 'infringing legal norms of good government'.[104] He concludes that this 'may yet be an area in which public law has to take an interest'.[105] If he is contemplating possible judicial action with regard to convention, intervention to provide principles for the operation of departmental rules would seem a possibility—particularly as in Europe these are a matter of concern for the courts. This would bring the courts into conflict with the new public management model which 'elevates economic rationality to primary status . . . and in so doing attempts to replace the legal and procedural framework of the classic model.'[106] Indeed, 'the discourse of management sits uncomfortably with, and by its logic tends to preclude, reference to substantive public service obligations like maintaining the rule of law . . .'[107] It has also shifted the emphasis from outputs to outcomes. This 'may have implications for judicial review and the context of the law which has hitherto matched the traditional ethos and tradition of government and the Civil Service by focusing on decision-making and policy making *processes* rather than "merits" or outcomes.'[108]

Perhaps the most fundamental challenge to judicial thinking and public law developments is the contractualization of government. This is a major feature of Government reforms and it is 'developing at a rate which outstrips the ability of public or administrative law to provide an adequate framework of regulation or supervision'.[109] Indeed, the Government 'finds itself able to draw on previously untapped springs of inherent discretionary contractual powers lying deep in the strata of the common law.'[110] So far it seems that the courts do not see these powers as being subject to judicial review. Indeed, the way in which they have dealt with the few cases brought before them suggests they view them as being 'almost non-justiciable'.[111] They are powers which are exercised in the private or commercial sphere not the public one. The courts at present do not seem to be prepared to distinguish between public contracts and commercial ones, yet there are frequently important differences. This suggests the need to develop a 'distinct body of public law contract'.[112] Moreover it is a pressing need if the judges are not to be 'left out of the picture altogether',[113] for the new public management's vision of the State of the future is grounded in the law of contract.

It is ironic that as the courts are engaging more fully with the principles of public law and their application, the executive is intentionally or otherwise

[104] Sedley (above, n. 42) at 41. [105] Ibid.
[106] A. Yeatman quoted in Bayne (above, n. 103). [107] Ibid.
[108] G. Drewry & D. Oliver, Memorandum to Pub. Serv. Cttee, HC 313–II, (1995–6).
[109] D. Faulker, C. Crouch, M. Freedland, & D. King, Memorandum to TCSC, HC 27–III, (1993–4).
[110] Ibid. [111] Birkenshaw (above, n. 14), 199.
[112] N. Lewis, Memorandum to TCSC, HC 390–II, (1992–3). [113] Ibid.

escaping the restraints of these principles, seeking refuge in the private law of contract. It is also ironic that as the Government seeks to reduce the public sector and to apply private sector methods in those areas that remain, the courts are increasing the scope and application of public law—or perhaps this is cause and effect.

6

DEVELOPING TENSIONS

Introduction

The coincidence of a new public management model of public administration and an interventionist judiciary has resulted in increasing tension between the executive and senior judges. This tension is apparent in the territorial claims, based on the separation of powers, made by both sides, and in the assertion of constitutional principle. From a judicial perspective it arises from Treasury interference in the administration of justice and from the Government's law and order policies, in particular those relating to sentencing. It would also seem to stem from an underlying concern that rights are being eroded or, at least, that concepts like fairness and reasonableness are taking second place to cost savings. From a political perspective it arises out of a belief that judges are 'soft' on crime and are frustrating Government 'get tough' policies, which, politicians argue, have the support of the electorate. Judges are seen 'as the last bastion of the liberal society'[1] and, as such, at odds with Government philosophy. Indeed, some senior administrators have suggested that their judicial counterparts 'have an extra-legal political policy agenda of their own'.[2] They are also seen as concerned to protect their own vested interests and those of lawyers in general, hence their resistance to change in the administration of justice and their increased willingness to find against ministers in judicial review cases.

The Administration of Justice and Efficiency

One of the areas where tension has been most evident is the administration of justice. The Lord Chancellor is responsible for ensuring that the system by which justice is administered is efficient, impartial and serves the interests of justice. In constitutional terms this means that the system should be administered without reference to political considerations and in such a way as to safeguard judicial independence. It should also be effective both in terms of cost and in the delivery of justice and it is its failure here that has been the focus of both judicial and executive concern. However, the appearance of a common cause is misleading. Both may seek increased effectiveness and the reduction of costs, but there the commonality ends, for whilst judges are concerned about effectiveness in terms of

---

[1] 'Whitehall officials' quoted in *The Times*, 3 Nov. 1995.
[2] A. Barker, 'The impact of judicial review' (1996) *PL* 612 at 616.

accessibility and availability, ministers are concerned about value for money and restricting the available funds.

During the 1990s senior judges became increasingly aware that the cost of lit-igation puts the civil courts beyond the reach of any but the very rich or those poor enough to qualify for Legal Aid, a shrinking group, and that a shortage of senior judges was causing often unacceptable delay in hearing both first instance and appeal cases. This resulted in expressions of concern that inadequate funding was undermining the system, and that costs and delays were 'a cancer eating at the heart of justice'.[3] In an attempt to improve the effectiveness of the system, senior judges have sought to find ways of reducing costs and speeding up the progress of a case through the court. To this end, the Lord Chancellor, Lord Mackay, appointed Lord Woolf to consider proposals for the reform of the civil court sys-tem.

The recommendations of his report, *Access to Justice* (1996), included raising the limit of the Small Claims Court to £3,000 (as from January 1996), and giving the system a more inquisitorial slant by making greater use of written evidence, tribunals, and alternative dispute resolution. He also set out a blueprint for a sys-tem of case management by the courts and for stricter control of both pre-trial pro-cedures and the hearing or trial itself, to prevent time-wasting. This concern to increase control had been reflected, indeed anticipated, in the Lord Chief Justice's Practice Direction and the Family Division Practice Direction (both January 1995) and the Chancery Guide (April 1995), an indication of judicial support for Lord Woolf. However, the Lord Chancellor's enthusiasm for some of the reforms would seem to have been dampened by their resource implications and in October 1996 Lord Woolf expressed his concern at Lord Mackay's failure to take the necessary action. For his part, Lord Mackay had indicated that he was looking to the judi-ciary and the legal profession to make economies and thus cut the costs of litiga-tion.

The measures proposed by Lord Woolf were intended to make litigation cheaper and speedier and thus to make the system more accessible. Efficiency is therefore a means to an end, not an end in itself. It is not a question of cost-saving to benefit the Treasury but of cost-saving to benefit the system and those who use it. Indeed, the delivery of a more efficient service in terms of the through-put of cases, has required an increase in Treasury expenditure on judicial personnel. From 1988 senior judges campaigned for an increase in the number of High Court judges, achieving some success in 1993 when a further ten were appointed. Ironically, however, the substantial increase in judicial review, which occurred in the 1990s, meant there was still a shortfall of senior judges, many of whom were diverted from hearing appeals to hearing applications for review. Hence the cam-paign, led by the Master of the Rolls, then Sir Thomas Bingham, continued and the appointment of three more senior judges was announced at the end of 1995.

---

[3] Sir Thomas Bingham MR, quoted in *The Times*, 27 Dec. 1994.

The problem is, of course, that judges cost money, and it is clear that in the prevailing economic climate, their 'value' has to be costed before the Lord Chancellor is able to make appointments.[4]

Thus the perspective taken by the executive is somewhat different and the Lord Chancellor has been under increasing pressure to improve efficiency in terms of value for money. This has produced concern that the executive function of the Lord Chancellor is becoming confused with his judicial role and that 'the two sides of the office of Lord Chancellor have at any rate converged, if not coalesced, in this matter'.[5] The Lord Chancellor is required to act 'as the buffer and the link between the judiciary and the other two branches of government'.[6] The duality of his position is clearly at odds with the separation of powers, a principle upon which the British Constitution is often said to be founded. In the past the need for the Lord Chancellor to fulfil executive and judicial functions has not presented too much of a problem because the judicial and legal roles have been predominant, but in the 1990s the Lord Chancellor has become 'a strongly political Minister'.[7] Moreover, some consider that 'it is the political and administrative functions of the Lord Chancellor and his officials which have become dominant'.[8]

The concentration upon political and administrative functions is seen as posing a threat to the independence of the legal system and increasing the tension between judges and the Lord Chancellor. Such tension is perhaps inevitable when account is taken of the substantial shift there has been in the control of the administration of justice from judges to civil servants in the Lord Chancellor's Department.[9] However, the increasing involvement of the Treasury in the detailed funding of the justice system means that the 'friction' between judges and the Lord Chancellor is in danger of becoming destructive rather than 'constructive',[10] as 'the executive seeks to restrain open-ended expense whilst ensuring at the same time fair, speedy and efficient service to the citizen.'[11]

It is to restrain open-ended expense that the Lord Chancellor's Department is required to formulate policy and to make determinations as to value for money according to financial yardsticks. However, there is little or no requirement for consultation with the judges.[12] Thus it would seem that in the Lord Chancellor's Department, as elsewhere, 'managerialism is, by stealth, and unnoticed, taking over from constitutionalism.'[13] This suggests constitutional change, whereby

---

[4] The cost would increase further if the Lord Chief Justice, Lord Bingham, has his way and the salaries of judges are brought more closely into line with those of top barristers and solicitors. From 1 December 1996 High Court judges were paid £104,415 while a leading commercial law QC could get £1m. Lord Bingham is concerned that such a difference could cause recruitment problems.

[5] Lord Glenamara, HL Debs., col. 775, 27 Apr. 1994.   [6] Lord Lester, ibid., col. 758.

[7] Ibid.   [8] Ibid.

[9] See Lord Browne-Wilkinson, 'The independence of the judiciary in the 1980s', 11th Francis Mann Lecture, 17 Nov. 1987.

[10] Lord Donaldson used the term 'constructive friction' in HL Debs., col. 761, 27 Apr. 1994.

[11] Baroness Elles, ibid., col. 772.   [12] Lord Lester, ibid., col. 758.

[13] D. Oliver, 'The Lord Chancellor's Department' (1994) *PL* 163, and see J. W. Raine & M. J. Willson, 'New public management and criminal justice' (1995) 15 *Pub. Money and Man.* 1.

instead of the system of justice being administered in a way that is independent of political considerations, it is now subject to political direction. If this is so, then constitutional amendment has been made without public debate and, it would seem, with little reference to the judges.

The culture of managerialism and market politics has extended from the Lord Chancellor's Department to the legal system, as evidenced by the fact that the courts are now subject to performance targets and standards provided by the Citizen's Charter. The problem is that such standards have to be measurable and there is concern that the focus is on value for money rather than the ability of the system to be fair, impartial and just, for such concepts are 'not capable of being measured out by an accountant's computer'.[14] Thus whilst key performance indicators include the average cost and length of time taken per case in the Magistrates' Courts which are clearly important, measuring the 'quality of service' in terms of the number of telephones available to court-users, the number of seats in the waiting-area, and the opening hours of the cash office would seem to trivialize the functions of the court and ignore the most important qualities.

In line with Government policy in April 1995 the administration of justice passed to an executive agency, the Court Service Agency, thus distancing the Lord Chancellor from the day-to-day running of the courts. He continues to set the broad policy objectives but the Agency under its Chief Executive[15] is responsible for their implementation. To counter judicial criticisms that judges themselves should be able to advise on how resources are to be used, consultative committees have been included within the Court Service Agency structure. These committees are designed to foster a closer link between the executive and the judiciary, and allow judges once more to have a say in the administrative process. However, judicial involvement in the administration of justice is unlikely to reduce tension if the real master is the Treasury.

The problem is that justice is expensive and its subsidization does not accord with a market economy. Hence the Government has indicated its belief that civil courts should cover their costs rather than relying on a subsidy from the Treasury and in 1997 the costs to court-users rose substantially,[16] which does little for the cause of wider accessibility. Moreover, according to the Vice-Chancellor, Sir Richard Scott, the decision that the civil courts should be self-financing was made without consulting the judiciary. He expressed the view that the policy was 'lamentable' and 'misconceived', believing that the civil justice system 'should be available for anyone who needs it'.[17] Lord Justice Saville also voiced concern that the independence of the judiciary would be put 'in jeopardy' if the salaries of judges 'are part and parcel of the money available to run the system'.[18] Thus, as

---

[14] Lord Lester, HL Debs., col. 758, 27 Apr. 1994.   [15] Michael Huebner.

[16] In December 1996 revenue covered about 80% of expenses. The aim is to raise an extra £50m to make the system pay for itself.

[17] Reported in *The Times*, 2 Dec. 1996 and 14 Jan. 1997. The policy had universal application, although the discretion of the court to waive charges was re-instated after *R.* v. *Lord Chancellor ex p. Witham*, (1997) *The Times*, 13 Mar.   [18] Ibid.

the system is further squeezed and resources are more tightly controlled by the Treasury, the relationship between the executive and the judiciary is likely to remain tense.

The episode of Mr Justice Wood

The focus for much of the tension is the Lord Chancellor, under pressure on the one hand to pursue efficiency objectives, and on the other to ensure that the interests of justice are served and judicial independence protected. There is little doubt that at times his position has been compromised and senior judges have expressed concern that his actions have been politically rather than judicially motivated. One particular episode, which came to light in 1994, made headline news and triggered an unprecedented debate in the House of Lords. It concerned correspondence between the Lord Chancellor, Lord Mackay, and the President of the Employment Appeals Tribunal, Mr Justice Wood, which seemed to suggest that the Lord Chancellor was interfering in the President's interpretation of the law and putting pressure on him to change his view in order to save money.

Lord Mackay first wrote to Mr Justice Wood on 18 December 1992, expressing concern over the growing backlog of cases faced by the Employment Appeals Tribunal and the practice of the court to allow some appellants a preliminary hearing to see if they had a case deserving a full trial, even though their notice of appeal showed no point of law. Lord Mackay wrote:

> I wish to ensure that public money is not wasted in preliminary hearings . . . I need hardly remind you that the backlog of cases started the year at an unacceptably high level and has continued to rise rapidly. I cannot sit by and watch the situation get worse. Equally, I am unwilling to commit more expensive resources in the way of judges to sit in extra courts, whilst procedural rules which allow for the cheap and efficient disposal of clearly unmeritorious cases might be used to greater effect.[19]

He urged Mr Justice Wood to use Rule 3, a procedural device and one used in the Scottish courts, which allowed for the dismissal of appeals without a hearing when there was no point of law shown in the notice of appeal. Mr Justice Wood refused to comply, explaining his reasoning both on paper and in person. He considered, firstly, that the hearings were justified in law, and, secondly, that in the interests of justice they were necessary in cases where it was not always clear whether or not the grounds for appeal were on a matter of law.

Lord Mackay wrote again on 5 February 1993, after he had met with Mr Justice Wood, and then on 19 March, expressing 'disappointment' at the judge's attitude. He stated,

---

[19] Extracts of the correspondence between Lord Mackay and Mr Justice Wood were published in *The Observer*, 3 Apr. 1994. All correspondence was made available to the House of Lords Library and extracts were printed in the Report of the debate (HL Debs., cols. 754–8, 27 Apr. 1994).

I did not seek further discussion of Rule 3 but had sought to make it clear to you that I was not prepared to accept preliminary hearings being held where Rule 3 provides a cheap and expeditious procedure for final disposal of a purported appeal.

I ask you again for your immediate assurance that Rule 3 is henceforth to be applied in full and that preliminary hearings are not to be used where no jurisdiction is shown on a notice of appeal. If you do not feel you can give that assurance, I must ask you to consider your position.[20]

Lord Mackay's letters raised a number of constitutional issues. Firstly, he, as Lord Chancellor, had no power to 'discuss with judges their stewardship of cases in relation to cost, conduct and the legal principles involved.'[21] He certainly could not order a judge with regard to his interpretation of the law and, if he required a different procedure to be followed, then he needed to legislate accordingly. Secondly, the Lord Chancellor's concern was clearly with cost not justice. Indeed, his approach 'demonstrated all the unattractive attributes of a Treasury-driven policy to achieve savings at any cost . . . even at the expense of abandoning a course which ensured that justice was not only done but was seen to be done'.[22] Moreover, it needed to be 'viewed against the background of what must have been a Treasury motivated policy to restrict the appointment of more High Court Judges'.[23] Thirdly, the phrase 'consider your position' raised a matter of considerable constitutional concern. In the subsequent debate in the House of Lords Lord Lester considered that he 'would have interpreted it as an official and formal invitation . . . to consider whether [he] . . . could properly continue in that office'.[24]

For Mr Justice Wood, Lord Mackay's last letter raised 'a constitutional issue in such stark form' that he needed 'to take time before replying'.[25] His reply came on 23 April. In his letter the judge stated that the views he had expressed had been reached after consultations with others on the Bench and that in their 'collective opinion' it was a correct statement of the law. He further argued that the axing of preliminary hearings would deny justice to 'members of the public, who are not familiar with the law or its processes; who are not able to express themselves on paper, who are deeply and emotionally involved in their cases; and whose case merits investigation.'[26] He added that many did not qualify for Legal Aid, which the Lord Chancellor had recently cut.

He then addressed the constitutional issue which he considered had been raised by Lord Mackay's interference with the way in which he ran his court.

I have, of course, given the most serious consideration to my position as you required of me. You have demanded that I exercise my judicial function in a way which you regard as best suited to your executive circumstances, but I have to say that . . . I cannot regard compliance with your demand as conducive to justice.

[20] HL Debs., col. 754, 27 Apr. 1994.
[21] Andrew MacKinley MP, writing in *The Times*, 26 Apr. 1994.
[22] F. Purchas, 'Lord Mackay and the judiciary' (1994) *NLJ* 6644.
[23] Ibid.   [24] HL Debs., col. 257, 27 Apr. 1994.
[25] HL Debs. col. 755, 27 Apr. 1994   [26] Ibid., cols. 755–6.

You express disappointment. I express profound regret that it has ever been the uncomfortable duty of a judge in this country, in compliance with the judicial oath, to write to a Lord Chancellor refusing a demand such as the one which you have made of me.[27]

A few months later Mr Justice Wood announced his retirement, although he subsequently insisted that he had already made the decision and notified others of it before the episode with Lord Mackay. He had not resigned in response to being asked to 'consider his position'.[28] The correspondence between Lord Mackay and Mr Justice Wood came to light in 1994, whereupon the Lord Chancellor made a statement in the House of Lords in which he insisted that what he meant was that the President of the Employment Appeals Tribunal should consider his 'intellectual' position. He should detail the reasoning for his decision not to use Rule 3.[29] Such an explanation was not universally accepted either in the House of Lords or outside. Lords Lester, Donaldson, Oliver and Glenamara all saw the phrase used as 'inappropriate',[30] while Sir Francis Purchas argued that 'an attempt to influence a judge, backed up with a threat, whatever the precise form it may have taken, was almost certainly an unconstitutional act.'[31]

The episode of Mr Justice Wood rang alarm bells as far as the judiciary was concerned, calling into question the whole issue of judicial independence. Lord Oliver expressed concern that the Lord Chancellor and his Department were interpreting 'judicial independence' more narrowly than previously and only considering it to be infringed 'if an attempt is made to dictate or influence the decision in a particular case'.[32] This concern would seem to be confirmed by a subsequent statement made by the Lord Chancellor in which he said, 'The essence of judicial independence is that the judge trying the case is free to decide it according to his judgment in the light of the existing law. This applies to the individual case and that is the essence of judicial independence'.[33] Such a narrow interpretation, in which judicial independence is confined to the individual case, may have serious constitutional implications, blurring even more the separation of powers and opening up the possibility of executive dominance not only over the legislature but also over the administration of justice. This was recognized by Sir Francis who noted the importance of a 'truly independent Judiciary' and the danger that 'the stability of the Constitution is threatened if that independence is in this respect subjected to pragmatic factors such as economic and political stresses and conflicts inherent in the market economy, now so fashionable in current political circles.'[34] His concern was shared by Lord Ackner and Lord Browne-Wilkinson, who, in addition, claimed that justice was being compromised by government spending curbs.[35]

---

[27] *The Observer*, 3 Apr. 1994.
[28] Reported ibid.
[29] HL Debs., cols. 498–500, 21 Mar. 1994.
[30] HL Debs., 27 Apr. 1994.
[31] Above, n. 22.
[32] HL Debs., col. 779, 27 Apr. 1994.
[33] HL Debs., col. 1308, 15 June 1996.
[34] Above, n. 22.
[35] *The Brief*, Channel 4, 26 Apr. 1994, and see Lord Akner on Government's failure to understand and protect judicial independence (HL Debs., col. 1285, 15 June 1996).

Despite the final acceptance by senior judges and others that Mr Justice Wood's decision to retire had been made prior to his argument with the Lord Chancellor, the bottom line concern remains, that the search for efficiency and value for money undermines the system that administers justice, and thus inevitably undermines justice itself.

Legal Aid

This concern arose with regard to Legal Aid, where once more Lord Mackay had to contend with Treasury demands to curb costs which conflict with judicial concerns to improve accessibility to the law, or at the least not see it further diminished. Access in civil cases was substantially reduced in 1993 when tighter qualifying regulations were introduced and those who did get assistance were required to pay an increasing share of the costs. However, Lord Mackay's Green Paper, published in May 1995, and the subsequent White Paper of 1996, heralded the biggest overhaul of Legal Aid since its inception in 1949.[36] The Green Paper proposed that Legal Aid would be cash-limited[37] and that the thirteen areas of the Legal Aid Board would be provided with budgets, based on past demand. These local boards would then award fixed-budget contracts to law firms and advice agencies which would be subject to strict quality control. These agencies would in turn contract out work to others, such as barristers.

The reforms therefore remove the franchises currently held by some 1,000 law firms to operate the Legal Aid Scheme. They also give a much bigger role to paralegal agencies and Citizens' Advice Bureaux, the stated aim being to give more people help at a lower cost. Access to justice may therefore increase in some areas of the law. However, the overriding concern is cost, and the prevention of a continued escalation of the Legal Aid budget beyond that which can reasonably be afforded. The Green Paper stated that costs were rising out of proportion to public benefit. Such concern is widespread and non-controversial, what is controversial is the new public management thinking behind the reforms. This is evident in the 'quality control' of contractors and in the stipulation that budgets will cover the anticipated volume of cases 'for the lowest price consistent with achieving quality and ensuring access.'[38] Thus the emphasis is on price first and 'quality', however this is defined and measured, second. Suppliers may find themselves required to represent people whilst rationing their entitlement, suggesting a possible conflict of interest.

Moreover, the setting of fixed regional budgets raises concern about what happens when the money runs out. The Green Paper stated that any capped system of criminal Legal Aid would have to ensure that 'no case can be refused for lack of

[36] Cm. 2854 (1995); Cm. 3305 (1996).
[37] Cash limits on a £1.4bn civil and criminal Legal Aid budget.
[38] Cm. 2854 (1995).

money alone'.[39] A refusal on such grounds would be likely to contravene Article 6 of the European Convention on Human Rights. This states

> Everyone charged with a criminal offence has the following minimum rights . . . to defend himself in person or through legal assistance of his own choosing or, if he has not sufficient means to pay for legal assistance, to be given it free when the interests of justice so require.

A capped system clearly presents the danger of money not being available for legal assistance when the interests of justice require and raises the spectre of the Social Fund and the inherent injustice of it administration, whereby the availability of money depends 'on where in the country an applicant lives and the time of year at which they apply'.[40]

It is perhaps not surprising that the reforms have brought the Lord Chancellor once more into conflict with senior judges and the legal profession, and whilst some of the criticisms suggest the protection of vested interests by those groups affected, there are valid concerns. The Lord Chancellor is accused of cutting costs for the Treasury and of succumbing to anti-Statist New Right thinking which opposes State aid and subsidization. Moreover, it is argued that by so doing, he is undermining the philosophical basis of Legal Aid which is as far as possible to ensure equality before the law and universal access.

Sentencing Policy: Executive versus Judicial Discretion

Government policies concerned with curbs on spending and value for money have created tension between the judiciary and the executive because of their effect upon the administration of justice. The tension has manifested itself in an unusual confrontation between senior judges and the Lord Chancellor. However, he is not the only Cabinet minister to have been subject to judicial attack. In 1995 the Home Secretary, Michael Howard, was also extensively criticized by senior members of the judiciary for his 'law and order' policies. The 'lock 'em up' and 'treat 'em tough' approach has not met with approval from many judges whose more liberal ideas conflict with right-wing Conservative ideology. However, the main conflict has arisen over discretion in relation to sentencing, and in particular life sentences.

The situations in which life sentences are applicable are laid down by statute. The Murder (Abolition of Death Penalty) Act 1965 provides for mandatory life sentences and the Criminal Justice Act 1991 for discretionary life sentences. However, during the 1990s senior judges have expressed concern both over the legislative framework and the discretion that surrounds their operation. A major concern is the rigidity of the mandatory life sentence which applies to all cases of murder. Judges argue that murders should not all be treated the same and that they should have the power to recognize distinctions in the sentences they pass down.

[39] Ibid.　　　[40] Charles Ely, President of Law Society, quoted in *The Times*, 18 May 1995.

This, they maintain, would prevent the repeat of situations like that of Private Lee Clegg, the paratrooper convicted of murder whilst on duty in Northern Ireland. Private Clegg was released by the Secretary of State for Northern Ireland in response to the public outcry at his imprisonment. He had served only four years of his sentence. For judges this demonstrates the illogicality of mandatory sentences, which they believe should be reserved for 'truly heinous murders', where 'life' should then mean life.[41]

A second concern of the judiciary is the anomaly that exists between discretionary and mandatory life sentences with regard to appeals against the recommended length of sentences. Under the Criminal Justice Act the judge, when passing a discretionary life sentence, has the power to stipulate the length of time that should be served for the purpose of punishment and deterrence.[42] This is part of the judge's order, not merely a recommendation, and is made in open court. It is therefore open to challenge. However, where a mandatory life sentence is concerned, the minimum recommendation made by the trial judge is not part of the sentence, rather it is advice and very often it is given to the Home Secretary privately in writing through the Lord Chief Justice. It is one of the considerations the Home Secretary should take into account when deciding the length of time a prisoner should serve. As a consequence it cannot be challenged directly through judicial review and the prisoner has to rely upon representations to the Home Secretary. Senior judges have expressed their dissatisfaction with this position, believing that mandatory 'lifers' should have the same rights as those whose sentences of life imprisonment are discretionary.

Thirdly, senior judges consider sentencing to be a matter for the courts and are concerned at the statutory provision for executive discretion. In cases of mandatory life sentences the Home Secretary has the power to add a 'public interest' tariff to a sentence recommended by the judiciary.[43] The existence of such a tariff and its use by politicians is unusual in a Western democracy and inevitably raises the question of whether it is the 'public interest' that the Home Secretary is considering or the 'political interest' of the Government. Thus the Home Secretary's announcement that the Moors murderer, Myra Hindley, would never be released from prison was attacked by Lord Donaldson, a retired Master of the Rolls, as a response to public opinion which was only one step removed from the lynch mob and did not equate with rational decision-making.[44]

The matter also arose in the case of John Venables and Robert Thompson who were eleven years old when sentenced to be detained 'during Her Majesty's pleasure'[45] for murdering a two-year-old boy. The trial judge recommended that they serve a minimum of eight years. This was increased to ten years by the Lord Chief

[41] Lord Lane, in evidence to Home Affairs Cttee, HC 111, (1995–6).
[42] S. 34 and see Pract. Dir. *(Crime; Life Sentence)* [1993] 1 WLR 223.
[43] Criminal Justice Act 1991, s. 35.   [44] Article in *The Guardian*, 28 Dec. 1995.
[45] Under Children and Young Persons Act 1933 as amended by s. 1(5) and s. 4 of the Murder (Abolition of the Death Penalty) Act 1965.

Justice. However, the Home Secretary announced they would be detained for a minimum of fifteen years. This led to concern that he had been overly receptive to public reaction immediately after the trial and that the adjusted tariff was motivated by the Home Secretary's desire for electoral popularity rather than by consideration of fairness, justice and the public interest.

The Court of Appeal subsequently ruled the fifteen-year tariff to be unfair.[46] The Master of the Rolls (Lord Woolf) considered that by taking into account petitions and other public demands for a higher sentence than that recommended by the judiciary, the Home Secretary had taken account of factors which were irrelevant to the fixing of the tariff and had departed from the standards of fairness required. He was also concerned that a series of policy decisions had removed the flexibility that Parliament had intended should apply in sentences of detention in such cases and that the effect of the Home Secretary publicly disagreeing with the judiciary over the length of the tariff would undermine public confidence in the criminal justice system. Judges have been particularly concerned that the distinction between the judicial and the political elements of a sentence should be known and, to this effect, have ruled that the Home Secretary should inform prisoners of the judicial or penal tariff and give reasons if the intention is to depart from it. A prisoner should then be given the opportunity to make representations to the Home Secretary.[47]

The Home Secretary's decision is challengeable by way of judicial review and in 1995 Mr Justice Turner quashed the Home Secretary's reaffirmation of the previous Home Secretary's decision, made in 1988, that John Pierson should serve twenty years for the murder of both his parents.[48] The trial judge had recommended fifteen years and the Home Secretary's justification for an additional five years had been that Pierson had committed two separate murders, a justification later challenged by Pierson who argued that the murders should be seen as part of the same act rather than two separate acts. The subsequent Home Secretary, Michael Howard, accepted Pierson's argument. However, despite this, he had confirmed the twenty-year sentence in 1994. Mr Justice Turner held it was not lawfully open to the Secretary of State to fix a longer term if no new adverse factor had emerged.

However, the decision of the High Court was overturned by the Court of Appeal which held that the Home Secretary had acted within the wide discretion provided by section 35 of the Criminal Justice Act.[49] Lord Justice Bingham MR, who gave the leading judgment, noted that the decision raised questions about the Secretary of State's powers, and expressed sympathy for the view that it was unacceptable for the Home Secretary to raise a penal term fixed by his predecessor on the

[46] *R. v. Sec. of State for Home Dept, ex p. Venables; R. v. Same, ex p. Thompson* [1996] 2 WLR 67.
[47] *R. v. Sec of State for Home Dept, ex p. Doody* [1993] 3 WLR 154, given effect by Home Secretary's policy statement (HC Debs., cols. W863–5, 27 July 1993).
[48] *R. v. Sec. of State for the Home Dept, ex p. Pierson* [1996] 1 All ER 837.
[49] [1996] 1 All ER 837.

grounds that it did not adequately meet the requirements of deterrence and retribution. However, he concluded that there was nothing in law to stop the Home Secretary from doing so. His decision could not therefore be challenged on grounds of rationality. The Court of Appeal drew comfort from the fact that a commitment had been given under oath on the Secretary of State's behalf that he was open to further representations from the applicant. The court made clear that it expected such representations to be given fair and careful consideration. Such a statement carried with it an implied willingness to review a future decision on grounds of fairness, if such a challenge was appropriate.

Where discretionary life sentences are concerned, the courts have moved to limit executive discretion by ensuring that it is exercised reasonably. Thus the Court of Appeal has ruled that it is not reasonable for the Home Secretary to reject the opinion of the Lord Chief Justice regarding the length of a sentence unless his recommendation is out of line with similar cases or is too lenient. This was held not to be the case on either count in *ex parte McCartney*.[50] The Court of Appeal also ruled that it was unreasonable or unfair for the Home Secretary not to give a life prisoner access to information that was made available to the Lord Chief Justice when the length of a prisoner's tariff was being reconsidered.[51]

The courts, it would seem, are concerned to prevent the possibility of an arbitrary use of power. To this end they have made the sentencing process more open and reasoned and have gradually reduced the power of the executive over sentencing. The gradual diminution of executive power was noted by Lord Windlesham, a former Home Office minister, when giving evidence to the Home Affairs Committee in February 1995. He considered that this reduction would continue and that eventually the mandatory life sentence, so disliked by the judges because of the fetter it placed on their discretion and the power it gave to the executive, would itself go. The Home Affairs Committee subsequently recommended the abolishment of the Home Secretary's discretion.[52]

Lord Windlesham's observations were made before the Conservative Party Conference in October of that year. During his speech to Conference the Home Secretary, Michael Howard, announced that he intended to increase the use of mandatory life sentences by making them automatic for second serious sexual or violent offences. He also announced the creation of stiff minimum sentences for burglars and drug-dealers. His announcement outraged senior members of the judiciary. The Lord Chief Justice, Lord Taylor, who had not been consulted by the Home Secretary, publicly condemned it for undermining judicial discretion. He further suggested that with detection rates so low, resources would be better employed catching criminals in the first place.

However, the strongest pronouncement against the Home Secretary's sentencing plans came from Lord Donaldson, who was Master of the Rolls from

[50] *R. v. Sec. of State for Home Dept, ex p. McCartney* [1994] The Times 25 May.
[51] *R. v. Sec. of State for Home Dept, ex p. Chapman* [1994] 42 LS Gaz. R. 38.
[52] HC 111, (1995–6).

1982–92. He questioned the motivation behind them, noting, 'There will be some who will wonder whether such proposed measures are dictated by an objective consideration of the public good, or by electoral imperative.'[53] He saw the measures as not only limiting judicial discretion to take individual circumstances into account, but also as 'limiting the powers of the courts to decide, by means of judicial review, whether the Government is exceeding the powers granted to it by Parliament,' and he concluded 'any Government which seeks to make itself immune to an independent review of whether its actions are lawful or not is potentially despotic.'[54]

Michael Howard had used sentencing for political purposes, as a demonstration that the Conservatives were still the party of law and order. This provoked a response from Lord Ackner, who had retired as a Lord in 1995, that Mr Howard's interference with sentencing was 'yah boo politics' and an attempt by the Home Secretary to prove he was 'tougher than the opposition'.[55] Judges were further alarmed by the call of the Party Chairman, Mr Brian Mawhinney, for members of the public to write and complain to judges and magistrates if they thought a sentence in a particular case was too low. This populist move, intended to distance the Government from the sentencing policies of the courts, was seen by judges as undermining their independence and questioning their motives and integrity.

Thus the executive and the judiciary appeared to be pulling in different directions. The executive sought to limit the discretion of the courts over sentencing while the judges sought to limit that of the executive. The dispute lies in a disagreement over sentencing policy and whether sentencing is a judicial matter, in which the executive should not interfere, or an executive one, and thus for ministers to decide. Despite the open opposition of the judiciary the Government continued to move towards the stipulation of minimum sentences for offences, presenting its Crime Bill to Parliament in the 1996–7 session. The minimalization of judicial discretion coincidentally accords with rational-choice thinking and the new public management model, reducing, as it does, the court's ability to think in terms of fairness and justice. However, its motivation has been political and the reaction of the Conservative Party Conference to the sentencing proposals indicated that it was in accord with the wishes of many Conservative supporters and thus a potential vote-winner.

The judicial viewpoint on sentencing was forcefully made by Lord Lane in a report to the Prison Reform Trust. Lord Lane saw executive interference as 'contrary to the deep-rooted concept of the common law and the European Convention on Human Rights, namely that the length of time a prisoner serves . . . should be determined by the courts not the executive.'[56] He was concerned that '[f]ailure to observe this precept can obviously lead to political consideration creeping into decisions where they properly have no place.'[57] The matter has in fact been taken

---

[53] Article in *The Guardian*, 1 Dec. 1995.
[54] Ibid.
[55] Reported in *The Sunday Times*, 5 Nov. 1995.
[56] The Lane Committee (1993).
[57] Ibid.

to the European Court of Human Rights (ECHR) on the basis that the existence of executive discretion breaches Article 4(4) which requires that persons detained are entitled to have the lawfulness of their detention determined by a court of law.

In February 1996 in the cases of Messrs Hussain and Singh[58] the ECHR made a decision on one aspect of that discretion. The applicants had been convicted of murder in the 1970s whilst in their teens and, because of their age, had been sentenced to be detained during Her Majesty's pleasure. They had served their tariff period and the Parole Board had recommended their release. However, the Home Secretary had not accepted this recommendation and had ordered them to be detained indefinitely on the grounds that they still presented a risk to public safety. The ECHR ruled that it was a breach of the Convention for the Home Secretary to order further detention once the tariff period had been served. If the matter of further detention arose, it should be considered by an independent tribunal or court before which prisoners would have the right to put their case and be legally represented. The application of this judgment by the ECHR does not affect the Home Secretary's discretion to increase the original tariff recommended by the trial judge, and only affects those technically detained during Her Majesty's pleasure, some 235 people, and not those serving mandatory sentences. However, further reductions in that discretion seem likely, which would be to the benefit of fairness and impartiality if not executive–judicial relations.[59]

Government Defeats in the Courts

The judicial–executive row over sentencing and the hostility shown by some ministers towards the judiciary needs to be seen against the background of a number of successful challenges of ministerial decisions in the courts. These had been given high-profile treatment by the media and reported as personal defeats for particular ministers. Moreover, at a time when Government popularity in the polls was at an all-time low, they further undermined public confidence in the Government and were seen to reaffirm political accusations of sleaze, moral corruptness and an abuse of power. In constitutional terms they suggested a change in the balance of power between the executive and the judiciary, a change that ministers sought to resist. Many of the rulings made during the period 1991–6 had financial consequences or affected the operation of government policies. Most were concerned with national law. However, a number of significant decisions came directly, or indirectly, as a consequence of European law, either from the Community or the Convention on Human Rights.

---

[58] *Hussain and Singh* v. *UK*, 21928/93 22 EHRR.

[59] The Home Secretary has moved to give effect to the ruling of the ECHR in the Crime Bill. This removes executive discretion in relation to Parole Board recommendations that a prisoner should be released. The cases of Venables and Thompson await judgment by the ECHR.

European Community law and sovereignty

In 1991 *ex parte Factortame* (Nos. 1 and 2)[60] made headline news. The case was brought by Spanish fishermen who claimed that regulations made by the Secretary of State under the Merchant Shipping Act 1988 contravened EC law and their rights under the doctrine of direct effect. The House of Lords sought a preliminary reference from the ECJ. It also sought a ruling on whether EC law gave it the power to grant interim relief, a power which it believed it did not have under national law because of the Crown Proceedings Act. The ECJ ruled that a national rule could not stand in the way of an effective remedy to enforce rights arising under EC law and the House of Lords 'disapplied' the relevant section of the Act.[61] Subsequently, the British Government was found to have contravened EC law, and in 1996 the ECJ delivered its opinion that Spanish fisherman could claim financial compensation.[62]

Factortame had considerable constitutional significance. It was the first time since Britain had joined the Community (subsequently to become the Union) that British judges had ruled that a section of an Act of Parliament, or rather the regulations made by the Secretary of State under that section, was incompatible with EC law. The House of Lords had done so only with the authority of the ECJ. By 1994 its confidence had grown and in *ex parte Equal Opportunities Commission*[63] it made a declaration without reference to the ECJ that parts of the Employment Protection (Consolidation) Act 1978 were incompatible with Community law. *The Times* considered that the House of Lords had 'in effect . . . struck down as "unconstitutional" an Act of Parliament' and suggested, 'Britain may now have, for the first time in history, a constitutional court'.[64]

Defeats for the Government with regard to EC law also came in two cases brought by women forced to resign from the armed forces when they became pregnant.[65] The Employment Appeals Tribunal ruled that the Minister of Defence's policy was unlawful and that compensation should be paid. The large amounts initially awarded provided uncomfortable headlines for the Government, the money coming, of course, from the taxpayer.

In 1995 the Government again found itself the subject of a ruling with regard to EC law which had financial implications, although this time the ruling was from the ECJ rather than the national courts.[66] The ECJ held that the EU equal

---

[60] *R. v. Sec. of State for Transport, ex p. Factortame* (No. 1) [1990] 2 AC 85, (No. 2) [1991] 1 AC 603.
[61] *Ex p. Factortame* (No. 2), above n. 60.
[62] *R. v. Sec. of State for Transport, ex p. Factortame Ltd* (No. 4) [1996] 2 WLR 506; the matter is now before the national court for resolution.
[63] *R. v. Sec. of State for Employment, ex p. Equal Opportunities Commission* [1994] 2 WLR 409.
[64] *The Times*, 5 Mar. 1994.
[65] *Ministry of Defence* v. *Sullivan* EAT [1994] 1 CR 193 and *Same* v. *Cannoch* EAT [1994] 1 CR 918.
[66] *R. v. Sec. of State for Health, ex p. Richardson*, C–137/94 [1995] All ER (EC) 865.

treatment Directive[67] meant that Britain could not provide for the exemption of women from prescription charges at sixty and for men at sixty-five. Moreover, the Directive, which was concerned with the progressive implementation of the principle of equal treatment for men and women in matters of social security, could be relied upon to support claims for damages in respect of the period before the date of the judgment. Thus the ruling had retrospective effect and the Government was obliged to make it known that there was an entitlement to damages for men who had been charged for prescriptions when they were sixty or over since the Directive's implementation date in 1979. Subsequently, the ECJ ruled that concessionary fares on public transport, which could be claimed by women at sixty but not by men until sixty-five, also breached the Directive.[68]

The ECJ also gave a ruling in the case brought by the Royal Society for the Protection of Birds (RSPB) against the Government.[69] The House of Lords had referred questions to the ECJ concerning the interpretation of the Council Directive on the conservation of wild birds.[70] The point at issue was whether economic considerations could be taken into account when designating wild bird protection areas. In 1993 the Secretary of State for the Environment had decided to designate the Medway Estuary and Marshes as a special protection area but to exclude an area of mud flats, which were adjacent to the Port of Sheerness, on the grounds that they were needed for the expansion of the port. He argued that the contribution this expansion would make to the local and national economy outweighed the nature conservation value of the mud flats. This was contested by the RSPB who considered the mud flats to be an important component of the overall estuarine eco-system, and they sought to have the decision quashed. The ECJ ruled that the Secretary of State was not entitled to take account of economic requirements when designating a special protection area for wild birds and defining its boundaries, a decision which has implications for economic development in the area and for more general economic development.

National law: cases of constitutional importance

Rulings by the national courts and the ECJ on matters of Community law are the direct effect of membership of the EU. Membership has also had an indirect effect upon judicial thinking, and judges have moved to minimize the operation of a dual system wherever possible. Thus once the House of Lords had recognized that Hansard could be used as an aid to interpretation in order to see if legislation was intended to give effect to EC law,[71] it was logical for their lordships to rule that it could be referred to in all cases of ambiguity, whether or not Community law was

---

[67] Council Directive 79/7/EEC.   [68] *Atkins* v. *Wrekin DC and Another*, Case C–228/94.
[69] *R.* v. *Sec. of State for Environment, ex p. Royal Society for Protection of Birds* HL [1995] 7 Admin. LR 434.
[70] Council Directive 79/409/EEC.   [71] *Pickstone* v. *Freemans plc* [1989] AC 66.

concerned.[72] The argument of the Attorney-General that such a move would impugn ministerial freedom of speech within the House was not accepted by the court as relevant in the 1990s.

The most significant case which appeared to bring the rules relating to national law into line with those operating in EC law was *M*. v. *Home Office*,[73] although the convergence of national and European Community law was secondary. The prime concern of the House of Lords was, it would seem, to reassert the constitutional authority of the courts in interpreting and applying the law and to remind ministers and departments that they were not above the law. The issue before the House of Lords was whether a minister of the Crown could be held in contempt of court for failing to obey an order made by a judge in the High Court. The Home Secretary, at that time Kenneth Baker, had ignored such an order which required him to return an asylum seeker, who was in the process of being deported, to Britain, pending the hearing of his application for judicial review. The Home Secretary argued that the judge had no jurisdiction to make an order against the Crown and thus he was under no duty to obey it. He further argued that he could not be held in contempt of court.

The House of Lords ruled that notwithstanding the Crown Proceedings Act, which had been the prohibitive national rule in *Factortame*, the courts could make coercive orders against the Crown, at least where judicial review cases were concerned, by virtue of the Supreme Court Act 1981 which, *inter alia*, allowed for a stay in proceedings. It further held that ministers could be separated from the personage of the Sovereign and that the failure to follow an order made by the court would render a minister in contempt of court.

The decision of the House of Lords can be seen as a message to ministers who, having been in power for so long, might be tempted to think themselves above the law and to be careless of legal constraints. Indeed, the *M*. case may be seen as a trend-setter for judicial–executive relations over the next few years. It demonstrated a ministerial arrogance with regard to the courts and a judicial determination to reign back the powers of an over-mighty executive.

It was followed in 1994 by the *Pergau Dam* case in which the High Court ruled that the Foreign Secretary had acted unlawfully in using funds from the Overseas Development Administration budget to help finance the construction of the Pergau Dam in Malaysia.[74] The Overseas Development and Co-operation Act 1980, which provides for the allocation of such funds, requires that they be used for 'promoting the development or maintaining the economy'[75] of the country concerned. The court held that the money allocated would not serve this purpose. It paid special regard to the advice given to the Foreign Secretary by his Permanent Secretary, who considered that the development was in fact

---

[72] *Pepper* v. *Hart* [1993] 1 All ER 423.   [73] *M*. v. *Home Office* [1993] 3 All ER 541.
[74] *R*. v. *Sec. of State for Foreign and Commonwealth Affairs, ex p. World Development Movement* [1995] 1 WLR 386.
[75] S. 1(1).

'economically unsound', and held that the aid had been granted for political purposes, namely honouring a pledge made by the Prime Minister, Mrs Thatcher.[76]
The Foreign Secretary subsequently told Parliament that the project would be paid
for out of Treasury reserves and not the Overseas Aid and Development (OAD)
budget.[77] This would also apply to three other contracts which were thought to be
illegal.[78]

Pergau Dam demonstrated the effectiveness of legal, as opposed to political,
action in securing a change in Government policy or action. Two Select
Committees had previously published Reports critical of the use of the funds[79] but
these had been ignored by Government. The difference is, of course, that while the
courts remain independent from the executive, the House of Commons is dominated by it. Thus, unlike Select Committee Reports, judicial decisions cannot easily be ignored. It is no wonder that the Government is alarmed at the increase in
judicial review.

The High Court decision on *Pergau Dam* had obvious implications for the
Government's budgetary plans, benefiting the OAD budget at the expense of the
Treasury. The decision came the day after the Court of Appeal had made another
ruling, this time about a new Criminal Injuries Compensation Scheme (CICS),
which had clear cost implications. The case, brought by the Fire Brigades Union
against the Home Secretary, Michael Howard, was appealed to the House of
Lords.[80] By a majority their Lordships confirmed the decision of the Court of
Appeal, holding that the Home Secretary had abused his powers by using the prerogative to introduce a new tariff scheme for compensating victims of violent
crime which was radically different from that approved by Parliament in the
Criminal Justice Act 1988. The statutory scheme was a codification of the CICS
which had been established under the prerogative and provided for claims to be
treated on a case-by-case basis. The Act gave the Home Secretary discretion to
decide when to bring the statutory scheme into operation, but he chose instead to
bring in a cheaper alternative which operated on a tariff rather than a case-by-case
basis. He argued that as the statutory provision had not been implemented, he was
entitled to use the prerogative to set up the alternative scheme. The House of Lords
accepted that the Home Secretary did not have to implement the statutory scheme
but held that he could not use the prerogative to devise one that was completely
different. To do so would be a fettering of his discretion with regard to his consideration of the statutory scheme. It would also ignore the will of Parliament and
give insufficient weight to its legislative role.

The *CICS* case raises several points of interest. First, it bears some comparison
with *M.* v. *Home Office*. The cases suggest executive arrogance and a lack of

---

[76] Above, n. 74.   [77] HL Debs., col. 773, 13 Dec. 1994.
[78] The other contracts affected were a British sub-contract for the metro system in Ankara, Turkey,
a contribution to the costs of a TV station in Indonesia, and a flight information project in Botswana.
[79] See Public Accounts Cttee, HC 155, (1993–4); Foreign Affairs Cttee, HC 271, (1993–4).
[80] *R.* v. *Sec. of State for the Home Dept, ex p. Fire Brigade Union* [1995] 2 WLR 464.

respect for the other institutions of government, hence the concern of the House of Lords in both cases to remind the minister of the constitutional relationships involved. In *M*. the relationship in question was that between the executive and the courts; in the *CICS* case it was that between the executive and the legislature. Different Home Secretaries had acted remarkably similarly in the way in which they had abused their powers.

Secondly, the decision of the House of Lords undermined the plans of the Home Secretary to reduce the amount of money spent on compensation and thereby contribute to the Government's cost-cutting exercise. It is interesting to note that the proposed tariff scheme accorded with the thinking behind the new public management model of administration, in which, wherever possible, decisions are made according to a fixed formula which allows no exceptions[81] and is therefore cheap to operate.

Cases brought against Michael Howard, as Home Secretary

A third point of interest is that the *CICS* ruling was one of a number of rulings made against the Home Secretary in the person of Michael Howard during the period 1994–6. These almost seemed to gain a momentum of their own, adding to the tension that was already developing over the Home Secretary's law and order and sentencing policies. Rulings against the Home Secretary covered the range of his responsibilities. In *ex parte Melari*[82] asylum-seekers secured a High Court decision that the Home Secretary had acted unlawfully when he refused asylum without considering the merits of the case. It made no difference that they were being returned to a safe third country, in this case Spain. In *ex parte Khan*[83] the High Court also ruled that immigration officers could not use their legislative powers to keep certain asylum-seekers in custody while their claim was being considered by the Home Secretary. Mr Justice Dyson reasoned that this power was intended for illegal immigrants and that the detention of asylum-seekers was only lawful when their claims had been rejected and directions had been given for their deportation.

The decision was controversial and had a direct impact upon Home Office policy. Millions of pounds had been spent securing accommodation in which to keep asylum-seekers. This included Campsfield House, the detention centre near Oxford. The ruling also raised the prospect of claims for compensation from the hundreds of those at present detained. To the undoubted relief of the Home Office, the Court of Appeal overturned the High Court decision four days later, holding that Parliament could not have intended to deprive the Home Secretary, and thus immigration officials, of the powers of detention.

---

[81] See ch. 3.   [82] *R.* v. *Sec. of State for the Home Dept, ex p. Mehari* [1994] WLR 349.
[83] *R.* v. *Sec. of State for the Home Dept, ex p. Khan and others* [1995] 2 All ER 540.

Despite the reverse suffered by the applicants in *ex parte Khan*, indeed despite the fact that most cases brought by asylum-seekers are unsuccessful, applications for judicial review of deportation decisions continue to rise. This trend is likely to continue as, in many instances, the removal of rights of appeal during 1995 makes judicial review the only mechanism available for challenging a decision. Moreover, the human rights issues involved and the highly political nature of immigration policy mean that successful challenges are likely to receive considerable publicity, thereby encouraging others to take the same route.

During 1994–6 the Home Secretary also faced a number of challenges to his penal policies and practices. The Government's policy to commit increasing numbers of offenders to prison seemed to be being met by a judicial determination to extend their rights once they were inside. Many of these rights relate to internal prison matters although, of course, applications for review still lie against the Home Secretary, even though the prison service has executive agency status. It is therefore his name that is in the frame. In *ex parte Leech* the concern was the censorship of a prisoner's correspondence with his solicitor, which the Court of Appeal held to be beyond that which was required for reasons of security.[84] In *ex parte Duggan* the court was concerned with Category A prisoners, who, it ruled, were entitled to know any facts or opinions which were relevant to their retention of that status.[85] The ruling resulted in an announcement from the Director General of the Prison Service that he was putting the necessary procedures in place to ensure that this information was made available.

The judicial requirement in penal cases that information be made available and reasons given for decisions stems from Lord Mustill's statement in *ex parte Doody*.[86] This was cited in *ex parte Hickey*, where it was held unfair for prisoners, who were seeking a referral of their case to the Court of Appeal on the basis of a miscarriage of justice, not to be given access to new expert evidence which the Home Secretary had received.[87] The High Court ruling that the Home Secretary should make such information available opened the way for some 200 offenders to request information on why their cases had not been sent to the Court of Appeal.

The Home Secretary was also held to have acted unlawfully in *ex parte McCartney*, while in *ex parte Pierson* the High Court held that the Home Secretary had 'failed to live up to the required standard of fairness.'[88] He was again criticized in *ex parte Norney*, a case where the applicants were five IRA prisoners. Mr Justice Dyson held that the Home Secretary's policy of refusing to refer the cases of discretionary life prisoners to the Parole Board until after the expiry of the 'tariff period' was unreasonable and produced manifestly unjust results.[89]

---

[84] *R. v. Sec. of State for the Home Dept, ex p. Leech* [1994] QB 198.
[85] *R. v. Sec. of State for the Home Dept, ex p. Duggan* [1994] 1 WLR 621.
[86] See *ex p. Doody* (above, n. 47), (1993) and *ex p. Chapman* (above, n. 51).
[87] *R. v. Sec. of State for the Home Dept, ex p. Hickey and others* [1995] 7 Admin. LR 549.
[88] Both cases are considered above, n. 50 and n. 48.
[89] *R. v. Sec. of State for the Home Dept, ex p. Norney and others* [1995] 7 Admin LR 861.

It resulted in a delay of twenty-three weeks in considering parole applications and in effect extended the 'tariff' by this time. This was contrary to the principles of the common law and the ECHR, Article 5(4). A declaration was therefore granted that the Home Secretary should have referred the cases at such a time as would have ensured a hearing immediately after the expiry of the tariff period.

A further ruling against the Home Secretary arose with regard to his decision to extradite a man to the United States for offences he had allegedly committed between nine and twelve years previously, without considering the enormity of the delay by the US authorities in seeking extradition.[90] The High Court held that he had failed to take account of relevant factors. He had simply complied with an American request without giving sufficient regard to the protection that the extradition process was supposed to provide.

However, particularly controversial with regard to the Home Secretary's powers of extradition and the granting of applications for entry, the other side of the same coin, was the decision of Mr Justice Sedley in November 1995.[91] He held that the Home Secretary's decision to ban the Reverend Moon, cult-leader of the Moonies, from entering the country was 'unlawful by reason of procedural unfairness'. The Reverend Moon had been allowed entry on two previous occasions, in December 1991 and July 1992, and Mr Justice Sedley considered that if this time the Home Secretary was considering refusing entry, Reverend Moon might reasonably expect the opportunity to state his case. He noted, 'This is precisely the unpopular applicant for whom the safeguards of due process are most relevant to a society which acknowledges the rule of law.'

The ruling brought an immediate response from Mr Howard, who disputed it on the basis of a lack of precedents and that an applicant stated his case when making the application. In an angry riposte he was reported as saying that it was hard to predict these days which way the judges will jump.[92] Moreover, he insisted that, regardless of the court ruling, the Reverend Moon would not be allowed admittance. It seemed as if Mr Howard was prepared to defy the High Court, an act that would have brought him into direct conflict with senior judges. However, he was not put to the test as the Reverend Moon cancelled his trip and thus his request for admittance.

Mr Howard's response to the High Court ruling was evidence of the tension that developed between judges and ministers, particularly Mr Howard, during 1995. It was heightened by the speeches at the Conservative Party Conference and the reaction of senior judges to these (see above), and also by the media portrayal of judicial decisions as being against Mr Howard personally rather than against the office of the Home Secretary. Such a portrayal is understandable where ministerial policy—proclaimed by Mr Howard as 'his'—is affected by court decisions, for instance with regard to some of the sentencing and prison rulings, the *CICS* case,

---

[90] *R. v. Sec. of State for the Home Dept, ex p. Patel* [1994] *The Times* 10 Feb.

[91] *R. v. Sec. of State for the Home Dept, ex p. Moon* [1996] 8 Admin LR 477.

[92] *The Times*, 1 Nov. 1995.

and asylum cases. However, it did not aid the cause of judicial–executive relationships.

The apparent concern of Mr Justice Sedley to protect the rights of an individual, no matter how unpopular he or she may be, was echoed subsequently in *ex parte Al Fayed*, which concerned an application for judicial review against the Home Secretary's decision to refuse an application for naturalization.[93] The Court of Appeal accepted that there was no obligation under the British Nationality Act[94] for the Home Secretary to give reasons for such a refusal. However, it held that fairness required that before reaching a final decision, he should inform an applicant of the nature of any matters weighing against the grant of the application so that the applicant had the opportunity of addressing them. Lord Woolf MR considered 'the fact that the Home Secretary might refuse an application because he was not satisfied that the applicant fulfilled the rather nebulous requirement of good character or "if [the Home Secretary] thinks fit" underline the need for an obligation of fairness'. Once more the Court of Appeal seemed to be imposing a high level of fairness, amounting to the right of an individual to know the case against him or her, in a situation where it had not previously been thought to apply.

Fairness or natural justice was also an issue in the ECJ ruling that Britain's exclusion procedures were contrary to EC law.[95] The decision, given shortly after that of Reverand Moon, concerned Mr Galligher, an Irish national, who had been served with an exclusion order by the Home Office and removed from Britain. Mr Galligher subsequently challenged the order and was interviewed in the British Embassy in Dublin by an official who refused to reveal his identity and gave no reason for Mr Galligher's exclusion. The ECJ held that procedures, whereby suspected terrorists were first expelled and only then allowed an interview with an adviser nominated by the Home Secretary, breached the right to freedom of movement guaranteed under Community law. It considered that Mr Galligher should have been allowed the opportunity to make representations before being expelled and the Home Secretary should have considered the opinion of the adviser who had heard them before making the exclusion order.

Mr Howard played down the significance of the ruling, saying it was only concerned with the procedure and not the substance of extradition and thus would make no difference. No doubt his intention was to pacify the anti-Europe lobby. Adverse rulings from Europe provide a focus for the Euro-sceptics in Parliament and for the tabloid press, giving them a cause around which to unite. Decisions from the European Court have resulted in complaints that the Court is usurping its powers and interfering with Parliamentary sovereignty. Such complaints were dismissed by Lord Justice Taylor, when Lord Chief Justice, as unjust, and he was quick to point out that it is Parliament that has limited its sovereignty with regard

---

[93] *R. v. Sec. of State for the Home Dept, ex p. Mohammed Al Fayed* [1996] *The Times* 18 Nov.
[94] S. 44(2).
[95] *R. v. Sec. of State for the Home Dept, ex p. Galligher* C–175/94 [1996] 1 CMLR 557.

to EC law not the courts.[96] Nevertheless the decisions of the ECJ on prescriptions and, subsequently, on concessionary fares[97] and its decision on the entitlement of Spanish fishermen to compensation[98] have resulted in predictable calls for the powers of the ECJ to be curtailed.

At around the same time as the *Galligher* decision, a ruling from the ECHR against the British Government produced an angry response from some politicians. The Court ruled by a majority of one, splitting 10–9, that the killing of three terrorists in Gibraltar in March 1988 was a violation of the right to life guaranteed by Article 2 of the ECHR.[99] The ruling was controversial and some lawyers considered the dissenting opinion of the ECHR to be more persuasive than the majority judgment.[100] It gave the tabloid press and politicians a chance to attack the judges. The *Daily Mail* described the rulings of the Court as 'veering crankily from the tragic to the farcical' and The *Sun* labelled the judges 'loony'.[101] For the Government Michael Heseltine, deputy Prime Minister, called the decision 'ludicrous',[102] while 'Whitehall sources' let it be known that the Government would consider not renewing the right of individuals to bring claims in Strasburg when the current right lapsed in January. There was even the suggestion that ministers might consider withdrawing from the ECHR altogether.

Such comments by the Government were to a large extent political posturing. They were necessary to placate the Conservative Right. However, they were at odds with the reality. In fact Britain had recently ratified Protocol No. 11 to the ECHR which, once ratified by other signatories, will make permanent the acceptance of the right of individuals to petition, and in January 1996 the Government quietly renewed the right of individual claim for another five years. Ministers recognize that a British withdrawal from the ECHR would be unacceptable internationally. Hence within a couple of months of the Gibraltar decision, Mr Howard was retreating from suggestions of withdrawal from the ECHR.[103] Nevertheless, political rhetoric, apparently supported by Ministers, which imputes blame upon European judges, whether from the European Court of Justice or that of Human Rights, undermines the relationship between the Government and national judges.

Judicial decisions: resource and policy implications

Judicial decisions that have financial consequences are obviously uncomfortable for any government. They are particularly uncomfortable for a government intent on value for money and cost-cutting. Compensation and damages arise in the European context in relation to rights under the doctrine of direct effect and to

[96] BBC 1 News, 26 Feb. 1995.
[97] *Ex p. Richardson* (above, n. 66) and *Atkins* v. *Wrekin DC* (above, n. 68).
[98] *Ex p. Factortame* (No. 4) (above, n. 62).
[99] *McCann and ors* v. *UK*, Case No. 17/1994/464/545.
[100] See, e.g., D. Pannick QC, article in *The Times,* 8 Oct. 1995.
[101] *Daily Mail*, 28 Sept. 1995 and *Sun.* 28 Sept. 1995.   [102] *The Times*, 28 Sept. 1995.
[103] *Breakfast with Frost*, BBC 1, 17 Dec. 1995.

breaches of the Convention. They can also arise in the national context in cases of wrongful imprisonment or when the length of a prison sentence has been wrongly calculated. In 1996 the High Court ruled that the way in which the Prison Service calculated release dates on concurrent sentences was unlawful because it did not make an adequate deduction for time spent on remand.[104] Lord Bingham stated, 'It appears that defendants are remaining in prison when the sentencing court did not intend that they should'. His comment raised again the matter of judicial discretion with regard to sentencing but, more seriously from the Government's point of view, the ruling resulted in the release of hundreds of prisoners earlier than expected and claims for compensation from ex-offenders and inmates which could cost £18m.[105] However,the financial implications of a judicial decision are not confined to compensation claims. There may be resource implications, as for instance in the cases concerning *Pergau Dam* and the *CICS*.

Traditionally the courts view the deployment of resources as 'policy' and non-justiciable. The tendency is to see statutes as imposing a target duty rather than an individual duty and thus to refuse to accept challenges which concern resource allocation. In *ex parte B* Mr Justice Laws strayed from the traditional line of reasoning when he ruled that the right to life, contained in the ECHR, was also a principle of domestic law and thus the refusal to provide treatment to a child dying from leukaemia was potentially unlawful.[106] Mr Justice Laws recognized the problem of resource-allocation when resources were limited and finite but refused to accept 'inadequate resources' as a sufficient argument. He held that a Hospital Trust 'must do more than toll the bell of resources': some evidence was required.

Mr Justice Laws' decision was reversed four hours later by the Court of Appeal which held that difficult clinical issues were not justiciable and that an authority could not be expected to provide detailed financial justification as to why it could not afford to provide treatment. The Court of Appeal's ruling was no doubt a relief to the Government and its agencies, who, on Mr Justice Laws' reasoning, were faced with the prospect of having to provide a full justification for any lack of provision across a range of services and, possibly, having to provide extra resources to met the requirements of the court.

The Court of Appeal was also concerned with the relevance of resources in *ex parte Barry*, where a local authority had withdrawn services because of a lack of resources from a person assessed as needing them.[107] It ruled that a local authority was not entitled to take account of the availability, or otherwise, of resources

---

[104] *R. v. Sec. of State for the Home Department, ex p. Reid, R. v. Same, ex p. Evans* [1996] The Times, 16 Nov.

[105] The court ruling was particularly embarrassing because it came shortly after the debacle in which 541 prisoners serving consecutive sentences were released early because Home Office lawyers advised that their sentences had been wrongly calculated. The advice proved to be erroneous, as confirmed in Aug. 1996 by the High Ct which, however, warned that there was ambiguity over the calculation of concurrent sentences.

[106] *R. v. Cambridge Health Authority, ex p. B* [1995] 1 WLR 898.

[107] *R. v. Gloucestershire County Council and Another, ex p. Barry* [1996] C.O.D. 387 CA; [1997] *The Times*, 21 Mar. HL.

when carrying out its duty to assess the needs of a disabled person and to make provision for those needs to be met.[108] They might be relevant to the way in which provision was made but it was unlawful not to provide a service at all or to withdraw it on financial grounds. This decision was subsequently overturned by the House of Lords which by a majority held that cost was a relevant consideration in the assessment of need, the weight it was accorded depending on the resources available.

The ruling of the House of Lords came as a relief to local authorities. The Court of Appeal decision would have had a direct effect on local authorities upon whom the duty lies but it also had financial and ideological implications for central government, appearing to undermine attempts to cut costs and reduce the support given to individuals by the State. Moreover, both the decision of the High Court in *ex parte B*[109] and that of the Court of Appeal in *ex parte Barry*[110] suggest a willingness by some judges to intervene in resource issues where they affect individuals. There have also been instances where judges have called for explanations of resource-based issues. There were several occasions during 1995 when the courts threatened to call the Secretary of State for Health before them to account for the failure of the Government to fulfil its statutory duty of accommodating a mentally-ill person, convicted of a criminal offence, in a mental hospital. Judges had been told that because of a bed shortage, the prisoner would have to go to prison. In the cases concerned the need for the minister to appear was averted by beds in appropriate institutions being found. Also in 1995 the Governor of Holloway Prison was called before the court to explain why a woman on trial was locked in a cell for twenty-three hours a day.[111] The Governor's response that this was because of lack of resources inevitably brought into question Government policy.

In 1996 the Court of Appeal made a ruling which fundamentally affected the Government's policy of discouraging economic migrants from making and pursuing asylum claims, thereby cutting the costs associated with asylum-seekers. The Joint Council for the Welfare of Immigrants sought judicial review of the regulations made by the Secretary of State for Social Security[112] which came into force in February 1996.[113] These removed all entitlement to income-related benefits from those who had failed to make a claim for asylum upon arrival in the UK and from those who were waiting appeal of the Home Secretary's decision. The aim of the regulations was to discourage false claims, thereby speeding up the system to the advantage of genuine refugees and saving the taxpayers some £200m a year.

The Court of Appeal recognized the desirability of the aim but held the

---

[108] The duty is contained in Chronically Sick and Disabled Persons Act 1970, s. 2(1).
[109] Above, n. 106. [110] Above, n. 107.
[111] Reported on *The Today Programme*, Radio 4, 19 Dec. 1995.
[112] Under the Social Security (Contributions and Benefits) Act 1992.
[113] *R.* v. *Sec. of State for Social Services, ex p. Joint Council for the Welfare of Immigrants* [1996] The Times, 29 June.

regulations to be unlawful. Lord Justice Simon Brown considered that they were 'so uncompromisingly draconian in effect that they must be ultra vires'. They rendered the rights conferred on asylum-seekers in the Asylum and Immigration Appeals Act 1993 nugatory, contemplating for some 'a life so destitute that no civilized nation could tolerate it'. Their effect was to present genuine asylum-seekers with the choice of remaining in the UK destitute and homeless until their claims were finally determined or abandoning their claims and returning to the persecution they sought to escape.

Lord Justice Simon Brown held that such 'a sorry state of affairs' could only be achieved by primary legislation, something the Government moved swiftly to enact in the Asylum and Immigration Act 1996. This has not, however, stopped effective challenges by those affected by the provisions, although the challenges have been against local authorities rather than Government ministers. In four cases against London Boroughs the Court of Appeal found for the applicants, that is to say that the local authorities had a duty to house them.[114] Lord Justice Neill reasoned that homeless asylum-seekers, who because of the denial of income support and housing benefit were completely without resources were 'vulnerable' as a result of some 'other special reason' within the meaning of the Housing Act 1985 (section 59(1)(c)). As a consequence they were in priority need of accommodation and had to be housed by the local authority. Three months later the High Court ruled that local authorities had a duty under the National Assistance Act 1948 to provide asylum-seekers at risk of destitution with emergency aid while their refugee status was being considered.[115] Mr Justice Collins said that he found it 'impossible to believe that Parliament intended that an asylum-seeker, who was lawfully here and who could not be lawfully removed from the country, should be left destitute, starving and at risk of grave illness and even death because he could find no one to provide him with the bare necessities of life.'[116]

The two rulings had implications for the estimated 8,000 asylum seekers denied benefits under the Asylum and Immigration Act 1996. Like *ex parte Barry*[117] their direct effect was on the resources of local authorities. However, they clearly acted to frustrate Government policy and the desire of ministers to reduce public expenditure. They also required the diversion of resources, thereby interfering with pre-determined priorities and policy choices. Interventions by the courts which run contrary to Government policy are not new:[118] memories of *Tameside*[119] still linger. However, such interventions are particularly unwelcomed by a

---

[114] *R. v. Kensington and Chelsea LBC, ex p. Kihara; R. v. Hammersmith and Fulham LBC, ex p. Ilunga-Ilunga; R. v. Westminster CC, ex p. Pavlov; R. v. Islington LBC, ex p. Araya* [1996] The Times, 10 July.

[115] Reported in *The Times*, 9 Oct. 1996.   [116] Ibid.

[117] Above, n. 106.   [118] See J. A. G. Griffith, *Politics of the Judiciary*.

[119] *Sec. of State for Education and Science v. Tameside MBC* [1977] AC 1014, where the House of Lords ruling in favour of the local authority's return to selective education was contrary to the Govt's policy of comprehensive schooling.

Government which is economically driven to cutting public spending and ideo-logically committed to reducing the role of the State in welfare provisions and to transferring public sector functions to the private sector, wherever possible.

The effect of the employment protection afforded by EC law[120] on contracting-out and market-testing has been underplayed and treated as an irritant rather than as possibly reducing the projected cost-savings of such exercises and, in general, successful challenges to aspects of privatization have done little more than cause delay. However, their political impact has been considerable, reflecting the unpop-ularity of some privatization policies and a growing popular perception that only the courts can stand up to an ideologically-driven government.

In 1992 a High Court decision delayed the closure of a number of coal pits, a prelude to selling off the coal-mining industry, when it quashed the decision of British Coal and the President of the Board of Trade, Michael Heseltine, with regard to the closures.[121] The decision had been made without consulting the min-ers and trade unions affected and without having followed an established colliery review procedure. The ruling by the High Court added to the problems already faced by Michael Heseltine, whose policy was strongly opposed by backbenchers from both sides of the House, and contributed to a reduction in the proposed clo-sures.

In 1995 a judicial ruling also delayed plans to axe the London to Fort William sleeper service which British Rail claimed was uneconomical and heavily subsi-dized by other services.[122] In the build up to privatization the Government seems to have considered that its inclusion within a rail franchise would reduce the value of that franchise. The High Court quashed the decision to stop the service on the grounds of failure to consult, and the delay this caused enabled supporters of the sleeper to win its reprieve. Later that year, the Pressure Group 'Save our Railways' successfully challenged the granting of franchises to a number of train compa-nies.[123] In the Court of Appeal the Master of the Rolls, Sir Thomas Bingham, held that minimum passenger service requirements for five of the first seven new train companies had been illegally set too far below the existing British Rail timetable. He accepted that the Franchising Director had acted contrary to instructions given in 1994 by the Secretary of State for Transport, then John MacGregor, to award franchises 'based on' those which then existed.

The effect of the ruling appeared to be that the franchising process would have to be delayed while contracts were renegotiated. Moreover, a higher service requirement would mean less money for the Exchequer as the franchises would be less valuable to the train companies whose potential profit would be cut. However, within days of the ruling, the Secretary of State, now George Young, indicated that he was 'clarifying' the instructions to the Franchising Director to read that the

---

[120] Transfer of Undertakings Directive 77/187/EEC.
[121] *R. v. British Coal Corp., ex p. Vardy* [1993] ICR 720.
[122] *Highland Regional Council v. British Railways Board* [1995] The Times 6 Nov.
[123] *R. v. Sec. of State for Transport, ex p. Save Our Railways* [1995] The Times 18 Dec.

service levels should be 'broadly similar to those operating immediately prior to franchising'.[124] The Government thereby demonstrated a determination to move ahead with its policy despite the Court of Appeal decision and was undeterred by accusations of going against the spirit, if not the letter, of the law. Indeed, ministers proffered counter-accusations, asserting judicial interference in matters of policy.

The above cases are by no means inclusive but they demonstrate the range of judicial review decisions. They stretch over most areas of Government policy and, even when the decisions relate to administrative procedures and policies, they frequently have a high political impact. This has become increasingly the case as the courts are seen as the only effective mechanism for holding Government to account and for checking its powers. The comparative 'newness' of judicial review, at least as it concerns central government, has also given it a novelty value, and, although some rulings concerning EC law and the ECHR are portrayed by the media, particularly the tabloid press, as an attack upon Parliamentary, and hence national, sovereignty, mainstream judicial review decisions are frequently reported as well-deserved Government defeats. At times it is almost as if a judicial ruling takes the place of a Government defeat in the House of Commons. It is perhaps not surprising that ministers have at times demonstrated irritation, even anger, with such reporting; after all in the scheme of things the number of successful challenges against central government are still comparatively small.

However, this irritation has not just been directed at the press for its reporting. It has also been directed at the courts, who are seen as acting to frustrate mainstream policies and as undermining cost-cutting and value-for-money exercises and the philosophy which supports the transfer of rights and obligations from the public to the private sector and the reduction of 'the nanny state'.

The Judicial–Executive Conflict

During 1995 the tension between the executive and the judiciary became increasing apparent. Senior judges, already concerned about executive encroachment into the administration of justice, the proposed reforms to Legal Aid, the exercise of executive discretion with regard to sentencing, and the apparent arrogance of some ministers with regard to the law and court decisions, were further disconcerted by the law and order policies, particularly concerning fixed sentences, announced by the Home Secretary at the Conservative Party Conference. It was this announcement that prompted the Lord Chief Justice and other senior judges to speak out (see above).

For their part, ministers were becoming increasingly frustrated with judicial opposition to reforms of the legal system and with judicial rulings which seemed

[124] Reported in *The Times* 18 Dec. 1995.

to undermine executive discretion. There was also concern that the courts had relaxed the rules of standing and were now prepared to accept what were seen as 'political' challenges, brought by pressure or interest groups, in a way that had not previously been the case. Successful challenges by groups, such as the RSPB, Save our Railways, and the World Development Movement, seemed to prove the point. In addition, a spate of articles, written by senior judges, seemed to suggest their desire for an extended constitutional role, seen as necessary to restore the balance lost through the executive domination of Parliament, and for a Bill of Rights.[125] There were also suggestions from some judges that they drop the fiction of the *ultra vires* doctrine, described by Lord Woolf as a 'fairy-tale' and by Sir John Laws as a 'fig leaf'.[126] This doctrine, based on the intention of Parliament, has acted in theory to limit the powers of the courts, although, in practice, judges have frequently found their way around it, and some commentators have for a number of years questioned its validity as a basis for judicial review.[127] Nevertheless, the acceptance or pretence by the courts that it forms this basis has continued to act as a check on judicial discretion. There was therefore political concern that its demise would open the way for the courts to extend further their jurisdiction in relation to judicial review.

This was the background against which the Government launched what judges perceived to be a political campaign to undermine the independence and reputation of the judiciary, with ministers making dismissive and derogatory comments about judges, suggesting they were stepping beyond the boundaries of constitutional propriety and acting 'politically'. This drew an outspoken response from Lord Donaldson. He wrote, '[I]n recent months we have seen an entirely new development. This is an attack by politicians on the Judiciary as a whole. This is without precedent in my lifetime and raises very serious constitutional issues.'[128] He continued, 'All governments believe that their actions are in the public interest and have no difficulty in persuading themselves that they must be lawful. To be told by judges that they are not in fact acting lawfully is an affront which they find hard to accept. Much easier to say, and sometimes believe, that the judges are entering the political arena and are disagreeing on policy grounds.'[129] Lord Donaldson attributed the 'concerted attack upon the Judiciary' to the Government's need to secure Parliamentary approval for its fixed-term sentencing policy. The policy would reduce judicial discretion with regard to sentencing; hence ministers were adopting the strategy of undermining its use by judges, suggesting that judges had their own political agenda.

On 7 December 1995 the front page headlines of The *Daily Telegraph* read 'Mackay lays down the law: Judges warned to keep in line'. The report stated that

---

[125] See, e.g., Lord Woolf, 'Droit Public—English Style' (1995) *PL* 57; J. Laws, 'Law and Democracy' (1995) *PL* 72; S. Sedley, 'Human Rights' (1995) *PL* 386.

[126] Lord Woolf, above n. 125; Laws, above n. 125.

[127] See D. Oliver, 'Is the *ultra vires* principle the basis of judicial review?' (1987) *PL 543*.

[128] *The Guardian*, 1 Dec. 1996.   [129] Ibid.

Lord Mackay, the Lord Chancellor, was to make a speech at the Guildhall that evening in which he would take the unprecedented step of reminding the judges 'that the courts were not superior to Parliament' and of warning them 'not to overstep their powers by using judicial review to challenge ministerial decisions'. It also said that he would make clear that judicial review decisions were not made against the minister personally. Interestingly, this was a point that the Master of the Rolls, Sir Thomas Bingham, had been at pains to make in a judgment a few days earlier.[130] He had said, 'The case involved no challenge to the Secretary of State personally. He was named in the application because he was responsible for the department within which the decisions were made and references to him were to be read as references to the relevant decision-maker.' The Secretary of State concerned was the Home Secretary, Michael Howard, and Sir Thomas' statement was no doubt a response to the media's tendency to report each case as a personal defeat for him.

The *Daily Telegraph* report further stated that Lord Mackay would 'stress that ministers are part of the elected government and must be allowed to propose policies as they think fit' and said that he was expected to state that it was 'dangerous and mistaken' to argue that there was some form of authority in the courts that was superior to Parliament. 'Rather it is the duty of the judges to apply the law as Parliament had enacted it—and the ultimate authority over the judiciary and the Executive is Parliament.' This reiteration of constitutional theory suggested adherence to the *ultra vires* doctrine (at least in name) and an end to creative judicial thinking. It failed, of course, to recognize the reality of executive dominance over the legislature. The *Daily Telegraph* report also stated that the Lord Chancellor was expected to remind judges that the imposition of limits on their discretion with regards to sentencing was neither new nor would it undermine judicial independence.

It seemed therefore as if the judges were about to be suitably chastised for perceived misdemeanours, the proposed speech by the Lord Chancellor alluding to judicial writings on the constitutional position of the courts, judicial review decisions which frustrated Government policies, and the sentencing controversy. However, the following day Lord Mackay wrote to The *Telegraph* refuting the front page story. The Lord Chancellor had in fact spoken at the Guildhall the evening before the story had been published (on 6 December), but his speech had been short and had not been about the judiciary or judicial–executive relations. It transpired that the document on which the report was based was a draft, which had not been approved by Lord Mackay, and it had been given to the paper by Conservative Party Central Office.

It therefore appeared to be a continuation of the feud between the Party Chairman, Brian Mawhinney and the Lord Chancellor, who had crossed swords over Mr Mawhinney's suggestion at the Party Conference that anyone dissatisfied

---

[130] *Ex p. Pierson* (above, n. 48).

with a lenient sentence should write to the judge and say so. Now it seemed that the Party Chairman was seeking to embarrass the Lord Chancellor publicly. It was subsequently reported that the Prime Minister was being 'urged to end the Cabinet feud'[131] and that he was to meet with the Lord Chief Justice to discuss the problems that were arising between the Government and the judges.[132]

The action of Conservative Party Central Office in leaking the draft document would also seem to have been an attempt to undermine the relationship of the Lord Chancellor with senior judges, a relationship that was already somewhat precarious. Putting such a document into the public domain not only allowed Government grievances to be given a public airing, apparently by the head of the judiciary, it raised the question of whether, given the opportunity, Lord Mackay would have given such a speech. 'Dirty tricks' are established practice in politics. They are used to undermine political opponents. Their use by the Government against the judiciary suggested executive anxiety which operated on two fronts. Firstly, the Government was concerned that judicial rulings would act to frustrate core policies aimed at cost-cutting, value for money and privatization. Secondly, the Government, increasingly desperate to regain its standing in the opinion polls, was intent on implementing law and order policies which had popular appeal. Its fear was that judicial opposition to fixed sentences might gain sufficient support in the House of Lords to delay the necessary legislation.[133]

The Inquiry into the Export of Arms to Iraq

The tension between the executive and the judiciary also became evident in relation to Sir Richard Scott's Inquiry into the export of arms to Iraq which arose out of the collapse of the Matrix Churchill trial in 1993.[134] Sir Richard was asked by the Prime Minister to investigate and report, *inter alia*, on whether Parliament had been misled over arms-export policy and on whether the use of public interest immunity certificates was appropriate. His Report was finally delivered in February 1996. However, long before it was complete, the Inquiry was subject to repeated accusations of unfairness. Some suspected that a 'whispering campaign' was being conducted to undermine the Inquiry's conclusions. This suspicion grew when parts of the draft report, concerning William Waldegrave, were leaked to the press. The Government insisted that it was not responsible for the leaks. However, leaking is a recognized, if seldom admitted, Government tactic and has been used before with regard to Inquiries. The premature disclosure of an Inquiry's conclusions allow denials and justifications to be made and previously-stated positions to be modified. The conclusions of the final Report are therefore undermined and their impact is considerably reduced.

---

[131] Reported in *The Sunday Times*, 10 Dec. 1995.   [132] Reported in *The Times*, 8 Dec. 1995.
[133] A fear that was realized in 1997.
[134] See (1996) *PL* 357–528 and (1997) 50 *Parl. Affs*. 1 (special edns. on Scott Report).

In the case of the Arms to Iraq Report[135] Sir Richard Scott's conclusion that William Waldegrave had misled Parliament was public knowledge more than six months prior to official publication. This enabled the Minister to 'utterly refute' the charge and to call into question the fairness of the Inquiry process and its conclusions. It also allowed the Prime Minister to indicate his support for Mr Waldegrave ahead of publication of the Report and to modify his position with regard to acting on the Report's findings.

The apparent coolness of the Prime Minister towards the forthcoming report suggested that a highly respected judge had been used for political purposes. In the aftermath of Matrix Churchill it had been politically expedient to announce full backing for an independent inquiry. The hope, no doubt, was that by the time Sir Richard Scott reported, public interest in the affair would have waned. Despite the delay in publication, caused in part by the tardiness of departments in giving Sir Richard documentation he required, public interest did not diminish and the Prime Minister was faced with the publication of a Report which was highly critical of ministers and of the workings of Government departments. He now found it expedient to distance himself from it.

Publication confirmed Sir Richard Scott's criticism of William Waldegrave. He was also critical of Sir Nicholas Lyell, the Attorney-General, particularly with regard to his handling of public interest immunity certificates. Both Ministers and their supporters contested the conclusions on the basis either that they were untrue and unfair, or were simply matters of opinion, or a reflection of the fact that Sir Richard did not understand the workings of Government and the technicalities surrounding public interest immunity certificates. In addition, the Government adopted a policy of extracting 'sound-bites' from the Report, which gave the impression that Sir Richard exonerated those concerned, or at least did not condemn them. Sir Richard thus found his recommendations ignored, his conclusions twisted for political advantage, and his integrity and intellectual ability questioned. His initial response was to hold a number of briefing sessions. Subsequently he gave talks and lectures on his findings and their political and constitutional implications.

Conclusion

The treatment afforded Sir Richard Scott by the Government was indicative of its mistrust of, and hostility towards, the judges and presented further evidence of a deterioration in the relationship between the Government and judiciary during the 1990s. The poor relationship can partly be attributed to particular personalities involved, and a change of government may result in an immediately improvement in that relationship. However, no government will feel comfortable with a judi-

---

[135] Sir Richard Scott, HC 115, (1996).

ciary which is intent on assuming a more interventionist role, as the Shadow Lord Chancellor, Lord Irvine, indicated in a debate in the House of Lords. He stressed that in exercising their powers of judicial review, judges 'should never give grounds for the public to believe that they intend to reverse government policies which they dislike'.[136] Nor should they in any way suggest that in exceptional cases they 'may be entitled to hold invalid statutes duly passed by parliament'.[137] To do so, he argued, would cause 'ordinary people . . . to believe that judges . . . are exercising a political function in judicial review cases instead of simply upholding the rule of law.'[138] He therefore called for 'self-restraint by the judges so as to conserve their reputation for political impartiality in the decisions they make according to the law.'[139] In addition, the position of the Lord Chancellor as a bridge between a partisan executive and an independent judiciary still remains open to question. Indeed, Lord Steyn has expressed the view that 'the proposition that a Cabinet minister must be head of our judiciary in England is no longer sustainable on either constitutional or pragmatic grounds'.[140] He has contested the notion that the Lord Chancellor is impartial, stating, 'the Lord Chancellor is always a spokesman for the government in the furtherance of its party political agenda'.[141] The continuing need of any government to reduce public expenditure suggests that, regardless of who holds office, there will be a continuing tension between judges and the executive. This tension may become less apparent as both sides strive to paper over the cracks in the relationship but it will remain in the realms of administration, if not obviously at the political level. The problem is that '[t]he function of the courts in controlling government activity is not to secure efficiency and value for money or the effective fulfilment of policy objectives, but to ensure that certain values or ideals are observed by government, that duties are performed, and that bodies with limited powers do not exceed these powers.'[142]

This is not to say that the courts ignore the requirements of efficiency and cost but the balance they use and the importance they attribute to them may be different to that of the government. Moreover, 'the values and ideals' which they uphold may get in the way of cost-effectiveness. What these values and ideals are, how they inform judicial thinking with regard to principles of good administration, and how they relate to the models of good administration is the subject of the next two chapters.

---

[136] HL Debs., col. 1255, 15 June 1996.   [137] Ibid.   [138] Ibid.
[139] Ibid., cols. 1259–60.   [140] Address to the Administrative Law Bar Association, Nov. 1996.
[141] Ibid.   [142] P. Cane, *Introduction to Administrative Law*, 392.

7

JUDICIAL PERSPECTIVES ON GOOD ADMINISTRATION: THE INDIVIDUAL INTEREST

Introduction

The belief that the courts play an active part in fostering principles of good administration is widely held.[1] Indeed, some commentators have argued that the substantive rules, broadly classified as legality, procedural propriety, rationality, and possibly proportionality,[2] themselves amount to principles of good administration, containing, as they do, requirements of fairness, reasonableness, the proper use of power and the absence of bad faith, capriciousness and arbitrary decision-making.[3] Moreover, it has also been suggested that how these rules are applied is determined by the judicial view of the proper scope of public administration in the particular case.[4] This may account for judicial dicta which sometimes sees good administration as protecting the individual (the main concern of this chapter) and sometimes as aiding administrators and the administrative process and hence the public interest (the subject of Chapter 8). However, the judicial perspective of good administration[5] is not limited to the content of the substantive rules or grounds for judicial review. It goes beyond the legal requirements.

The Legal Status of Good Administration

An obvious starting-point for an analysis of judicial perspectives on the concept of good administration is its position in law. In the absence of a statutory code which lays down the principles of good administration, the concept has no legal status. This does not prevent some of the requirements of good administration from being legally enforceable when 'the law and good administrative practice is in accord'.[6] Moreover, this coincidence of standards may even be expressed in

---

[1] See D. Oliver, 'Is the *ultra vires* rule the basis of judicial review?' (1987) *PL* 543; D. Galligan, 'Judicial review and the textbook writers' (1982) 2 *OJLS* 257.

[2] As per Lord Diplock in *Council for Civil Service Unions* v. *Minister for the Civil Service* [1984] AC 374.

[3] Oliver (above, n. 1), and J. L. Jowell & A. Lester, 'Beyond Wednesbury' (1987) *PL* 368.

[4] P. Bayne, 'Administrative Law' (1988) *Aust. Law Journal* 1043.

[5] In order to determine this perspective, extensive use was made of Lexis, initial 'good administration' searches listing nearly 300 cases.

[6] McNeill J., *R.* v. *Sec. of State for Education, ex p. Hardy* CO/354/88 (Lexis).

such a way as to suggest an equal validity of law and good administration in the eyes of the court. In *Conway* v. *Rimmer*,[7] Lord Reid, commenting on the case of *re Joseph Hargreaves*[8] which had concerned the use by the state of confidential material, appeared to suggest this equality when he said, 'The state must not, backed by compulsory powers, obtain information from the citizen for one purpose and use that information for another. It does not matter whether this is seen as a principle of good administration or statutory construction or ordinary morality or all three.'[9] Such a statement demonstrates the importance of 'good administration' and 'ordinary morality'. However, neither have been upheld in their own right by the courts, for they do not impose, nor take precedence over, legal obligations.

As a consequence, the courts will not limit a common law principle in the interests of good administration.[10] Neither, according to Lord Bridge, will they use the concept of good administration as an aid to statutory interpretation, even in order to avoid a possible injustice. In *Griffith* v. *Secretary of State for the Environment* Lord Bridge held that 'when one finds . . . numerous provisions imposing an express obligation to give notice it is impossible to imply a statutory duty (as opposed to a duty in the cause of good administration) to give notice, where no express obligation is imposed.'[11] Thus the failure to give notice, in this case of the Secretary of State's decision to dismiss an appeal over planning permission, was not unlawful even though it might offend against the concept of good administration and cause injustice by depriving the applicant of the opportunity to instigate further appeal proceedings.

The restrictive approach of Lord Bridge in *Griffith* was followed in *ex parte Birmingham City Council*.[12] Mr Justice McNeill held that the practice adopted in previous years by the Secretary of State of laying Rate Support Grant Reports before the House early in the year was obviously good practice and in the interests of good administration, as it enabled local authorities good time to set their precepts and rates before 1 April. However, it was neither an express obligation under the relevant legislation nor could it be implied as an obligation. Thus, once again, a clear distinction was made between lawfulness and the standards of administrative practice, the latter not being a matter for the courts.

Similarly in *Khan* v. *Secretary of State for Home Department* the Court of Appeal was critical of the Home Office for its failure to notify Mrs Khan, who was being prosecuted for passport infringements, of its view with regard to her immigration position.[13] Lord Justice Bingham noted that the lack of communication

---

[7] [1968] AC 910.   [8] *Re Joseph Hargreaves* [1900] 1 Ch 347.
[9] At 946, referred to by Sir Thomas Bingham in *Lonrho plc* v. *Fayed and Ors* [1994] 2 WLR 209 at 218–9.
[10] See Lord Slynn, *Woolwich Equitable Building Society* v. *IRC* HL [1993] AC 70.
[11] HL [1983] 1 All ER 439 at 446.
[12] *R.* v. *Sec. of State for the Environment, ex p. Birmingham CC* CO/72/87 (Lexis).
[13] *Fauzia Wamar Din Bagga Khan* v. *Sec. of State for the Home Department* CA [1987] Imm. AR 543.

was 'an unfortunate feature of this case since it would appear to be an elementary precept of good administration that public authorities who are involved with decision-making should inform interested parties where they stand and what decision, if any, is under consideration.' However, this departmental failure to comply with good administrative practice did not constitute an infringement of the law and thus the application for judicial review was unsuccessful.

Good administration may therefore impose higher standards than the law, suggesting a particular process or course of action additional to the legal requirement. This was the case in *Hussein* v. *Secretary of State for the Environment* which concerned compulsory purchase.[14] There was a legal requirement for notice to be served and a dispute arose over whether it had been. The Court of Appeal took an instrumental approach considering that 'as a matter of good administration', although not law, it would have been 'prudent' to have asked the Council to deliver the notice, 'bearing in mind the uncertainties of the post.' Good administration was therefore concerned with ensuring that the purpose of the procedure was fulfilled and a satisfactory outcome achieved.

The courts would also seem to see good administration as being concerned with filling in any gaps in the legal framework and with providing the framework itself when the law is silent. Thus unless there is a statutory provision that requires the investigation of complaints and the remedying of grievances, the courts will not impose such a duty. Yet they recognize that good administration requires that such investigations are undertaken.[15]

The attitude of the courts would therefore suggest that the principles of good administration are seen as a luxury, much to be desired and recommended but in legal terms not essential and certainly not accorded the status 'of a rule of law'.[16] As a consequence a remedy will not be granted merely on the basis of an infringement of good administration.[17] However, contravention of the principles underlying good administration may be used by the courts as evidence that the Government has not exercised its powers properly. This was a view expressed by Lord Justice Woolf in *ex parte London Borough of Greenwich*.[18] The case concerned the distribution by the Secretary of State for the Environment of a leaflet entitled *The Community Charge (the so-called 'Poll Tax'): How It Works For You*. Greenwich LBC objected to the leaflet on the basis that it contained misleading information, and that it was party political and thus represented a departure from the standards of good administration as reflected in the convention, published by the Government, on government publicity.

---

[14] CA [1984] JPL 431.
[15] See Lord Denning, *Padfield* v. *Minister of Agriculture, Fisheries and Food* [1968] AC 997 at 1006.
[16] See *R.* v. *Deputy Governor of Parkhurst Prison, ex p. Hague* CA [1990] WLR 1210.
[17] *R.* v. *Monopolies and Mergers Commission, ex p. Ecando Systems Ltd* CO/1227/90 (Lexis).
[18] *R.* v. *Sec. of State for the Environment, ex p. London Borough of Greenwich* CO/731/1989 (Lexis).

Lord Justice Woolf was critical of the distribution of the leaflet but held that the 'convention' referred to did not have the force of law. The application for judicial review was therefore unsuccessful. However, he noted that 'the court in exercising its role of judicial review can regard the conventions as providing guidance as to what are the proper standards and if the government has not complied with the convention that may be an indication that the government has not exercised its powers properly.' This suggests that the interests of good administration may be a factor considered by the courts and, whilst the concept has no legal validity, its requirements may be utilized as a limitation upon discretionary powers.

Openness

Not only do the standards of good administration, whether given form in conventions or left as underlying assumptions, help to provide a judicial yardstick for what constitutes the proper exercise of power in a legal sense, they also excite certain expectations within the courts. The most common expectation that arises is openness, described in *ex parte TSW Broadcasting* as 'one of the keys to good administration'.[19] In an application for judicial review the Independent Television Commission was found not to have acted unlawfully in the grant of television franchises but was criticised for its lack of openness.

Such a criticism was also levelled against a Social Fund Inspector in *ex parte Connell*.[20] The Inspector was legally required to take account of Guidance from the Secretary of State and Mr Justice Brooke considered that good administration required an open application of this consideration. In finding against the Independent Review Service, he stated, 'Good administration is founded on good law, and if the law requires the Social Fund Inspector to take account of guidance given by the Secretary of State, in my judgment, the way he takes account of that guidance should be made transparent.' He was particularly critical of the consequences of the lack of transparency which had resulted in it being left 'to distinguished legal counsel and a High Court Judge to have to puzzle out, between themselves', whether the Social Fund Inspector did in fact go through the processes required by the Act and by the Social Fund Guidance. The conclusion they reached was that he did not and *certiorari* was granted on the grounds of failure to take account of a relevant consideration of which the Inspector was 'statutorily bound to take account'.

This judgment suggests that where a wide discretionary power is concerned, particularly one as judicially unpopular as the Social Fund,[21] the courts will insist

[19] *R.* v. *Independent Television Commission, ex p. TSW Broadcasting Ltd* CA [1992] The Times, 7 Feb.
[20] *R.* v. *Independent Review Service, ex p. Connell* CO/1811/94 (Lexis).
[21] See judicial comments in *R.* v. *Sec. of State for Social Services, ex p. Stitt* [1991] 3 Admin LR 169.

that the exercise of the power clearly and obviously conforms to such rules as there are, this being the only way to control the discretion. Mr Justice Brooke was not, of course, upholding a legal requirement of openness but the ruling indicated that a secretive process was not only against the interests of good administration but might result in an adverse inference being made by the courts for lack of evidence to the contrary.

Openness is therefore an aid to the legal determination of the lawfulness or otherwise of an administrative decision. It is particularly desirable when the issue before the court is concerned with relevant or irrelevant considerations. This was made clear in *ex parte Huddleston* by the Master of the Rolls, Sir John Donaldson, who considered that a local authority whose decision was challenged by way of judicial review should, in the interests of high standards of public administration, assist the court by disclosing, as far as necessary, such reasons as were adequate to enable the court to ascertain whether the authority was in error in reaching its decision by taking into account irrelevant considerations or not taking into account relevant ones.[22]

Sir John Donaldson made the optimistic assumption that public bodies were as concerned as the courts to determine the legality or otherwise of a decision and that they were capable of standing back from their decisions and actions and considering impartially what had happened. There may be occasions when this is true, when public bodies welcome legal guidance on how they should exercise their statutory powers, particularly if these powers have not yet been tested in the courts. This accords with the need for both citizens and public authorities to know their legal position and thus where they stand, an important aspect of good administration. Such guidance from the courts would be most useful if given before the exercise of discretion rather than afterwards, when its attachment to a remedy suggests administrative wrong-doing rather than uncertainty as to the law. However, judicial review is remedy-based and the courts have ruled that they have no jurisdiction to grant a declaration in the form of an advisory opinion of the state of the law at the time.[23] Thus any guidance from the courts remains retrospective and, as a consequence, is more likely to be seen as a hindrance to the administrative process than as an aid to good administration.

Not all judges have shared Sir John Donaldson's optimistic view that public administration is concerned with the objective truth or legality of its actions, nor do they agree with his expectation of openness. Indeed, there are times when they recognize that openness may conflict with the requirements of confidentiality. Such requirements are, where appropriate, respected by the courts (see below), but in any case, the extent to which the courts have forced the issue of openness has not significantly affected the administrative process. Some commentators see this as an area in which the judges should be active, suggesting that British courts

[22] *R.* v. *Lancashire County Council, ex p. Huddleston* CA [1986] 2 All ER 941 at 945.
[23] See Brooke J., *R.* v. *Sec. of State for Education, ex p. Birmingham City Council* [1991] The Times 14 May.

should look at the development by the United States' courts of the 'hard-look' review.[24] This requires reasonable access to decision-making processes so that the basis of the decision is clear and it can be seen that all relevant factors have been considered. Baldwin suggests that, in the context of rules, the courts should be 'concerned to see that rule-makers have been open about their proposed rules, that they have given proper attention to opposing arguments, that they have taken all relevant factors into account, and that the rule produced can be justified.'[25]

A development of this nature would conflict with the instinctive desire of public administration to keep the courts at arm's length, an outcome better achieved by secrecy than by openness and one which accords with its traditional attitude to political accountability. This attitude and predilection to secrecy still remains, despite the establishment of Next Steps agencies, which promised a transparency previously lacking, and John Major's commitment to more open government, which includes the Code of Practice on Access to Government Information.[26] Moreover, whilst the new public management model might see transparency as an important management tool and thus as a feature of good administration, it would be unenthusiastic about its development as a legal principle with application across the range of decision-making processes.

Confidentiality

Judicial support for openness as a principle of good administration may conflict with the need of public administration for confidentiality. This need was recognized in *ex parte Huddleston* by Lord Justice Parker when he took a different view from the Master of the Rolls.[27] Whether the courts allow the protection of information in the interests of confidentiality depends upon the particular circumstances, a point developed in *ex parte TC Coombs* by Mr Justice Schiemann Mr Justice Schiemann saw no obligation of disclosure imposed by the concept of good administration and was concerned that a lack of openness should not automatically be seen as the administration hiding its wrongdoing.[28] However, he was also concerned that the needs of good administration should not be used as an excuse for non-disclosure. He said, 'An unwillingness on the part of the administrator to disclose the factual basis for his decision may be, but need not be, because there is no factual basis for his decision, or because the factual basis evidences some illegality which he wishes to keep from the court. It is, however, perfectly understandable for an administrator not to be prepared to disclose the factual basis for his decision because to do so would in his eyes prejudice good administration.' In the case before Mr Justice Schiemann the tax inspector would not reveal his

---

[24] E.g. R. Baldwin, *Rules and Government*, 80; S. Breyer and R. B. Stewart, *Administrative Law and Regulatory Policy*.
[25] Baldwin (above, n. 24), 80.   [26] See ch. 4.   [27] [1986] 2 All ER 941.
[28] *R. v. IRC, ex p. TC Coombs & Co.* [1989] STC 104 (Lexis).

sources of information on the grounds that the interests of good administration required the preservation of confidentiality to prevent these sources from drying up, an argument accepted by the court.

Confidentiality was also the issue in *ex parte Sheffield City Council*.[29] Both sides were seeking documents concerning the interpretation of regulations on rent subsidies. Mr Justice McNeill having 'regard to the interests of justice and the interests of good administration', refused to order discovery. He reasoned that decision-making would be 'almost intolerable if informal exchanges of provisional views . . . of the elected members of a local authority between themselves and their officers were, save in extreme cases, to be subject to disclosure'. He was persuaded by the argument of Counsel, Mr Stephen Sedley, that if such documents were ordered to be disclosed, 'the shredders in every council office in the United Kingdom would be working overtime', and he added his own thought that this would no doubt also apply to the offices of central government.

Mr Justice McNeill's ruling clearly gave support to the 'candour argument'[30] and the view that the requirements of good administration for confidentiality between elected representatives and their advisers should outweigh the requirements of openness and the provision of information, unless the interests of justice are overwhelming. This was a view which was supported in *ex parte US Tobacco International*, at least with regard to 'political' advice given by civil servants to the minister.[31] However, it was not seen as appropriate in the context of scientific advisers. The case concerned regulations banning the trading in oral snuff, which the Tobacco Company challenged as being unfair. The company had received planning permission to build a factory to manufacture the product but had then been refused a licence on the basis of new scientific advice. It argued that fairness required that it should have been given an opportunity to dispute the expert advice on which the refusal of the licence was based but that this opportunity had been denied.

In the Divisional Court Mr Justice Moorland did not accept the submission made on behalf of the Secretary of State that it was not in accordance with good administration to reveal technical advice given to Ministers by scientific experts because to do so might inhibit the giving of candid advice. He commented,[32] 'For my part I regard the submission as having no realistic basis at all . . . I cannot believe that scientists of the quality to be expected to be serving on a committee of this kind would be in any way inhibited if their conclusions were revealed to interested parties.'[33]

---

[29] *R. v. Sec. of State for Social Services, ex p. City of Sheffield* CO/346/85 (Lexis).

[30] See *Duncan* v. *Cammell, Laird & Co. Ltd* [1942] AC 624, where it was used in relation to public interest immunity.

[31] *R. v. Sec. of State for Health, ex p. US Tobacco International Ltd* [1992] 1 All ER 212.

[32] At 229.

[33] Despite judicial support for access to the information, US Tobacco's application was unsuccessful, the CA holding that the Govt could not be fettered by a moral obligation to a company which was contrary to the public interest ([1992] QB 353).

Giving Reasons

Closely related to openness is the giving of reasons, which in the context of good administration has generally been viewed positively. However, the courts have been concerned not to impose or support too high a requirement. In *Impey* v. *Secretary of State for the Environment* a planning decision made by the Secretary of State was unaccompanied by an appropriate explanation, despite a statutory requirement for reasons.[34] Mr Justice Hodgson held that the Secretary of State was bound 'to provide all parties concerned with sufficiently detailed reasons to enable them to be advised of whether he is right or wrong and to take such further proceedings as they think appropriate.' As in *Connell*[35] and *Huddleston*[36] the requirement was for those concerned to know their position. This time the interests of good administration coincided with a statutory duty and thus could be given legal effect. However, Mr Justice Hodgson was concerned that his ruling should not be seen as requiring too high a standard of elaboration, which if very detailed would be neither in the interests of good administration nor, because of the manpower involved, in 'the national interest'. He considered that the level of detail required should be sufficient to make clear in what way the Secretary of State 'is directing himself': in other words, for the parties to know what he had and had not taken into account.

His reasoning would appear to accord with the 'hard-look' doctrine which 'presents judicial review as a mechanism for ensuring rational decision-making'.[37] However, for judicial review to fulfil this function, it is necessary for judges to have 'the expertise, experience and information appropriate to the task of identifying, and then imposing, standards of rationality'.[38] Without this, 'judicial review cannot be expected to perform at anything other than a symbolic level'.[39] Judges also face the challenge, when ruling on the detail required in giving reasons or notice or in allowing comments in individual instances, of trying 'to achieve gains under the accountability and due process headings whilst avoiding the efficiency losses associated with . . . the over-inclusive application of notice and comment requirements.'[40] In other words, judges have to balance gains in accountability and fairness against losses in efficiency.[41] This was clearly Mr Justice Hodgson's concern. In making this balance, judges are considering good administration in relation to the individual on the one hand, and the administrators and the public, or as Mr Justice Hodgson called it 'national', interest on the other.

The amount of detail required when the giving of reasons is a statutory duty will depend on the issue involved. In *ex parte Mellstrom* the judgment suggested that when there is also a right to make representations, the courts will consider there is an 'obligation to set out . . . [the] reasoning process with sufficient particularity to

---

[34] [1980] P & CR 157. [35] Above, n. 20. [36] Above, n. 22.
[37] G. Richardson & M. Sunkin, 'Judicial review' [1996] *PL* 79 at 80. [38] Ibid.
[39] Ibid. [40] Baldwin, above n. 24, at 79.
[41] See below on 'fairness' for further discussion of gain-cost analysis.

enable the persons affected to comment meaningfully'.[42] Mr Justice Schiemann said, 'The very fact that a person or institution affected is given the right to know the grounds and to make representations on them, points to the fact that Parliament must have intended that person or institution to know the factual basis of the ground to be relied upon . . . The right to make representations is meaningless unless the alleged factual basis of the value judgment is disclosed. This interpretation is required not merely in the interests of the person affected but for good administration generally.'

This statement by Mr Justice Schiemann suggests that the courts are prepared to use 'the intention of Parliament' to support the principles of good administration.[43] The case concerned the withdrawal of authorization to accept deposits from Mr Mellstrom on the basis that he was not a fit and proper person to hold the position of executive controller. Once again the court would seem to assume that good administration is concerned not just with process but with the process producing the outcome intended. In this case, where the loss of a substantive right was involved, a full explanation of the decision involved was considered necessary, Mr Justice Schiemann demonstrating how the statutory basis and the facts of the case impact upon what the courts consider to be in the interests of good administration.[44]

In the cases of *Impey*[45] and *Mellstrom*[46] there was a statutory requirement to give reasons and thus the courts could insist the duty should be fulfilled to the standard they deemed appropriate. However, in the absence of a statutory duty to give reasons the courts consider that they cannot impose a general obligation on administrative authorities to that effect. This position was confirmed by the Court of Appeal in *ex parte Grillo*,[47] which specifically rejected Mr Louis Blom-Cooper's assertion in the High Court that there was a general duty to give reasons for administrative decisions. Mr Blom-Cooper had made reference to his previous decision in *ex parte Walters*[48] in which he had stated, 'It seems to me that English law has now arrived at the point where there is at least a general duty to give reasons whenever the statutorily-impregnated administrative process is infused with the concept of fair treatment to those potentially affected by administrative action.'[49]

In the Court of Appeal Lord Justice Neill was sympathetic to the view but stated, 'There may come a time when English law does impose a general obligation on administrative authorities to give reasons for their decisions. But there is no such requirement at present.'[50] He cited Lord Mustill in *ex parte Doody*, who said, 'I accept without hesitation . . . that the law does not at present recognize a

---

[42] *R. v. Bank of England, ex p. Mellstrom* CO/2529/92 (Lexis).
[43] Although see Lord Bridge in *Griffith* (above, n. 11).
[44] See also *ex p. TC Coombs & Co.* (above, n. 28).   [45] Above, n. 34.
[46] Above, n. 42.
[47] *R. v. Kensington and Chelsea Royal LBC, ex p. Grillo* CA [1996] 8 Admin LR 165.
[48] *R. v. Lambeth LBC, ex p. Walters* [1993] 26 HLR 170.   [49] Cited in CA at 178.
[50] Ibid. at 177.

general duty to give reasons for administrative decisions.'[51] The Court of Appeal did, however, concede that explanations in the form of reasons may be required for decisions which on their face appear absurd. Moreover, there was clear judicial support for the giving of reasons as a principle of good administration, here as part of a sensible and sensitive policy on the accommodation of the homeless with which the case was concerned, Lord Justice Neill commenting, 'One may applaud the giving of reasons for an administrative decision as a sign of good and courteous administration.'[52]

This acceptance of the importance of reasons in terms of good administration echoed dicta from Lord Denning, who as long ago as 1971 in *Breen* v. *Amalgamated Engineering Union* considered that, 'the giving of reasons is one of the fundamentals of good administration'.[53] More recently, Lord Woolf has also been outspoken on the matter, stating that he regarded 'the giving of satisfactory reasons for a decision as being the hallmark of good administration'.[54] Indeed, he has suggested that 'the most beneficial improvement which could be made to English administrative law' would be 'the introduction of a general requirement that reasons should normally be available, at least on request, for all administrative actions.'[55]

Openness and reasoned decision-making are, of course, proclaimed virtues of the English justice system. It is therefore not surprising that judges seek to apply the principles to public administration as well. Reasoned decision-making is also a feature of any model of good administration, and 'part of the morality of aspiration (if not practice) of any decision-maker'.[56] It means that relevant considerations are taken into account and irrelevant considerations are rejected. There would therefore seem 'no harm in judges adopting and applying these values as part of the basis on which to assess the legal propriety of administrative action.'[57] Moreover, the fact that discretion operates within a statutory framework suggests that there should be a high degree of coincidence in administrative and judicial consideration of what is relevant.

Where differences do arise, this, to a large extent, is because public administration and the courts have different views on decision-making. Public administration is concerned with the 'generality' of decision-making whereas the courts' interest is with the 'particular' or the individual decision.[58] Thus officials may be making a broader assessment of what is relevant than the courts, looking at the interests of the wider public rather than the individual. This assessment may include a consideration of cost and efficiency, both as factors in their own right and as factors militating against the consideration of another factor, which

[51] [1994] 1 AC 531 at 564.   [52] Above, n. 50 at 178.
[53] [1971] 2 QB 175 at 195.   [54] H. Woolf, *Protection of the Public*, at 92.
[55] Ibid; and see also JUSTICE, *Administration under Law* and JUSTICE–All Souls, *Review of Administrative Law*.
[56] D. Feldman, 'Judicial review: a way of controlling government?' (1988) 66 *Pub. Admin.* 3 at 26
[57] Ibid.
[58] R. Cranston, 'Reviewing judicial review' in Richardson & Genn (eds.), *Administrative Law and Government Action* at 64.

although relevant is expensive to determine, perhaps because it requires the collection of considerable data. The result may be that the individual is disadvantaged, sacrificed to the public interest in the efficient spending of public money. However, the courts will not generally accept arguments of expense as an excuse for the failure to consider a relevant factor, although this may be a matter of degree and if it would have been 'very expensive' to gather the necessary information, this may be accepted.[59] Nevertheless, there is some discrepancy over what public administration sees as relevant in relation to good administration and what the courts consider necessary. Much may depend on how the judges see their role and what purpose they consider administrative law should serve, whether they see it as protecting the individual or facilitating the administrative process. It also depends on whether they see good administration as benefiting the individual or the public interest.

Consistency

Just as openness and reasoned decision-making are proclaimed by the courts as in the interests of good administration, so too is the need for consistency. Consistency is a major feature of precedent-based common law and is assumed by the courts to be a principle of good administration. This was illustrated in *ex parte Ramanathan*, an immigration case in which the applicant was granted a visa but then refused entry because a different view was taken by another official of the same documentation.[60] Such inconsistency was considered by Mr Justice Collins to be 'contrary to good administration', as well as unlawful, and he held that only fresh material, not a reappraisal of the original material, could justify a refusal once a visa had been granted. Judicial assumptions about consistency are largely uncontroversial, consistency being supported by both the public service model of good administration and the new public management model. As a principle, consistency, together with certainty, encourages forward planning, seen by Mr Justice Woolf as 'an integral part of good administration'.[61] It therefore might be considered to aid efficiency.

Legalistic models of public administration consider that consistency requires the imposition of a structure upon the decision-making process to prevent discretion being exercised in an arbitrary manner and encourage the adoption of rules.[62] In the context of good administration rules are advocated both as an alternative to discretion and as a means of controlling it.[63] It is through rules that the courts

[59] P. Cane, *Introduction to Administrative Law*, 392.

[60] *R. v. Sec. of State for Foreign and Commonwealth Affairs, ex p. Ramanathan* CO/3600/93 (Lexis).

[61] *R. v. Sec. of State for Health, ex p. Keen* [1990] 10 BMLR 13.

[62] For the rules vs. discretion debate, see R. Baldwin (above, n. 24); K. Hawkins (ed.), *Uses of Discretion*; D. J. Galligan, *Discretionary Powers*.

[63] See K. C. Davis, *Discretionary Justice*.

traditionally exert influence on the administrative process. Thus the adoption of administrative rules, whether concerned with procedure or substance, are likely to be supported by judges as being in the interests of good administration. In theory they prevent power being exercised in an arbitrary manner and thus accord with the Diceyian exposition of the rule of law. However, they can also provide a shield for the mechanization of decision-making and for the protection from political pressure of those who make the decisions.[64] Moreover, any system of rules is only as good as those who operate it[65] and no system can improve the substance that is on offer, although an elaborate mechanism may suggest better substantive rights than are actually available. In any case, rigid rules are not always appropriate in the context of social welfare, where a looser framework with adjudicating procedures may be required.

Thus whilst judicial support for consistency as a principle of good administration may be uncontroversial, the belief that this requires an underpinning rigid structure of rules is less so. Much depends on how the courts consider administrative rules; whether they see them as having legal force to the exclusion of other considerations, being a factor to take into account, or an internal management mechanism. Judicial attitudes vary depending on the type of rule and its originating authority.[66] However, the development of legitimate expectations indicates a judicial belief that good administration requires a consistency, bordering on rigidity, which is unlikely to be welcomed by those who administer the system (see below).

Equity and the Need for Administrative Policies

Consistency serves the interests of equity, ensuring that like cases are treated alike. This is a fundamental principle of the public service model and of any judicial view of good administration. The importance of equity of treatment was indicated by Mr Justice Henry in *ex parte Islington LBC* when he said, 'I take it to be a precept of good administration that like cases should be treated in like manner unless there are good reasons for a differentiation of treatment.'[67] Similarly, in *ex parte Misra* Mr Justice Latham accepted that whilst not necessarily unlawful, there was 'considerable force in the argument that it is poor administration for the State to come to two different conclusions in respect of the same issues.'[68]

Treating like cases in a uniform way requires a policy framework to guide the exercise of discretion. The courts have consistently accepted the use of policies in the decision-making process. In *British Oxygen* v. *Minister of Technology* Lord Reid made the link between having a policy and good administration when he

---

[64] J. L. Jowell, *Law and Bureaucracy*.   [65] As the experience of the CSA suggests (see ch. 4).
[66] For a full discussion see Baldwin (above, n. 24).
[67] *R. v. Sec. of State for Environment, ex p. Islington LBC* CO/914/90 (Lexis).
[68] *R. v. Sec. of State for Health, ex p. Misra* CO/2844/91 (Lexis).

said, '[I]f the Minister thinks that policy or good administration required the operation of some limiting rule, I find nothing to stop him.'[69] In this context Lord Reid seems to have seen the adoption of a policy as benefiting those who operate the system,[70] making the exercise of discretion easier and more efficient. However, policies also benefit those to whom they apply. In *ex parte Stroud* Mr Justice Brooke considered that 'properly implemented, such policies or practices lead to like justice in like cases, and to the consistency and predictability that are both attributes of good administration.'[71] The adoption of policies was therefore seen as beneficial to those who used the service, ensuring equitable treatment and a predictable outcome, as well as to administrators. A similar view was taken in *ex parte Mohammed Manzur*, an immigration case, where Mr Justice Simon Brown was concerned with the policy adopted to help determine who should be allowed to settle in Britain.[72] He noted that 'the administration of a scheme of this character requires, for the sake of consistency, fairness and good administration, that criteria are evolved as to how competing applications, for such they essentially are, are to be treated.'

The use of policies helps to protect decision-makers from suspicions or accusations of bias. If all users of the system are subject to the same criteria, then a 'real danger of bias'[73] is less likely to arise. Whilst the courts have accepted the use of policies, they have always stipulated that no policy should be so rigid as to prevent an applicant or claimant from showing that his case is exceptional. This requirement was clearly established in *ex parte Kynoch* in which a distinction was made between policies which guided the exercise of discretion and rules which fettered it, preventing consideration of an individual case.[74]

The distinction between 'policy' and 'rule' was subsequently blurred by Lord Reid's use of the phrase 'limiting rule' in *British Oxygen*.[75] However, this has not diminished the requirement that regardless of what the guiding framework is called, it must provide for exceptions to be made. This preserves the legal principle that discretion has to be actively exercised by those to whom is it granted, whilst recognizing the practicality of the situation. Thus in *Stroud* Mr Justice Henry was concerned to stress that whilst policies contribute to good administration, it was impermissible 'when an over-rigid application of the policy or practice prevents proper appreciation and treatment of the distinguishing features of the individual case in question.'[76] Similarly in *Phil Shaw Ltd* it was held that where there was a statutory discretion to consider late claims for purchase tax rebates, the Commissioners could not institute a policy which put a time limit

[69] *British Oxygen* v. *Minister of Technology* HL [1970] 3 All ER 165 at 170.
[70] See also *R.* v. *Sec. of State for Trade, ex p. Chris International Foods Ltd* CO/1020/82 (Lexis) and *Sir Brandon Meredith Rhys Williams* v. *Sec. of State for Wales* CA [1985] JPL 29.
[71] *R.* v. *Sec. of State for the Home Department, ex p. Stroud* [1992] The Times 19 Aug.
[72] *R.* v. *Sec. of State for the Home Office, ex p. Mohammed Manzur Yakub* [1986] Imm. AR.
[73] The test laid down in *R.* v. *Gough* [1993] AC 646.
[74] *R.* v. *Port of London Authority, ex p. Kynoch Ltd* [1919] 1 KB 176.
[75] Above, n. 69.
[76] Above, n. 71.

upon the consideration of such claims.[77] To do so would be to fetter their discretion which imposed a duty to consider every late claim notified in order to decide whether or not to accept such late notification.

This need to make exceptions, whilst clearly important for the individual with something different to say, imposes a burden on the administration which adds to costs and is unlikely to provide value for money. As a consequence, the legal requirement does not accord with the new public management model of good administration, which, whilst allowing considerable discretion at the management level, favours a rigid framework at lower administrative levels with the removal of all discretionary elements and the mechanization of decision-making.

Making exceptions may also conflict with the judicial rule that a discretionary public law power must not be exercised arbitrarily or with partiality between individuals or classes.[78] As noted by Mr Justice Sedley in *ex parte Hamble Fisheries*, 'The line between individual consideration and inconsistency, slender enough in theory, can be imperceptible in practice.'[79] Moreover, making an exception carries the risk of 'justified accusations of partiality or arbitrariness.' There is therefore a potential conflict between two legal rules as well as between the new public management model of good administration and the judicial view.

Mr Justice Sedley suggested that possible conflict between making exceptions and arbitrariness might be averted by the 'inclusion of thought-out exceptions in the policy itself'.[80] This he believed 'may well be exhaustive of the obligation [to make exceptions]. While any further candidates for exception must be considered, it will always be a legitimate consideration that to make one such exception may well set up an unanswerable case of partiality or arbitrariness.' Thus Mr Justice Sedley advised not just a policy which guided the exercise of discretion but a framework that determined the exercise of discretion in cases to which the policy applied and in those where it did not. This avoided the charge of fettering as it still provided for the consideration of the exceptional case, although, in practice, additional exceptions were unlikely to be made. Including 'thought-out exceptions' within the policy would seem to go some way to satisfying the requirements of the new public management model. It allows decision-making to be strictly regulated and, as a consequence, for decisions to be made at a low level with a minimal need to refer cases upwards for a ruling on their exceptionality. Moreover, generally, it also satisfies the requirements of equity and consistency, preventing charges of partiality.

---

[77] *Phil Shaw Ltd* v. *Commissioners, London VAT Tribunal* [1976] VATTR 86.

[78] See *Kruse* v. *Johnson* [1898] 2 QB 1.

[79] *R.* v. *Minister for Agriculture, Fisheries and Food, ex p. Hamble Fisheries Ltd* [1995] 7 Admin LR 637 at 645.

[80] At 646. The CA subsequently held Sedley J's ratio in *Hamble* (above, n. 79) to be wrong in so far as he propounded a balancing exercise to be undertaken by the court. The CA stated that where there are public interest reasons for refusing a legitimate expectation, the courts cannot look at a change of policy other than for *Wednesbury* unreasonableness (*R.* v. *Sec. of State for the Home Dept, ex. p. Hargreaves & ors* [1996] The Times 3 Dec. 1996.

Fairness

There may, however, be occasions when, as far as the individual is concerned, the operation of a policy is unfair. Fairness differs from equity in that it is concerned with the way the individual is treated in his or her situation rather than with treating like cases in a like manner. Thus whilst having a policy may support the principle of equity, it does not necessarily ensure the fair treatment of each individual. The right to a fair hearing, upon which the concept of fairness centres, is a fundamental legal principle and one which, Wade suggests, has been 'used by the courts as a base on which to build a kind of code of fair administrative procedure'.[81] Thus, he argues, 'the law makes its contribution to good administration.'[82] How judges see this contribution depends on which approach they adopt to fairness.

Within the legal literature two distinct approaches are discernable.[83] These can be described simply as instrumental and non-instrumental approaches. The instrumental approach centres on the protection of the individual from wrongdoing and on the role played by the procedures in ensuring the correct decision is reached. The rationale of this approach is that hearing representations encourages informed decision-making, thereby protecting the individual and assisting the efficient functioning of the administrative process in carrying out its required tasks. The instrumental approach suggests that the individual and good administration have separate interests and accrue separate benefits from the right to a hearing. It carries with it the implication that the substance of a decision may be as important as the process and thus that a remedy can be refused if the courts consider that a hearing would have made no difference to the outcome.

Such an approach is seldom acknowledged but would seem to have been taken in *Glynn* v. *Keele University* where the court ruled that a student should have been allowed a hearing before being disciplined, but refused a remedy on the basis that it would not have affected the outcome.[84] There have also been occasions when the courts have denied that fairness required the opportunity to make representations or even that the situation in question gave rise to the duty to act fairly, when they consider that finding otherwise would not affect the final outcome.[85] Rulings such as these suggest that where a hearing presents no tangible benefit to the individual, and, perhaps, when the individual is seen not to deserve any favours, the courts are reluctant to impose unnecessary burdens on the administrative process. It is clearly inefficient, both in cost and time, to have to re-make decisions which will have the same outcome and might be seen as a waste of public money when the individual's case has little merit.

---

[81] H. W. R. Wade & C. F. Forsyth, *Administrative Law*, 494. [82] Ibid.
[83] For full discussion see G. Richardson, 'The legal regulation of process' in Richardson & Genn (eds.), *Administrative Law and Government Action*.
[84] [1971] 1 WLR 487.
[85] See, e.g., *Cinnamond* v. *British Airways Authority* [1980] 1 WLR 582.

However, any consideration of the substance of a decision, even if covertly made, is contrary to legal authorities who have ruled that in judicial review the outcome is irrelevant.[86] It also underplays the importance within the public service model of good administration of fair procedures for their own sake, a factor recognized by non-instrumental approaches to fairness, such as the dignity[87] and process values[88] rationales. These consider that the primary function of procedures is to protect individual dignity and autonomy and to legitimate the administrative process. Thus procedures are required which ensure fairness, providing individuals with the opportunity to participate in decisions affecting them and to know why decisions are made against them. Such procedures may result in improved decision-making but, even if they do not, there is still administrative gain, for their existence increases confidence in the system and results in the acceptance of decisions which might otherwise be contested.

Both instrumental and non-instrumental approaches have their place in the context of good administration which is concerned to balance efficiency, fairness to the individual and the need for confidence in the system. They are also apparent in judicial rulings. The dominance of the instrumental approach is evident in statements such as that made by Lord Bridge in *Lloyd* v. *McMahon* when he said, 'what the requirements of fairness demand . . . [in making a decision] which will affect the rights of individuals depends on the characteristics of the decision-making body, the kind of decision it has to make and the statutory or other framework in which it operates.'[89] In other words in determining what procedures are appropriate, the interests of the individual is balanced against the purpose of the administrative process and the effect of procedures upon the final decision.[90]

Frequently judgments display a combination of instrumental and non-instrumental approaches. Richardson suggests that while in practice the approach is instrumental, '[o]rthodox judicial rhetoric . . . displays an additional concern for process, possibly dignity, values.'[91] This implies that at times the judges expound the virtues of procedural protection as an end in itself whilst actually upholding procedures as a means to an end. Certainly both approaches may be evident in the same ruling, as in Lord Mustill's statement in *ex parte Doody*.[92] Lord Mustill held that a prisoner, sentenced to life imprisonment, was entitled to be given reasons for the length of his sentence. He considered that such a person would want to know why a particular number of years had been chosen 'partly from an obvious human desire to be told the reason for a decision so gravely affecting his future,

---

[86] See, e.g., *Johns* v. *Rees* [1970] Ch 345; *R.* v. *Board of Prison Visitors of Hull Prison, ex p. St. Germain* (No. 2) [1979] 1 WLR 1401; *R.* v. *Chief Constable of Thames Valley Police Force, ex p. Cotton* [1990] IRLR 344.

[87] See J. Mashew, 'Administrative due process' (1981) 61 *Boston Univ. LR* 885 id., *Bureaucratic Justice*; id., 'Dignitary Process' (1987) 39 *Univ. of Florida LR* 433.

[88] See M. Bayles, *Procedural Justice*.   [89] [1987] AC 625 at 702.

[90] And see *Hussein* v. *Sec. of State for the Environment* CA [1984] JPL 431.

[91] Richardson (above, n. 83) at 117.

[92] *R.* v. *Sec. of State ex p. Doody* [1993] 3 All ER 92 at 98 and see P. Craig, *Administrative Law*, 282.

and partly because he hopes that once the information is obtained he may be able to point out errors of fact or reasoning and thereby persuade the Secretary of State to change his mind, or if he fails in this to challenge the decision in the courts.' His lordship's approach therefore incorporated process or dignity values, in which the giving of reasons was an end in itself, and instrumentalism, where they were a means to an end.

The support of the courts for process values is also evident in the judicial rules against bias, which ensure impartiality, an important characteristic of the administrative system. They are concerned not just with actual bias but with the appearance of bias, recognizing that it is as important for there to be public confidence in the system as it is for the individual to be confident of an impartial decision. However, the support shown by judges for process values has its limitations. In most instances when such values are emphasized, they are 'firmly linked to the possession by an individual of a substantive interest worthy of protection; the obligation to provide fair procedures and to treat a person with dignity may be independent of the direct outcome of the decision, but it only arises when the person's recognized substantive interest is at stake.'[93] This was evident in *ex parte Doody* where the substantive interest was the person's liberty. Such a link would suggest that in the context of good administration the possession of a sufficient substantive interest will result in the duty to act fairly being upheld over other principles, such as equity and consistency, regardless of whether the courts consider the resulting procedures to be concerned with the making of correct decisions or the legitimization of the process.

Both instrumental and non-instrumental approaches to procedural fairness raise the question of how extensive should procedural protections be. Procedures are not cost-free and it is necessary for the courts to engage in a balancing exercise between the individual's interest and the benefit and cost to the administration, and hence the public interest, of instigating process rights.[94] The problem arises in assessing both benefit and costs. Taking a law and economics or efficiency approach, 'the ideal level of procedural regulation will be that which minimizes both the cost of the procedure itself (direct costs) and the costs of reaching a wrong i.e. inaccurate decision (error costs).'[95] Such a calculation also has to consider the extent to which procedural protections will reduce the possibility of error.[96]

The law and economics calculation is concerned with balancing benefit to the individual with benefit to the administration such that '[p]rocess rights are accorded insofar as they constitute an efficient mechanism for ensuring correctness of the substantive outcome'.[97] Such a calculation may find some favour with rational-choice theorists for whom procedures are mechanisms for providing measurable gain and benefit accruing from procedural protection is costed in terms of efficiency. However, it fails to recognize that at times there may be a 'moral cost',

---

[93] Richardson (above, n. 83) at 118.
[94] Above, n. 34.
[95] Richardson (above, n. 83) at 111.
[96] See B. Posner, *Economic Analysis of Law*.
[97] Craig (above, n. 92), 299.

for example when a person's liberty is at stake, which outweighs considerations of economic factors.[98] Moreover, in the context of good administration, the law and economics approach ignores the public interest dimension, taking no account of the claims of society nor of the interest of the public at large in the promotion of process benefits. Assessing the level of procedural protection on the basis of an economic judgement alone is therefore limited. An alternative approach is to make a fuller assessment which takes account of error, moral and direct costs, and the promotion of process benefits. This in some ways is compatible with the public service model of good administration.

Just as the evidence suggests that courts take both instrumental and non-instrumental approaches to fairness, it not surprisingly indicates that in the context of good administration they make both cost-benefit and process-values calculations. In some instances there is a judicial separation of 'fairness' and 'good administration' which suggests a weighing of the procedural benefit against the benefit to efficiency. In other cases 'fairness' is expressed as part of 'good administration', thus indicating a fuller assessment which takes account of process values.

However, some commentators consider that the concern for the individual, endemic in both instrumental and non-instrumental approaches to fairness, fails to take sufficient note of the public interest, regardless of the type of cost-calculation that is made. Baldwin, for instance, suggests that 'a model of justice built on fairness to individuals looms sufficiently large to obscure such values as efficiency in the public interest, since it focuses on procedures rather than substantive rights.'[99] In the context of good administration this may be too extreme. There are judicial attempts to balance fairness with efficiency (see Chapter 8). In addition, the concentration on fair procedures, whilst at times obscuring efficiency, may contribute to the legitimacy of the administrative process, thereby working in the public interest as well as for the individual. As Baldwin also comments, 'The real test of a governmental process should be whether it furthers recognized and accepted values'.[100] Fairness would seem to be one of those values.

The underpinning case with regard to the concept of fairness in the context of good administration is *Re HK*.[101] This was an immigration case where the point at issue was whether an immigration officer was acting in a judicial capacity, and thus had to follow the rules of natural justice, which here meant allowing the would-be immigrant a full opportunity to convince him of the virtues of his case. Lord Parker gave the leading judgment in which, having considered that the immigration officer was acting as an administrator, he looked to the concept of good administration to determine the behaviour that was required.

He said, 'Good administration and an honest or bona fide decision must, as it seems to me, require not merely impartiality, not merely bringing one's mind to

[98] See R. Dworkin, *A Matter of Principle*, 80 and his consideration of bare harm and injustice harm.

[99] Baldwin (above, n. 24), 18.   [100] Ibid.   [101] [1967] 2 QB 617.

bear on the problem, but acting fairly; and to the limited extent that the circumstances of any particular case allow, and within the legislative framework under which the administrator is working, only to that limited extent do the rules of natural justice apply, which in a case such as this is merely a duty to act fairly.'[102]

Acting fairly was therefore seen as being on the lower slopes of natural justice. What it meant depended on the situation but it did not involve the full procedural might of natural justice. Lord Parker's statement suggested a process-value approach in which fairness was seen as an underlying principle of good administration and thus sustainable in its own right, not simply as a means to an end. This removed the problem of the administrative–judicial divide which had resulted in a correlation between natural justice and acting judicially, and thus in the artificial classification of many situations, depending on whether the courts wanted to quash a decision for a breach of natural justice or leave well alone.

In *Re HK* the duty to act fairly was used to limit the obligations of the immigration officer whilst still allowing judicial control of immigration procedures. On the facts the officer was held to have complied with the requirements of fairness, which was all that was necessary, and the application therefore failed. The procedural protection afforded by the court was minimal, and subsequently criticized, but fairness as an aspect of good administration, recognized and upheld by the courts, was established.

Whilst the duty to act fairly initially arose as a limitation to procedural expectations, a kind of lesser natural justice, it has subsequently developed an equivalent status. In *ex parte Sayda Fataha Khanom*, *Re HK* was cited not as a limitation but in support of the finding that the immigration officer had not fulfilled the requirements of fairness.[103] He had denied the applicant the opportunity to give explanations. Similarly in *Mamei Gaima* v. *Secretary of State for the Home Department,* an asylum case, *Re HK* was used to support the contention that the Home Secretary had acted unfairly in failing to give the applicant a sufficient opportunity to make representations.[104] Thus the linkage between acting fairly and good administration which was made in *Re HK* is retained and these cases imply, like *Re HK*, that fairness is a concept in its own right and not simply a means to an end. This is supported by the change in terminology from natural justice to the duty to act fairly, for whilst an entitlement to natural justice only arises in certain situations, a duty to act fairly suggests an ever-present obligation. What it requires in any situation will be different and at times it may be overridden by other considerations, but as a value underlying the administrative process it is constant.

In *ex parte Hardy*, a case concerning the leaking of the Secretary of State's decision to reject the proposal of the Local Education Authority (LEA) regarding a school in its area, Mr Justice McNeill held that there had been procedural

[102] Ibid. at 630.
[103] *R.* v. *Sec. of State for the Home Department, ex p. Sayda Fataha Khanom* CO/676/86 (Lexis).
[104] CA [1980] Imm AR 205.

impropriety, arguing that 'the LEA—and in due course the objectors—were entitled as a matter of good administration, of fairness and in fulfilment of a legitimate expectation to have from the Secretary of State that which would in law be
regarded as an approval (or, as the case may be, a rejection or a modification) of
the LEA's proposals, not a mistaken, unauthorized and confidentially expressed
telephone message.'[105] A properly authorized response was obviously necessary
to enable the parties concerned to make representations, if these were appropriate,
and to enable the administrative process to operate effectively. It was also necessary so that those involved felt they had been fairly treated.

Judicial expectations with regard to fairness are not simply determined on the
basis of the individual. They are also affected by the needs of the administrative
process. Indeed, it is the totality of the situation that the courts consider in determining what procedures are appropriate. This was implied by Lord Parker in *Re
HK* and subsequently developed by Lord Diplock in *CCSU* when he said, 'in any
event what procedure will satisfy the public law requirement of procedural propriety depends upon the subject matter of the decision, the executive functions of
the decision-maker . . . and the particular circumstances in which the decision
came to be made.'[106] This suggests that the requirements of good administration
inform judicial thinking on fairness, a supposition that will be expanded in the
next chapter when detriment to good administration is considered.

Legitimate Expectations

The instigation of the duty to act fairly has been accompanied by the development
of the doctrine of legitimate expectations.[107] Just as the concept of fairness allows
a more flexible application than the rules of natural justice, so legitimate expectations provides more room for judicial manoeuvre than a strict rights- or interests-
based approach. In the context of good administration 'legitimate expectations'
has assumed particular importance, administrative rule-making becoming largely
dominated by the doctrine.[108] The duty to act fairly has been extended in the procedural sense to public promises made by public bodies, which create an expectation that they will be fulfilled, and to previous practices, which may create an
expectation that they will continue to be followed. An area of debate is the extent
to which legitimate expectations go beyond an expectation of procedural protection and thus fair treatment to an expectation in the substantive sense, which
moves controversially from a regulation of policy application to a regulation of
policy formulation.[109] Clearly, the development of the concept has considerable

---

[105] *R. v. Sec. of State for Education and Science, ex p. Hardy* CO/354/88 (Lexis).

[106] *Council of Civil Service Unions* v. *Minister for Civil Service* HL [1984] 3 All ER 935 at 1411.

[107] For a discussion of the concept see P. Craig, 'Legitimate Expectations' (1992) 108 *LQR* 79; and
C. Forsyth, 'provenance and protection of legitimate expectations' (1988) 47 *CLJ* 238.

[108] Richardson (above, n. 83) at 118.

[109] But see *R. v. IRC ex p. Unilever* [1996] STC 681 CA, which Richard Gordon QC suggests provides a positive answer as to whether legitimate expectations can provide a substantive benefit.

implications for public administration and may explain why judges have sought to link legitimate expectations through fairness to the interests of good administration.

This link was established in the *Hong Kong* case.[110] It concerned a change in Government policy in Hong Kong in relation to illegal immigrants and the promise that accompanied it. Previously, illegal immigrants who had managed to get to the city were left alone. The Hong Kong Government announced that such immigrants would now be interviewed and, whilst stating that no guarantees could be given that they would not subsequently be removed, it undertook to treat each case on its merits. Ny Yuen Shiu reported to immigration, whereupon he was detained and a removal order was made against him. He was only allowed to answer questions and given no opportunity to state his case. He applied for judicial review on the grounds that he had been denied a fair hearing. The case reached the Privy Council which quashed the order on the basis that the applicant had a legitimate expectation that he would be treated fairly and he had not been. Lord Fraser examined the way in which the expectation arose, stating that it 'may be based on some statement or undertaking by, or on behalf of, the public authority which has the duty of making the decision, if the authority has through its officers, acted in a way that would be unfair or inconsistent with good administration for him to be denied such an enquiry.'[111]

Thus it would seem Lord Fraser considered that failing to honour an undertaking was either unfair or inconsistent with good administration. However, he made a closer linkage suggesting that the failure to honour a promise was contrary to good administration because it was unfair. He said, 'when a public authority had promised to follow a certain procedure, it is in the interests of good administration that it should act fairly and should implement its promise, so long as implementation does not interfere with its statutory duty.'[112] This suggested a recognition of the importance of process values in providing confidence in the system as well as protecting the individual.

More controversially the keeping of a promise or undertaking has extended to published policies and guidelines, which the courts consider create an expectation that they will be followed, and thus present the possibility of unfairness or unreasonableness if they are not. The matter arose in *ex parte Khan*.[113] The Home Office had issued a circular letter which gave guidance on immigration for adoption. Subsequently the guidance was departed from. Lord Justice Parker held that the Secretary of State was entitled to change the policy but that such a change could only be implemented 'after the recipient of such a letter had been given a full opportunity to make representations, and only after full and serious consideration whether there was some overriding public interest which justified a departure from procedures stated in the letter'.[114] Thus a legitimate expectation had

---

[110] *Attorney-General of Hong Kong* v. *Ny Yuen Shiu* PC [1983] 2 All ER 311.
[111] Ibid. at 350. [112] Ibid. at 351.
[113] *R.* v. *Sec. of State for the Home Department, ex p. Khan* [1985] 1 All ER 40.
[114] Ibid. at 48.

been created by the letter which meant that any departure from the policy within it was unfair or unreasonable unless representations were allowed and unless the change was necessary in the public interest.

In *ex parte Ruddock* Mr Justice Taylor held that there was a legitimate expectation that the Home Secretary would follow published criteria with regard to telephone tapping and that this imposed a duty to act fairly.[115] The application for review was in fact dismissed, national security considerations being accepted as paramount. However, Mr Justice Taylor cited Lord Fraser's ruling from the *Hong Kong* case and thus once more the link was made between implementing a 'promise', here published criteria, and the interests of good administration. The implication would seem to be that public administration benefits from being fair, consistent and honest. This accords with the public service ethos, which underlies the public service model of good administration, and gives public administration legitimacy in the eyes of the public.

Clearly the development of legitimate expectations impacts upon the adoption of policies. It also imposes a restraint on the way policies are changed. Sudden changes, which do not give sufficient notice, may attract the charge of unfairness. This does not, however, apply when the change is made to rectify a mistake. In *Jaramillo-Siva* v. *Secretary of State for Home Department* the Home Secretary had wrongly told two brothers, convicted of drug smuggling, that they had a right to appeal against the judge's recommendation that they be deported after serving their sentences.[116] In fact whilst there was a right of appeal under the Immigration Act 1971 against a deportation decision of the Home Secretary (section 3(5)(b)), there was no such appeal against the recommendation of the court (section 3(6)). The Home Secretary corrected his mistake, but the brothers made an application for judicial review on the basis that they had a legitimate expectation of a right to appeal. The Court of Appeal rejected their submission, Lord Justice Simon Brown stating that for there to be a legitimate expectation, it is 'necessary for the applicant to establish that it was unfair or inconsistent with good administration for the Secretary of State, following his mistake, to pursue the section 3(6) route'. He continued, 'I for my part, am wholly unpersuaded that that was unfair or that good administration required him, so to speak, to stand by his mistake, and regard himself as inhibited from following what otherwise must inevitably have been the appropriate route, namely deportation under 3(6).'

Again there is the implication that good administration is concerned with trust and integrity. The judgment accords with the *Hong Kong* case with its reference to the need to establish that the decision or action was unfair or inconsistent with good administration, and suggests that if the Home Secretary's actions were established as being inconsistent, in the sense described, this might be seen as evidence of unfairness or unreasonableness and upheld on that basis. Lord Justice Simon Brown was not implying that acting in a way that was inconsistent with good

---

[115] *R.* v. *Sec. of State for the Home Department, ex p. Ruddock* [1987] 2 All ER 518.
[116] CA [1994] Imm AR 352.

administration would itself provide a ground for challenge. He had already ruled out this possibility in a case against the Monopolies and Mergers Commission in 1990, where an application for judicial review had been made on the basis that the Commission had failed to comply with expressly-stated guidelines, and had therefore failed to fulfil a legitimate expectation.[117] The applicants argued that they were entitled to a remedy even though they had suffered no detriment. Mr Justice Simon Brown rejected the argument, stating that it was necessary to show 'objective unfairness', not just that there had been 'a free-standing procedural failure . . . for which the Report should be impugned essentially to further the principles of good administration'. Thus the applicants needed to have been detrimentally affected by non-compliance with the guidelines. This accords with the rules relating to *locus standi* which do not afford standing on the basis of the interests of good administration, even if these interests incorporate the need for fairness.

The courts have also ruled that a legitimate expectation cannot arise that a normal procedural requirement will not be enforced. Such an expectation would clearly be at odds with principles of good administration which relate to equity of treatment and consistency. The matter arose in an immigration case where the applicant had tried to obtain entry clearance once he was in Britain.[118] The rules stipulated that such clearance should be obtained from outside the country but the applicant claimed that he had been led to believe that the Home Office would waive the rule in his case. His argument was dismissed by Mr Justice Kennedy who said, 'It is quite impossible to spell out . . . the proposition that it would be unfair or inconsistent with good administration to allow the Home Office to act in the way in which they did act.'

In the landmark *CCSU* case,[119] which concerned the removal of the right to belong to a trade union, the House of Lords recognized that an established practice could also give rise to a legitimate expectation. In this case there had been an established practice of consultation and the failure to consult was held to have been unfair, although the application was unsuccessful for reasons of national security. In determining whether there was a duty to consult Lord Fraser stated, 'the test . . . is whether the practice of past consultation of the staff on significant changes in their conditions of service was so well established by 1983 that it would be unfair or inconsistent with good administration for the government to depart from the practice in this case.'[120]

Consultation is related to the right to a fair hearing but because it frequently focuses on the group and representative interests, rather than the individual, and is always prior to a decision being made, it suggests participation in the decision-making process. This serves to legitimate both the decision that is made as well as the administrative process. In a case brought by the Law Society against the Lord

[117] Above, n. 17.
[118] *R. v. Sec. of State for the Home Department, ex p. Mohammed Tahseen Sheikh* CO/648/87 (Lexis).
[119] Above, n. 106.   [120] At 944.

Chancellor the firm link was made between consultation 'as part of good admin-istration' and as a legitimate expectation which was capable of being upheld by the courts (although in the case concerned no remedy was granted).[121] This link and the apparent extension by the courts of the expectation to be consulted does not accord with the new public management model's preoccupation with value for money. Consultation, other than by a routine paper exercise in the form of a mar-ket survey, is costly in time and money and raises questions about how extensive it should be.

The development of the concept of legitimate expectations has extended the control of the courts over the administrative process, such that where good admin-istration demands the observance of a right to be heard or consulted the individ-ual or group may legitimately expect to be treated fairly. In addition, the concept impacts upon the ability of public administration to make policy changes. Some commentators suggest that legitimate expectations could make a contribution to 'structuring administrative discretion', its 'easily accessible values' of 'honesty, open-mindedness and consistency' meaning that it is easily absorbed by the administrative process.[122]

However, the concept present a number of problems. Firstly, it has much in common with Davis' concern for individual justice[123] and thus runs into the same criticisms of minimizing the importance in decision-making of efficiency, adapt-ability, and public, rather than private, interests. Secondly, it sits astride two conflicting legal principles, the principle of consistency and rationality, and the principle that a public body cannot fetter its discretion. These principles also com-pete in the public service and new public management models of good adminis-tration. Both models aspire to consistency as an aid to administration and to the public at large. Both also assert the importance of retaining the ability to make changes to administrative policies. For the public service model this accords with the constitutional position of the Civil Service, as accountable through the minis-ter to Parliament, and the need to respond to changes in political direction, 'the lib-erty to make such changes [being] . . . something that is inherent in our constitutional form of government'.[124] As far as the new public management model is concerned, the need is in relation to the demands of efficiency, value for money and meeting performance targets. This suggests a possible conflict between the courts and either model of good administration. However, such conflict is more likely with the public management model for whilst the courts are deferential in their attitude towards ministerial responsibility and constitutional accountability, they do not accord the same respect to value for money and are unlikely to yield to arguments related to performance targets.

Thirdly, even if the values which inform the doctrine of legitimate expectations are, as Feldman suggests, 'easily accessible', the situations in which a legitimate

---

[121] *R.* v. *Lord Chancellor, ex p. The Law Society* [1993] The Times 25 June.
[122] Feldman (above, n. 56) at 27.   [123] See Davis (above, n. 63).
[124] Lord Diplock, *Hughes* v. *Dept of Health and Social Security* [1985] AC 776 at 788.

expectation will be found are not always self-evident. There is indeed an unpre-dictability about the concept and an elasticity in its application by the courts, which does little to aid administrative confidence. Mr Justice Sedley described legitimate expectations as 'in effect a term of art, reserved for expectations which are not only reasonable but which will be sustained by the court in the face of changes of policy'.[125] He continued, 'whether this point has been reached is deter-mined by the court, whether on grounds of rationality, of legality or of fairness, all of which the court, not the decision-maker, is the arbiter'. This is not likely to be a popular contention as far as the new public management model is concerned, containing as it does variables which cannot be quantified or accurately predicted. It suggests that it is what the court with hindsight sees as being inconsistent with good administration which needs to be determined, not what officials at the time believed.

Fourthly, in relation to policies, legitimate expectation may only arise with regard to those that have been published or made known. This suggests an incen-tive not to publish rules and policies and 'hardly . . . encourages Ministers and officials to indulge in open structuring of their discretionary powers'.[126] Baldwin suggests that what may be required is the development of 'a rule of unfair non-disclosure' which 'will make it a duty to publish a rule where it is in operation'.[127] Such a duty is founded in the notion of fairness and in the case of policies it is nec-essary for an individual to show he or she is an exception. It also accords with Davis' thesis that 'as soon as discretion gives way to rules, the rules should be available to affected parties'. He argues that 'precedents and rules provide a beneficial structure of discretion, but not if they are kept secret, for the adminis-tration can then ignore a precedent or violate a rule, engaging in discrimination and favouritism without detection.'[128] Thus the argument returns to the need for openness which the courts, if not public administration, see as fundamental to good administration.

Conclusion

The judicial perspective on good administration and the interests it serves has con-siderable influence in shaping the administrative process, a process which the courts see as requiring equity, consistency, fairness, honesty, justice, openness, and rational decision-making. There is also increasing judicial pressure for public administration to adhere to human rights. Over twenty years ago Lord Reid expressed the opinion that it was 'hardly credible' that Parliament or any govern-ment department would act contrary to those rights. This view has been echoed subsequently by a number of judges.[129] Moreover, there is dicta to suggest that the

---

[125] *Ex p. Hamble Fisheries* (above, n. 79) at 657.   [126] Baldwin (above, n. 24), 114.
[127] Ibid.   [128] Davis (above, n. 57), 110.
[129] See, e.g., Lord Browne-Wilkinson, 'Infiltration of a Bill of Rights' (1992) *PL* 397 and J. Laws, 'Law and Democracy' (1995) *PL* 72.

courts might be prepared to give effect to human rights even though the European Convention is not incorporated into English law. In *ex parte Bennett*, Lord Griffith considered that it was the responsibility of judges 'to refuse to countenance behaviour that threatens either basic human rights or the rule of law'.[130] The case was concerned with unlawful extradition, not the administration of government departments. However, Lord Griffith's comments have a general application and, even if not given effect, demonstrate the strength of feeling amongst senior judges for the protection of human rights. Thus any judicial perspective on good administration will include a consideration of human rights.

The values recognized by judges as underlying good administration may at times conflict. However, all are portrayed positively, as being necessary for those affected by decisions and as affecting the operation of the administrative process for the better. Good administration therefore requires compliance with them. Such a perspective on good administration suggests adherence to the rule-of-law ideal, criticized by some commentators for being too narrow.[131] In particular, critics argue that it takes little account of the public interest or of the participatory aspects of a modern democracy, Jowell suggesting that the rule of law is 'large, but not, however, large enough to serve as a principle upholding a number of other requirements of a democracy'.[132] A further criticism is voiced by Cranston, who sees the focus on the individual and his or her interaction with public administration to be at the expense of the public interest.[133] As it is this interest that is the dominant concern of administrators, Cranston reasons that the courts frequently work against the interests of good administration rather than for them.

Such criticism would seem to suggest that the concept of good administration is only relevant in the context of the public interest. However, the individual, who comes into contact with the administrative process and is personally affected by the way in which decisions are made, also has a valid interest in good administration. The task of the courts is to balance this interest, which centres on fairness and justice, with the public interest in certainty and efficiency and, as the next chapter shows, this balance does not always favour the individual.

---

[130] *R.* v. *Horseferry Road Magistrates Court, ex p. Bennett* [1994] AC 42 and see *R.* v. *Lord Chancellor, ex p. Witham,* [1997] *The Times,* 13 Mar.
[131] See, e.g., N. Lacey, 'The jurisprudence of discretion' in Hawkins (ed.) (above, n. 59).
[132] J. Jowell, 'The rule of law today' in Jowell & Oliver (eds.), *Changing Constitution* at 76.
[133] Cranston, (above, n. 58) at 64.

8

JUDICIAL PERSPECTIVES ON GOOD ADMINISTRATION: THE PUBLIC INTEREST

Introduction

The use of the public interest by the courts in the context of good administration has a number of interpretations. Sometimes it recognizes a public interest in the individual being treated fairly. At other times it is concerned with the wider public, which includes the taxpayer. Usually, however, it is expressed in terms of there being a public interest in administrators being able to operate efficiently and effectively, unhampered by unpredictable challenges which bring into question the validity of decisions and result in uncertainty and a lack of confidence in the system.

Speed and Certainty

One of the key requirements of the public interest in good administration is certainty which is frequently linked with the need for speed in the decision-making process. Inevitably there are times when the courts have to balance these requirements with the needs of fairness. In the context of good administration, much depends on the individual case but Richard Gordon QC has commented generally that 'legal certainty is trumped by greater considerations of fairness'.[1] In *ex parte Banham* which concerned a challenge to the Secretary of State's decision regarding the future of the area's schools,[2] objectors complained that they had not received a copy of the 'statement of case' submitted by the local authority to the Home Secretary and that it was a requirement of the departmental Circular 3/87 that they should do so. Mr Justice Macpherson dismissed the application on the grounds that a failure to formally disclose a document could not amount to unfairness when the views it expressed were well known.

In his opinion good administration did not require the Secretary of State or the local authority 'to conduct the process as if it were litigation', and he quoted approvingly from Circular 3/87 which said, 'It would not be compatible with good administration and the speedy resolution of the uncertainty surrounding the future of a school . . . if there were to be a continuing exchange of argument and

---

[1] At Sweet & Maxwell Conference on Judicial Review, Dec. 1996, with reference to *R.* v. *IRC, ex p. Unilever* [1996] STC 681 CA.
[2] *R.* v. *Sec. of State for Education, ex p. Banham* [1992] The Times 9 Mar..

counter-argument over every issue involved'. As in many instances, there were competing requirements (in this case fairness and the right to consultation versus certainty and efficiency), all of which could lay claim to being principles of good administration. The function of the court was to strike the right balance between them. In its opinion the balance tipped in favour of certainty, a decision that would also benefit the interests of efficient administration.

Certainty was also paramount in *O'Reilly* v. *Mackman*.[3] Lord Diplock confirmed the decision of the lower courts to strike out an action for abuse of process, upholding the need 'in the interests of good administration and of third parties who may be indirectly affected by the decision, for speedy certainty as to whether it has the effect of a decision that is valid in public law.'[4] Clearly in this case as in the previous one there was a recognition not just of the need to make decisions as quickly as possible so that individuals and the public at large know their position but also so that those engaged in public administration could get on with the business in hand. Thus quick decision-making becomes in itself an aspect of good administration.

The dual need for speed and certainty, of which finality is a prerequisite, was expressed by Lord Justice Donaldson in *ex parte Argyll*, a case concerning the Commissioner's handling of a take-over bid.[5] He undertook an extensive examination of the competing requirements of good administration, accepting that, when the court sat as a public law court, it had to have a 'proper awareness of the needs of public administration' and he outlined some of these needs. He noted that good administration was concerned 'with substance rather than form' and 'with speed of decision', and that it required 'a proper consideration of the public interest' and of 'the legitimate interests of individual citizens'. However, he recognized that 'in judging the relevance of an interest, however legitimate, regard has to be had for the purpose of the administrative process concerned.'

Thus it was the outcome and the speed in producing it that were ultimately important, not who made the decision or how it had been made, and although the interests of individual citizens should be properly considered, this consideration was limited by the purpose the administrative process was required to fulfil. It was also limited by the fact that 'good administration requires decisiveness and finality, unless there are compelling reasons to the contrary.'

Lord Justice Donaldson's approach was instrumental and selective in the needs of good administration, including no consideration of process values. However, his outline was used to support the Court of Appeal's ruling that the consent of the Secretary of State to the decision of the Monopolies Board not to take further action should not be quashed. The Court of Appeal accepted that the Secretary of State had acted *ultra vires* in giving consent because the decision had been made by the Chairman alone and not the full Board. However, it considered that the need for finality and thus certainty overrode other considerations. Good administration

³ [1982] 3 All ER 1124.   ⁴ At 1133.
⁵ R. v. *Monopolies and Mergers Commission, ex p. Argyll Group plc* [1986] 1 WLR 763 at 774.

was therefore used to excuse the original decision-maker, on the basis that the decision had to be taken quickly, and to justify the court's refusal to grant a remedy, which, it believed, would lead to uncertainty and, in the context in which it was set, possible large financial loss.

A remedy was also refused in a case brought by British Telecom.[6] Here the court accepted that a limited time-scale meant that procedures and processes might need to be curtailed, possibility to the detriment of fairness. Mr Justice Auld expressed the view that 'the Secretaries of State had to do the best with what they had; they had to try to achieve as fair a solution as they could, concerning themselves with the substance and not the detailed form of the matter, and they had to achieve finality in time for a new system to come into effect on 1st April 1990.'[7]

There are some cases where judges have 'gone out of their way to acknowledge the boundaries set by financial and time constraints'.[8] These are frequently cases concerning local authorities. However, in *ex parte Datafin* the Court of Appeal stated that it would use its discretion in granting remedies in such a way as to underpin and not undermine the operation of the Take-over Panel, a body where speed and finality in decision-making were of the essence in order to provide the necessary certainty in take-over situations.[9]

The requirement for certainty is one with which the courts are particularly familiar and comfortable. It is an important principle in most legal systems. Indeed, some jurisdictions see legal certainty as being of paramount importance and allow no judicial discretion with regard to challenges brought outside strict time-limits. This is the case with EC law, where legal certainty is one of the general legal principles under which the Community operates.[10] Thus decisions of Community institutions cannot be challenged once they are formally recognized as valid, which is usually between one and three months of their publication or notification to affected parties. However, most jurisdictions allow judicial discretion with regard to delay in recognition that the substantive interests of an individual may at times outweigh the public interest in certainty or can be upheld with a minimum effect upon the wider community. In this respect the procedure under Order 53 offers the same balance of protection to the individual and the public interest as is found in many other jurisdictions.[11]

[6] *R. v. Sec. of State for the Environment and Sec. of State for Wales, ex p. British Telecommunications plc* [1991] RA 307.

[7] At 353–4.

[8] R. Cranston, 'Reviewing judicial review' in Richardson & Genn (eds), *Administrative Law and Government Action* at 68.

[9] *R. v. Panel on Takeovers and Mergers, ex p. Datafin plc* [1987] QB 815.

[10] See T. C. Hartley, *Foundations of European Community Law*, 149.

[11] Law Commission, *Administrative Law, Judicial Review and Statutory Appeals*, ch. 3.

Undue Delay

The recognition that speed and certainty are important aspects of good administration is apparent in the rules governing the procedure under which applications for judicial review are made. These are laid down in the Supreme Court Act 1981 and Order 53. The Supreme Court Act 1981, section 31(6), is concerned with 'undue delay' in making an application for judicial review and provides the High Court with discretion to refuse to grant leave or any relief 'if it considers that the granting of the relief sought would be likely to cause substantial hardship to, or substantially prejudice the rights of, any person or would be detrimental to good administration.' It is necessary to read this in conjunction with Order 53 section 4(1) which states, 'An application for leave to apply for judicial review shall be made promptly and in any event within three months from the date when grounds for the application first arose unless the Court considers there is good reason for extending the period within which the application shall be made.'

In relation to good administration the combination of these two sections has been interpreted by the courts to mean that they have discretion to refuse leave or relief in cases where an application was not made promptly if they consider that to proceed would be detrimental to good administration. Moreover, even where there is a good reason to extend the period beyond three months, the courts retain the discretion to refuse either leave or the relief sought on the same basis.[12] The courts are therefore engaged in determining whether the lack of promptitude was deliberate or in any way culpable and whether, in the circumstances, the length of the delay was undue. They then have to consider the effect on the administrative process of granting the relief required and be convinced that any detriment is as a result of delay, for, according to Mr Justice Sedley, 'detriment to good administration is not free-standing but arises only in the context of undue delay'.[13]

Such considerations are balanced against the interests of the individual and the need for fairness. In *ex parte Hussain* Mr Justice Taylor was persuaded that the extreme importance of the case to the applicant and his family, who faced deportation, eclipsed any argument of detriment on the grounds of delay.[14] He used his discretion to grant leave, saying, 'I cannot imagine any circumstances more compelling to the grant of discretion than those that apply in the present case'. In *ex parte Campbell*,[15] Mr Justice Woolf held that the applicant, a prisoner, should be given leave on the basis that he had been denied legal representation and that this went against a previously decided case.[16] Moreover, at the leave stage he considered that on the information he had the need for fairness outweighed any detriment

---

[12] *R.* v. *Dairy Produce Quota Tribunal, ex p. Caswell* HL [1990] 2 WLR 1320.
[13] *R.* v. *Sec. of State for Health, ex p. Willan* CO/2040/95 (Lexis).
[14] *R.* v. *Immigration Appeal Tribunal, ex p. Hussain* [1986] Imm AR 353.
[15] *R.* v. *Board of Visitors of HM Prison Gartree, ex p. Campbell* CO/1472/83 (Lexis).
[16] *R.* v. *Sec. of State for the Home Dept, ex p. Tarrant* [1985] QB 251.

to good administration, although he pointed out that it would be open to the respondents to put forward any detriment arguments at the full hearing.

This was a recognition that the balance can change when the evidence is presented by both sides, a point confirmed by Lord Goff in the House of Lords in *ex parte Caswell*.[17] Lord Goff examined the different considerations made by the court in determining the outcome in matters of delay. He said, 'I imagine that, on an ex parte application for leave to apply before a single judge, the questions most likely to be considered by him, if there has been such delay, is whether there is good reason for extending the period under rule 4(1). Questions of . . . detriment under section 31(6) are, I imagine, unlikely to arise in an ex parte application, when the necessary material would in all probability not be available to the judge.'[18] He also thought that even on a contested application for leave, it may be better to leave questions arising under section 31(6) 'to be explored in depth in the hearing of the substantial application'.

The need for time limits and the prompt making of an application, required by the Supreme Court Act and Order 53, were designed, according to Lord Justice Simon Brown, to 'promote sound administration',[19] whereby the administrative process could continue unimpeded, thus providing the certainty necessary for public confidence in administrative decisions. The courts are reluctant to accept late applications which upset this confidence. They are particularly reluctant if the requested remedy will also have implications that extend to third parties or the wider community. This was evident in a case brought by Oxford County Council against the Secretary of State for the Environment where the local authority had made a late application for leave to quash the report in which the Secretary of State set out transitional arrangements for local tax.[20] Mr Justice Pill accepted the argument put forward on behalf of the Secretary of State that 'any order would have serious implications, not merely for the Secretary of State and not merely for tidy administration, but for other chargepayers', and he refused to grant leave. He considered that to do otherwise would be prejudicial to good administration, commenting, 'This was a case where . . . speed was essential and should have been appreciated as essential by a public authority.'

A similar ruling was made against the London Boroughs of Hammersmith and Fulham at around the same time.[21] Again the case concerned a late application which, if relief were granted, could have a considerable impact upon other boroughs as well as the Secretary of State. Mr Justice Simon Brown held that 'any such challenge needs to be made with particular promptitude, and at the very least the Secretary of State should have been on early notice of it.' Granting leave in such circumstances was therefore seen as detrimental to good administration, the

---

[17] [1990] 2 WLR 1320. [18] At 1326.

[19] *R. v. Ministry of Agriculture, Fisheries and Food, ex p. Live Sheep Traders Ltd* CO/554/93 (Lexis).

[20] *R. v. Sec. of State for the Environment, ex p. Oxford City Council* CO/893/90 (Lexis).

[21] *R. v. Sec. of State for Transport, ex p. Hammersmith and Fulham LBC* CO/2614/90 (Lexis).

implication being that it would offend against the requirements of certainty and finality. In both these cases there was the implication that the applications had been motivated by a desire to embarrass the Government by causing administrative inconvenience and that the delay in making the applications was in line with this desire. It was thus a culpable delay. The local authorities should have known better.

Similar motives were suspected for the Prison Officers' Association's delay in applying for leave to challenge the decision of the Home Secretary which concerned the transfer of duties between prisons.[22] Mr Justice Otton refused leave, stating, 'It must have been abundantly clear to the Prison Officers' Association that by delaying and making their application at the last minute that leave (if granted) would lead to disruption and uncertainty within the prison service to a quite devastating extent.' He added that where applications could offend against the interests of good administration, they needed to be made with the 'utmost promptitude', thus echoing the dicta of Mr Justice Simon Brown.

Mr Justice Otton also refused leave in *ex parte Hebron*, where a prison officer sought review of a decision which had resulted in his dismissal two years previously.[23] He commented, 'We are dealing with the administration of the prison service, a public service, and to seek now to re-open the decision and procedures which were adopted some two years ago would be wholly undesirable.' The underlying premise would seem to be that it is detrimental to good administration for there to be unpredictable and unexpected forays into the decision-making process. Public administration should, as far as possible, be unhindered by the possibility of challenges to past decisions, for such possibilities result in uncertainty and administrative expense.

The courts are particularly reluctant to re-open decisions, made a number of years previously, by domestic tribunals, such as Boards of Prison Visitors. The reasons for this reluctance were outlined in *ex parte Chesterton*, where the applicant claimed a breach of procedure in a disciplinary hearing some years earlier and sought to have the decision of the Board quashed.[24] The court considered that allowing such a challenge would be detrimental to good administration on three grounds. Firstly, because of the time lapse, it would be difficult for the individuals, alleged to have breached procedures, to have a full recollection of exactly what had happened. Secondly, if the challenge were allowed, it would increase the expectation of similar challenges in the future and, as a consequence, encourage detailed record-keeping and the over-formalization of the proceedings. Thirdly, if the application were to be accepted or relief subsequently granted, the prisoner would be subject to a re-trial on the charges, something that could not be under-

---

[22] *R. v. Sec. of State for the Home Dept, ex p. Prison Officers' Association and Goodman* CO/2946/92 (Lexis).

[23] *R. v. Sec. of State for the Home Dept, ex p. Hebron* CO/1455/90 (Lexis).

[24] *R. v. Hull Prison Board of Visitors, ex p. Chesterton* CO/324/82 (Lexis).

taken fairly because of the lapse of time. Thus the charges would have to lie on the file undetermined, an unsatisfactory position.

In *ex parte Chesterton* the interests of good administration were underpinned by concerns about efficiency and certainty. Likewise in *ex parte Fraser*, another Board of Visitors case, an application was dismissed for similar reasons.[25] A prisoner sought leave after a three year delay on the basis that he had been denied legal representation when on a disciplinary charge, and that this was unfair. The prisoner had lost nearly a year's remission. In the Divisional Court Mr Justice Mann outlined the requirements placed upon him. He said, 'I have to balance the interests of good administration and the particular interest of the applicant, especially the 330 days, practically a year's loss of liberty.' He noted that it was not until October 1978 that it was known that prisoners had a remedy against the refusal of legal representation but continued, quoting Lord Justice Donaldson, in *ex parte Herbert William Coster*,[26] 'clearly a time must come, even for a man who is arguing for the best part of a year's freedom, when the court has to say "I am sorry; this is too late".' Mr Justice Mann believed this to be the case here and that the application should therefore be dismissed. He considered that to do otherwise would be detrimental to good administration, largely, as in *Chesterton*, because the passage of time made it difficult to discern what had happened.

Mr Justice Mann approach was confirmed by the Court of Appeal which also refused to grant leave. It upheld Mr Justice Mann's reasoning, in addition expressing doubts as to whether the applicant had in fact asked to be allowed legal representation at the time. The merit or rather lack of merit of the case therefore shifted the balance away from the need for fairness and justice to the requirement for finality which had been strengthened by the length of the delay.

Delay was also the key factor in *ex parte Caswell*, although the situation was somewhat different.[27] The applicants, who were dairy farmers, challenged the decision of the Dairy Produce Quota Tribunal on the grounds that it had misinterpreted the regulations and, instead of adjusting their quota when the size of their dairy herd increased, had wrongly imposed a super levy. In the High Court Mr Justice Popplewell allowed the application. Moreover, he recognized that the wrongful imposition of a super levy had caused financial hardship to the applicants. However, because of the undue delay of two years, he used his discretion to refuse relief on the basis that the relief sought would be likely to be detrimental to good administration.

The decision was upheld by the Court of Appeal whose main concern was that if relief were granted, other applications would follow and 'the problem of re-opening those claims, going back over three years . . . [would] be very great'.[28] In addition, the Court of Appeal was concerned that if relief were granted to Caswell

[25] *R.* v. *Leicester Prison Board of Visitors, ex p. Fraser* CO/582/84 (Lexis).

[26] In *R.* v. *Board of Visitors of Hull Prison, ex p. Herbert William Coster* (1983) (unreported).

[27] *R.* v. *Dairy Produce Quota Tribunal, ex p. Caswell* [1989] 1 WLR 1089.

[28] [1989] 3 All ER 211.

but other applicants were subsequently refused because of evidential problems, 'this would be contrary to one of the basic principles of good administration that like cases should be treated alike.'[29] The detriment to good administration was therefore not seen simply in terms of hampering the administrative process. It was joined by concerns about equity.

The case went to the House of Lords where Lord Goff took the opportunity to consider the factors that should be taken into account when determining the balance between competing interests in delay cases.[30] He considered that relevant factors included 'the harm suffered by the applicant by reason of the decision which has been impugned', the rights of third parties, and the likely detriment to good administration of granting relief.[31] However, in considering detriment, Lord Goff went on to say, 'the court is at that stage looking at the interests of good administration independently of matters such as these [harm to the applicant and hardship and prejudice to the rights of third parties].'[32]

He considered that in the *Caswell* context 'the interest lies essentially in a regular flow of consistent decisions, made and published with reasonable dispatch, in citizens knowing where they stand and how they can order their affairs in the light of the relevant decision.'[33] He noted that apart from the fact that there had been a two-year delay in bringing the application, the other matters which were particularly important in the case were 'the extent of the effect of the relevant decision, and the impact which would be felt if it were to be reopened'. He found that both factors suggested that granting relief after the delay would be detrimental because the re-opening of this decision about the allocation of quotas would 'lead other applicants to re-open similar decisions which, if successful, would lead to re-opening the allocation of quotas over a number of years.' The appeal was therefore rejected and the approach of Mr Justice Popplewell approved, Lord Goff noting that he 'took into account the relevant factors, including in particular the financial hardship suffered by the appellants . . . He then balanced the various factors and . . . came down firmly against the view of the applicant.'[34]

It seems therefore that the courts determine what factors in the applicant's case are relevant and what weight should be attached to them and then balance these factors with the interests of the administrative process and others who are affected by it. This includes the public interest, not just the interests of identifiable third parties. In *Caswell* it was the public interest's requirement for certainty, predictability and finality, and the need for efficiency in decision-making that 'won' over the substantive rights of the applicant, despite the financial hardship that had been suffered.

The public interest was also seen as paramount in *ex parte Farooq Azam*, despite the likely consequence for the individual concerned.[35] The applicant was seeking an extension of time to challenge the failure of the Immigration Appeal

[29] At 213.   [30] 2 WLR [1990] 1320 at 1328.   [31] Ibid.   [32] Ibid.
[33] Ibid. at 1329.   [34] Ibid.
[35] *R. v. Immigration Appeal Tribunal, ex p. Farooq Azam* [1994] Imm AR 193.

Tribunal to take notice of a solicitor's letter asking for more time to prepare the case because of new grounds. Mr Justice Owen stated, 'It seems to me that the question I must ask is: would it be detrimental to good administration of immigration control to allow this application for leave in respect of a decision in August 1993? I am bound to say that I have come to the conclusion that it would.' He noted that the Tribunal had actually considered the new grounds and that it was still open to the applicant 'to bring his circumstances to the attention of the Home Secretary for consideration to be given to them', although he stressed that he 'did not place any more reliance upon that factor than is right'. He then continued: 'Nevertheless, it is, as I see it, of the greatest importance in immigration matters that there should be finality. That is for the benefit of the general public and also for those who are seeking leave to stay in this country. Any delay which is avoidable indicates defect in the system.'

Mr Justice Owen therefore followed Lord Goff's outline in *Caswell*. He considered the factors that were relevant to the applicant's case, namely the new grounds and the right of the applicant to refer the matter to the Home Secretary. He then considered the interests of good administration, which he perceived lay in finality, and any detriment that these interests would suffer if relief were granted. Finally he balanced the applicant's case against that of the possible detriment to good administration, coming to the conclusion that if the applicant were granted leave, when the substance of his case was so weak, the interests of good administration would be detrimentally affected. Immigration decisions would lack finality and the system of immigration control would be seen as defective. This would undermine public confidence in the system.

Caswell and *Azam* demonstrate that the courts are concerned with balancing competing interests in good administration, namely the individual interest and the public interest, which includes the interests of the administrative process. How they do this depends on the particular circumstances but also on the view individual judges take of the public policy interests in judicial review, for here too there is competition. These interests include upholding the rule of law to ensure public bodies take lawful decisions and that reliance is not placed on invalid ones; supporting the requirement for speed and certainty in administrative decision-making where the whole community, or large sections of it, will be affected by the decisions of the public law bodies; and providing the individual litigant with a remedy where he or she has a grievance.[36] Such public policy considerations are imposed upon the requirements of good administration and, although they compete, it is evident that some judges consider the interests of good administration to be served by a recognition of all three. Thus good administration requires a clear basis of legality, including rulings on the extent and exercise of administrative powers, and a balancing of the public interest in speed and certainty with the individual interest in fair procedures and processes.

[36] Law Commission (above, n. 11), ch. 2.

Efficiency

The public interest in good administration also requires that it is carried out efficiently. This is implied in the need for it to be unhampered. Efficiency, in the public service model sense of being done as well and as quickly as possible at the least possible cost, is recognized by the courts in their acceptance of policies and also in their consideration of procedural fairness. They accept that public administration needs to channel the exercise of discretion in a way that not only adheres to principles of equity and consistency but also improves effectiveness. They are also concerned that it should not be overburdened with procedural protections which are costly and time-consuming.

The interests of efficiency are also recognised in the acceptance by the courts of the need for delegation. In *London Governing Board* v. *Arlidge* Lord Haldane, the Lord Chancellor, recognized that 'to insist that he and other members of the Board should do everything personally would be to impair his efficiency'.[37] Thus delegation was acceptable, providing that the person in whom the power was invested retained an ultimate discretion. Similarly in *Carltona Ltd.* v. *Commissioner of Works* Lord Greene implicitly recognized the needs of efficiency when he said, 'The duties imposed upon ministers and the powers given to ministers are normally exercised under the authority of ministers by responsible officials of the department. Public business could not be carried on if that were not the case.'[38]

The courts are not concerned with forwarding the cause of efficiency as an end in itself. However, they consider it as a relevant factor, balancing its needs with competing requirements.[39] This suggests recognition of the fact that if judicial decisions were in constant conflict with the needs of efficiency, the credibility of these decisions would be undermined and the part played by the courts in maintaining the standards of public administration would be reduced. Decisions that do have a noticeable impact upon efficiency, particularly on resource distribution, are likely to be portrayed by administrators and politicians as judicial interference in the political process. However, resource implications may be an increasingly important consideration in the courts and, in the context of undue delay, are weighed against other factors, occasionally triumphing.

This was the position in *ex parte Bullock*, a case which concerned a challenge of an order to destroy a dog, found to be dangerous under the Dangerous Dogs Act 1991.[40] The dog had spent three years in kennels at public expense while the case was heard and appeals made. The applicant was now seeking an order from the High Court for a fresh appeal hearing. Lord Justice Simon Brown gave the judgment in which he said: 'Given that this is a discretionary jurisdiction and given that, in my view, there was here substantial delay which is plainly detrimental to

---

[37] [1915] AC 120 at 133.   [38] [1943] 2 All ER 560 at 563.
[39] P. Cane, *Introduction to Administrative Law*, 380.
[40] *R.* v. *Teeside Crown Court, ex p. Bullock* CO/739/94 (Lexis).

good administration, even were there merits in the substantive application one would pause before granting relief. However, one asks, can it be other than detrimental to good administration to allow a dog to remain in kennels at public expense for three years and then ask the court, in its discretion, to order a fresh appeal hearing?'

The ruling of Lord Justice Simon Brown was clearly grounded in considerations of cost. However, there was the implication that had the merits of the case been better, the balance might have been finer with the consideration perhaps being whether the cost was disproportionate. When cost arises as a direct result of a statutory requirement, it cannot be given the same consideration. In *Phil Shaw Ltd* the VAT Tribunal Commissioners had discretion to allow late claims but had decided to impose a closing date for such claims as a matter of good administration and the saving of public expenditure.[41] The tribunal held that the Commissioners could not refuse to deal with claims on the grounds that they were administratively inconvenient or involved them in expenditure. Such a refusal might seem to be sensible and of benefit to the public at large if it saved money but where primary legislation was concerned, its implementation needed to come via Parliament.

The primacy of legislative requirements was reinforced by Mr Justice Woolf in the *Child Poverty Action Group* case, where his ruling had considerable financial implications.[42] The case concerned uncertainty as to whether some 16,000 unemployed people had received their full entitlement to Supplementary Benefit. The Secretary of State had been requested by the applicants to carry out a search through the non-current files to determine the monies owing. He refused on the basis of substantial expense, estimated to be £4.8m, and administrative inconvenience. He also considered that the welfare of those currently affected by the supplementary benefit system, some 4.74m people, would be prejudiced by the disruption this would cause to the administration of benefits.

Mr Justice Woolf held that such considerations could not excuse a department's failure to carry out a statutory duty. However, he implied that had the duty not been a statutory requirement he might have accepted financial considerations and administrative inconvenience as a limiting factor. He said, 'On purely financial and administrative convenience grounds, a strong case can be made for saying that, if the complainants who have been deprived do not come forward, then the department should not go to the expense and considerable inconvenience of tracing the claimants when this would result in current claimants being prejudiced.'

Even when there is a statutory duty, there may still be some room for manoeuvre. The courts have ruled that the requirement to consult is not open-ended.

---

[41] *Phil Shaw Ltd* v. *The Commissioners, London VAT Tribunal* [1976] VATTR 86.

[42] *R.* v. *Sec. of State for Social Services, ex p. Child Poverty Action Group* [1984] The Times 16 Aug. The CA subsequently reversed the decision in part, holding that the Sec. of State was not in breach of his statutory duty, although he might be open to a challenge on *Wednesbury* principles ([1985] The Times 8 Aug.).

The expense entailed, together with uncertainty regarding the outcome and the need to start work, means there have to be limitations.[43] Similarly, the duty to give reasons does not require a detailed elaboration which would be costly in terms of manpower,[44] and a decision will not necessarily be quashed for failing to follow a statutory procedure, if this has not disadvantaged the applicants. In addition, statutes, which have considerable resource implications, may be interpreted as resource-rather than needs-based, thereby limiting their financial effect.[45]

Financial implications were a factor in *ex parte Seymour-Smith*.[46] The applicants sought judicial review of the Unfair Dismissal (Variation of Qualification Period) Order 1985, which increased the qualifying period for obtaining employment rights from one to two years service, on the basis that the Order was indirectly discriminatory to women and thus infringed the EU Equal Treatment Directive.[47] Although there had been a delay of several years, the court in this case had no discretion to refuse leave or a remedy on the basis of detriment. A challenge by judicial review of the Government's failure to implement an EU directive is not affected by national time limits. However, the Court of Appeal in its judgment still took account of the detriment to good administration. Lord Justice Neill held that quashing the Order would be inappropriate, not only because of the constitutional relationship between the courts and Parliament but also because if it were quashed, 'countless past transactions might have to be re-opened'. This, he considered, 'would be likely to cause financial hardship and would be detrimental to good administration'. As a consequence, the Court of Appeal confined itself to making a declaration that the Order was discriminatory and that there was no objective justification for this discrimination, its expectation being that the Government would subsequently change the law.

Seymour-Smith had financial implications because of the knock-on effect of granting a remedy. In this it was similar to *Caswell*, where there was no specific mention of cost but the failure of the Court of Appeal to grant a remedy was in part because of the possibility of a large number of claims which would, by implication, be expensive to process and difficult to manage. The reasoning in *Caswell* and *Seymour-Smith* suggests a policy decision on the part of the court on the basis of floodgates. This too would seem to have played a part in *ex parte Davis*.[48] The applicant was a prisoner serving a life sentence, who had worked in prison for nearly thirty years. During this time he had paid into a 'general purpose fund', which he thought was obligatory. Another prisoner, who was studying law, ques-

---

[43] See, e.g., *R*. v. *Sec. of State for Health, ex p. Natural Medicines Group* [1991] COD 60; *R*. v. *Thames Regional Health Authority* [1993] The Times 22 June, and see P. Craig, *Public Law and Democracy in the United Kingdom and the United States of America*.

[44] *Impey* v. *Sec. of State for Environment* [1980] 47 P & CR 157.

[45] Baldwin suggests this could be an aspect of the legislative mandate (*Rules and Government*, 46) and see HL decision in *R*. v. *Gloucester CC, ex p. Barry* [1997] *The Times*, 21 Mar.

[46] *R*. v. *Sec. of State for Employment, ex p. Seymour-Smith and Perez* [1995] IRLR 464.

[47] Directive 76/207.

[48] *R*. v. *Sec. of State for the Home Dept, ex p. Davis* CO/2612/90 (Lexis).

tioned the constitutionality of the fund in an article in The *Guardian,* following which the Home Office issued a circular abolishing the fund. The applicant wanted his payments for the last thirty years returned. They amounted to £67.

His claim for relief was dismissed, Lord Justice Watkins stating, 'To grant this kind of relief with all its ramifications would, it seems to me, be absolutely absurd. When one thinks of the many prisoners who have been in our jails during the relevant period of time, and the possibility that if the applicant here was to be successful, thousands and thousands of claims for work might be brought for very, very trifling sums.' It was not therefore the finances involved in the particular case that prevented relief being granted but the cumulative effect and particularly the cost to the administration in determining the amounts owing. The court therefore appeared to support the need for efficiency within the administrative process, or rather the inefficiency or impracticality of having to process such a large number of claims spread over such a time scale. Such support is normally of the negative kind, arising because the case has little merit. This too was a feature of *Davis* where the individual sums involved were very small. The consequence of the relief sought was thus disproportionate to the harm suffered by the individuals.

Administrative Inconvenience

A principle that the courts have adopted with regard to detriment is that administrators cannot claim that delay is detrimental to good administration if the detriment is of their own making. This has arisen in cases where public bodies have known that an application for judicial review was pending but have continued with disputed plans regardless. The attitude of the courts suggests an expectation by the courts of loss mitigation similar to that arising in private law. The position was explained by Lord Wilberforce in *Secretary of State for Education* v. *Tameside MBC* when he said, 'The LEA is not fettered but we can hardly regard it as conducive to anything but the prospect of administrative chaos to press on with substantial educational changes in the teeth of a challenge to the validity of the authority under which it is acting.'[49] *Tameside* was subsequently followed by Mr Justice McNeill in *ex parte Hardy.*[50] He cited Lord Wilberforce and commented, 'As far as good administration is concerned, the LEA has only itself to blame if it went ahead with its proposals in the teeth of an application for judicial review.'

Administrative chaos is the big brother of administrative inconvenience. Sir Stephen Sedley has suggested that section 31 of the Supreme Court Act was an intervention by Whitehall in the process of judicial review to introduce a provision 'which tended to prioritize administrative convenience over justice where the

---

[49] [1977] AC 1014 at 1047.
[50] *R.* v. *Sec. of State for Education, ex p. Hardy* CO/354/88 (Lexis).

two came into conflict'.[51] If this was so, then according to the Law Commission, it has been unsuccessful. The Commission claims that 'where there is delay the courts are, in the exercise of their discretion, attempting to weigh not administrative convenience, but the impact of further litigation on the public in general and the practicality of turning back the clock.'[52] This accords with the reasoning in *Caswell*, where justice to the individual was denied because of the uncertainty that would arise from the granting of relief and the effect of this on public confidence. Administrative inconvenience was not considered as a factor although undoubtedly a ruling in favour of the applicants would have been extremely inconvenient for the administration.

Other cases also support the Law Commission's contention that administrative inconvenience is not a factor, or at least that the courts are unlikely to consider inconvenience as detrimental to good administration. This is particularly so in cases concerning liberty or fundamental rights and was evident in *ex parte Oyeleye*.[53] This concerned a delayed application for judicial review of a deportation order. The case rested on whether the applicant had renewed her application to stay in the country in time. Previously she had done this by sending in her passport which had been accepted as an application. On this occasion it had not been accepted. Mr Justice Dyson held that the Secretary of State could not reasonably have considered the submission of the passport as anything other than an application. Moreover, he dismissed the argument that the delay in challenging the decision was detrimental to good administration, stating, 'It may well be an inconvenience . . . to have to consider the case . . . that, however, is not enough'.

The matter of administrative inconvenience was prominent in *ex parte St. Germain*.[54] A central issue was whether prisoners, subject to disciplinary proceedings before the Board of Visitors, were allowed to call witnesses. Lord Justice Lane held that the Board had a discretion whether or not to allow witnesses, but that this discretion had to be exercised reasonably, in good faith, and on proper grounds, not 'merely on the grounds that it would cause administrative inconvenience'.[55] He stated that it would be acceptable to limit the number of witnesses called if there were good reasons for believing that the prisoner was attempting to render the hearing of the charge 'virtually impracticable' or where the number of witnesses called were more than was necessary to establish the point at issue. However, he stated, that 'mere administrative difficulties, simpliciter, are not in our view enough'. The attitude to the courts was further demonstrated in *ex parte Tarrant*, which ruled similarly that legal representation could not be denied merely on the basis of inconvenience.[56]

Both these cases were concerned with the application of the rules of natural

---

[51] S. Sedley, 'Governments, constitutions and judges' in Richardson & Genn (eds.), *Administrative Law and Government Action* at 42–3.

[52] Law Commission (above, n. 11), ch. 4.3.

[53] *R. v. Sec. of State for the Home Dept, ex p. Oyeleye* CO/1899/91 (Lexis).

[54] *R. v. Hull Prison Board of Visitors, ex p. St. Germain* [1979] 3 All ER 545.

[55] Ibid. at 550.   [56] Above, n. 16.

justice in situations where, because of the substantive rights involved, a high level of fairness was required. Moreover, the cases had considerable merit. Thus, in balancing justice with the detriment to good administration, justice was likely to be the winner, regardless of whether the detriment was expressed in terms of inconvenience or in other more acceptable terms. Even more certain is the reaction of the court to a claim of administrative inconvenience for the non-fulfilment of a statutory requirement. Regardless of how well intentioned such a claim may be, it will not be accepted. Thus in a case concerning the General Medical Council Lord Atkin held that the well intentioned refusal by the Council to hold an inquiry at which fresh evidence could be presented was unlawful.[57] He commented, 'If this is inconvenient, it cannot be helped' and added, 'Convenience and justice are often not on speaking terms'. This statement does much to explain the inherent tension between those engaged in public administration and the courts.

Similarly in *Phil Shaw Ltd* claims of administrative inconvenience were not accepted for fettering a discretion to allow late claims.[58] While in the *Child Poverty Action Group* case, despite obvious sympathy, Mr Justice Woolf held that where there was a statutory duty the court had 'a primary obligation . . . to ensure that Government departments carry out their legal obligations, no matter how inconvenient it may be'.[59] Sympathy was also evident in Mr Justice Taylor's adverse judgment against an LEA.[60] The LEA's proposed education plans included closing a girls-only school whilst retaining the boys' school and were held by Mr Justice Taylor to be contrary to the Sex Discrimination Act 1975. He quashed the plans despite pleas from the LEA that this would be administratively inconvenient but noted, 'I have considerable sympathy with the Education Authority who I have no doubt pondered long and conscientiously to produce the proposals for reorganization. [However] if the court were to decline its discretion to grant relief simply on the grounds of good motives or resultant administrative inconvenience, the bite of the [Sex Discrimination] Act would be seriously impaired.'

Thus while the courts might be sympathetic with arguments of administrative inconvenience, these can never take precedence over statutory requirements. However, they might be persuasive in situations where the remedy sought is the quashing of a decision for lack of adequate reasons or procedural unfairness. Certainly in *ex parte Natural Medicines Group* Mr Justice Pill indicated that he would 'give some weight' to the administrative inconvenience and financial embarrassment caused by quashing regulations.[61]

---

[57] *General Medical Council* v. *Spackman* [1943] 2 All ER 337 at 341.
[58] [1976] VATTR 86. [59] [1984] The Times 16 Aug.
[60] *R.* v. *Sec. of State for Education and Science, ex p. Keeting* [1985] The Times 3 Dec.
[61] *R.* v. *Sec. of State for Health, ex p. Natural Medicines Group* [1991] COD 60.

The Requirement of Leave: the Order 53 Procedure

Recognition and protection of the public interest is not confined to delay situations. It is fundamental to the requirement that leave must be obtained. The need for leave reflects the fact that public bodies exist to perform functions for the benefit of the public at large. It follows from this that the public interest should be taken into account when applications for leave are considered, the interest being that the administrative process should, as far as possible, continue unhampered. This relates again to the need for certainty so that decisions can be given effect as quickly as possible without fear of a subsequent challenge and its effect.

The need for 'speedy certainty' was the base line of Lord Diplock's development of the exclusivity principle in *O'Reilly* v. *Mackman*.[62] He considered that the interests of good administration were served by ensuring that all applicants making a claim which related essentially to a public law matter should proceed by way of Order 53. It was not acceptable in such instances for declarations or injunctions to be obtained in ordinary civil proceedings, for this bypassed the procedural protections afforded public bodies in Order 53 and could result in delay and uncertainty. Lord Diplock stated, 'The public interest in good administration requires that public authorities and third parties should not be kept in suspense as to the legal validity of a decision the authority has reached in purported exercise of decision-making powers for any longer period than is absolutely necessary in fairness to the person affected by the decision.'[63]

The need for fairness to the individual therefore still qualifies the public interest. However, it is the public interest that is the prime consideration. Lord Diplock's exclusivity rule was criticized for disadvantaging the individual in situations where both public and private law rights were involved and there has been a move by subsequent courts away from the exclusivity of the Order 53 procedure which suggests a realignment towards the interests of the individual.[64] However, in *Mercury Communications Ltd.* v. *Director-General of Telecommunications* the House of Lords, while continuing the trend towards the use of ordinary civil proceedings in certain instances alongside Order 53, stated that the protections afforded by Order 53 should still be applied.[65] Thus the courts are still concerned with balancing the individual interest with the public interest.

The rules concerned with delay, which allow the court to exercise its discretion if it considers that the granting of leave or the giving of relief would be detrimental to good administration, provide protection for public bodies and the administrative process. Administrators need to know that they are safe from challenge, unless an exceptional circumstance arises, and can therefore proceed to give effect to decisions. If this were not the case, officials would spend more time looking

---

[62] 3 All ER 1124.   [63] Ibid. at 1144.
[64] *Roy* v. *Kensington and Chelsea and Westminster Family Practitioner Cttee* [1992] 1 AC 624.
[65] [1996] 1 WLR 48.

over their shoulder than proceeding with the work in hand. It is also not in the interests of good administration if cases brought by 'busybodies, cranks, [or] mischief-makers'[66] are allowed to proceed. Hence the protection afforded against such cases by the need to seek leave which also protects against unmeritorious and groundless cases. Thus, 'in the interests of good administration, cases cannot be brought and fought so as to frustrate administrative action in hopeless cases.'[67]

As a further means of preventing the frustration of administrative action by 'hopeless cases', the courts will consider, amongst other things, whether, even if the applicant is successful, his or her position will be changed by the outcome. This is relevant when a decision is being challenged on grounds of procedural unfairness or for failure to take account of relevant considerations. In *Sutton LBC v. Secretary of State for the Environment* Mr Justice Schiemann refused an application from a planning authority against the Secretary of State's decision to allow an appeal against the authority's refusal to grant planning permission.[68] The authority claimed procedural unfairness because the Inspector had refused to reopen the enquiry to allow them to include further evidence. Mr Justice Schiemann considered whether there was 'a perceptible chance' that the Inspector would, in the light of the new evidence, come to a different conclusion and believed that he would not. He therefore concluded that it 'would not be conducive to good administration to re-open the enquiry' — in effect seeing the application as unmeritorious.

In *ex parte Hussain* Mr Justice McCullough similarly found a delayed case to have no merit, stating, 'In my judgment it is not in the interests of good administration that leave should be given. Were it granted, it would mean that a grossly delayed application had been allowed in on the back of . . . a hopeless challenge.'[69] He was clearly concerned to prevent judicial review being used as a mechanism for delaying deportation by challenging a decision which, he considered, to be 'unassailable'.

The interests of good administration are therefore used to restrict challenges and to require that challenges as a general rule proceed by way of an application for judicial review under Order 53. This enables the courts to act as the 'door-man',[70] protecting the administrative process from harassment and late challenges.

Conclusion

The role of the courts in relation to the principles of good administration is limited by the fact that there is no code of good administrative practice. Whilst it may

---

[66] Lord Scarman, *R. v. IRC, ex p. National Federation of Self-Employed and Small Businesses* [1982] AC 617 at 653.
[67] Taylor LJ, *R. v. Sec. of State for the Home Dept, ex p. Muboyayi* CA [1991] All ER 72 at 90.
[68] CO/86/85 (Lexis).   [69] CO/1353/86 (Lexis).   [70] Cane (above, n. 39).

be accepted that the substantive rules which govern the review of administrative decisions support, even provide, principles of good administration, they are too broadly formulated to make an obvious contribution. This situation contrasts with that in Australia where the grounds for review are detailed in authorising legislation.[71] It is because of the lack of a positive framework in the United Kingdom that much of the detailed discussion of what constitutes good administration takes place in the negative framework of Order 53 and the Rules of the Supreme Court and is addressed in terms of detriment.

Nevertheless it is apparent that good administration is frequently seen as being at the luxury end of the spectrum. As such it may require more than is required by law. Moreover, in some respects good administration seems to have a role not dissimilar to that of conventions in that it is seen as filling gaps, where legal requirements are absent, adding flesh to the bones of statutory provisions, and making sure that those provisions are operable and that their purpose is fulfilled.

The courts attribute different values to good administration depending on the circumstances before them and which interest, public or individual, they judge to be paramount. Indeed, as Galligan argues, as part of 'the political and social composition of society . . . [the courts] can be made instrumental in upholding values several and diverse'.[72] In a modern, liberal democracy such values centre upon stability in legal relations, rationality in decision-making, fair procedures and 'a rather loose residual category of moral and political principles'.[73] These translate into the requirement for legal certainty, consistency, reasoned decision-making, equity, fairness, honesty and integrity and are evident in the judicial acceptance of administrative policies, the application of the duty to act fairly, and the development of legitimate expectations.[74] They are also apparent in the support given by judges to openness and the giving of reasons.

Many of the values upheld by the courts are evident in the public service model of good administration, hardly surprising as this model is itself a reflection of the concerns of a liberal democracy. However, judges bring other values to the administrative process and have their own goals, 'which include upholding metaprinciples, such as the Rule of Law, and providing remedies for those who are aggrieved by an excess of power.'[75] These may take precedence over those values shared with the administration and may clash with the goals and particular values of administrators which are more concerned with wider aspects of efficiency and the public interest. Moreover, critics argue that judicial deference to the specialist skills of the administrator is rare.[76] Indeed, Cranston suggests that the courts 'in

---

[71] See ch. 9.   [72] D. Galligan, *Discretionary Powers*, 89–90.   [73] Ibid., 90.

[74] They have much in common with Davis' justice model, which emphasises individual rather than collective rights and the public interest, and which centres on the legal values of fairness, openness, predictability and rationality at the expense of efficiency and adaptability (see K. C. Davis, *Discretionary Justice*).

[75] D. Feldman, 'Judicial review: a way of controlling government?' (1988) 66 *Pub. Admin.* 3 at 32. This suggests support for Mashew's model of bureaucratic rationality and moral judgement (see J. Mashew, *Bureaucratic Justice*).

[76] Suggesting little judicial support for Mashew's professional model (see *Bureaucratic Justice*).

their concern to protect individuals rarely defer to administrative expertise' or 'acknowledge the sometimes delicate balance between the needs to protect individual interests on the one hand and the need for effective administration on the other.'[77] Rather their preoccupation with the individual is at the expense of the public interest, a concept they do not understand. As a result, they do not appreciate that the judicial requirement that a case be re-heard in the interests of fairness 'may be at the expense of the services which could be provided to others'.[78] It may also be at the expense of efficiency, in that it is costly in time, effort and resources and may undermine value-for-money strategies.

Such criticisms of the preoccupation of the court with the rights of individuals, regardless of the effect on the administrative process and the public interest, are supported to varying degrees by case law. However, there are clear indications that in the context of good administration judges do balance the interests involved. They are particularly concerned to promote confidence in the administrative system and uphold the principles of certainty and speedy finality in the public interest. There is also evidence to suggest that they do recognize some of the problems of administration and that there is a 'substantive judicial impression'[79] that judicial review can increase these problems.[80] The problem is that the lack of empirical evidence, regarding the impact of judicial review, makes it difficult for the court to determine how the individual interest and the interest of public administrators should be balanced. It has 'to rely on its own intuition, supplemented in many cases by the fears expressed by respondents'[81] rather than on actual data on administrative reactions. Thus, 'the interests of good administration' becomes an all-embracing term which has different applications depending not only on the circumstances before the court but also on the individual judge. Sometimes judicial reasoning suggests that the interests of the individual compete with those of good administration and at other times it suggests that the interests of the individual are served by it.

The courts are also concerned to legitimize their decisions with reference to public administration. How they do this also gives rise to differences in the application of 'the interests of good administration'. Baldwin identifies five different claims.[82] The first is the legislative mandate claim. This shares some features with Mashew's bureaucratic rationality in that it is concerned with giving effect to the legislative will. Its basis for legitimacy is the democratic authority implicit within the objectives set by Parliament. Judicial use of this claim is widespread, and is notably apparent in judicial pronouncements concerning the legislative purpose or objective. The second claim is the accountability or control claim, which is similarly based on democratic authority. However, rather than the authority flowing through Parliament, it flows through interest groups or representative bodies and

[77] R. Cranston (above, n. 7) at 63.   [78] Ibid., at 54.
[79] Lord Bridge in *Leech* v. *Governor of Parkhurst* [1988] 1 AC 533 at 568.
[80] See G. Richardson & M. Sunkin, 'Judicial review' (1996) *PL* 79 at 83.
[81] Ibid. at 84.   [82] Baldwin (above, n. 45), 43–6.

the claim manifests itself in support for consultation and openness in decision-making. It may also be indicated by the acceptance of public-interest applications for judicial review such as that brought by Greenpeace when it challenged the decision of British Nuclear Fuel to test its new reprocessing plant at Sellafield.[83]

Third is the due process claim, central to which is respect for individuals and fairness. This claim may combine with the legislative-mandate claim such that judges may impose a duty to act fairly on the basis that Parliament must have intended power to be exercised in such a way. Fairness thus becomes an implied statutory requirement. However, fairness as a requirement of the administrative process, fostered by the courts, is frequently proclaimed alone. Fourth is the expertise claim, in which the expert nature of decisions are stressed, as is the trust that should be placed in them. Such a claim is largely absent as a judicial justification in relation to public administration, where administrators are not classed as 'specialists' or 'experts' as they might be in other situations.[84] Finally, there is the efficiency claim, which is concerned with achieving stated objectives effectively and making good use of public money. Like the due-process claim, this is frequently related to the legislative mandate.

The concern of the courts that their rulings are seen as legitimate or justifiable in the context of public administration suggests a recognition that if they are to play a constructive and open part in upholding good administration, they need to be accepted by the public and by the administration. Judicial success in this area depends considerably on the receptiveness of Government to judicial review. In *ex parte Huddleston* Sir John Donaldson suggested that the post-war development of an administrative law court had 'created a new relationship between the courts and those who derive their authority from the public law, one of partnership based on a common aim, namely the maintenance of the highest standards of public administration.'[85]

Such a partnership has not been apparent, despite the fact that the public service model and the judicial perspective on good administration have much in common and share the same underlying values. There are inevitable differences in the weight attached to competing principles and in the balance accorded the individual and the public interest which produce tension between the courts and the administrators. This is perpetuated by the remedy-based and retrospective nature of judicial review. Moreover, tension seems likely to be increasing with the move towards a new public management model which distrusts the soft, unquantifiable principles applied by the court and focuses on the customer rights of the individual rather than process rights, and fairness and equity. Good administration in this model is therefore seen as benefiting customer relations, efficiency, and cost-

---

[83] *R.* v. *Inspectorate of Pollution, ex p. Greenpeace Ltd* (No 2) [1994] 4 All ER 328. On public interest cases see JUSTICE and Public Law Project, *A Matter of Public Interest*.

[84] Although it is possible to see the non-interventionist approach prior to the 1980s as a manifestation of the expert claim.

[85] *R.* v. *Lancashire County Council, ex p. Huddleston* CA [1986] 2 All ER 941 at 945 and implied in *ex p. Argyll Group plc* (above, n. 5).

effectiveness. This suggests that any idea of partnership is unsustainable, for whilst the courts are concerned to balance the individual interest with the needs of efficiency, there is no evidence to suggest that they recognize cost-efficiency or value for money as part of the equation. Moreover, whilst they may take account of the expenditure involved, considering excessive expenditure to be contrary to the public interest,they are unlikely to see value for money as a concern of judicial review. Such a consideration is more easily associated with private law than with public law and it is perhaps ironic that at a time when those engaged in the reform of public administration are emphasizing private law rights, the courts are becoming more comfortable with public law rights.

Part III

COMPARISONS AND CONCLUSIONS

Parts I and II of this book have been concerned with an examination of perspectives of good administration in the British context. However, the traditions and developments that provide this context are not unique to Britain. The move to a market economy, together with a fundamental review of the role of the state and the operation of the Civil, or in some countries Public, Service, has been a feature of many western democracies. Comparisons in relation to the concept of good administration can therefore be made and are particularly useful when the constitutional framework in which the government operates is similar to that in Britain.

The following chapter is therefore concerned with an examination of the Australian position, for whilst Australia has a federal rather than a unitary structure, in many respects its system of government corresponds to that in Britain. Like its British counterpart, Australian public administration operates through departments staffed by impartial and permanent officials, who are accountable through the minister to Parliament. Also in line with Britain, and important for comparative purposes, Australia operates under the common law and broadly speaking under the doctrine of Parliamentary sovereignty. The chapter centres on judicial perspectives on good administration and the tension between the reform of administrative law, undertaken in the 1970s, and the more recent reform of the Public Service.

The final chapter, Chapter 10, includes a consideration of judicial developments in relation to good administration both in Britain and Australia. It also examines the code of good administrative practice under which local government operates and considers the case for a code of good administration which applies in the context of central government.

9

AUSTRALIAN COMPARISONS

Public Sector and Administrative Law Reforms

Australia, like Britain, has also been engaged in the reform of the Public Service. However, the first phase of reform in the early 1980s was concerned with the improvement of public administration rather than with a reassessment of its role or with rolling back the frontiers of the State. The impetus for reform came from public and political dissatisfaction with the way in which the Public Service (the Australian equivalent of the Civil Service) was operating. There was concern about the efficiency and effectiveness of service delivery and, in this respect, the motivation for reform had a similar basis to that in Britain and elsewhere. Moreover, it resulted in similar changes within public administration, such that managerial responsibilities have been increasingly devolved, the central personnel functions abolished, procedures to measure performance and review programmes introduced, and top public service positions have become subject to open competition.

However, there was an additional, in many respects more important, concern which in some ways conflicted with the needs of efficiency and which had a fundamental effect on the emphasis of the reforms undertaken. It centred on the extent and nature of bureaucratic power and increasing public disquiet that the Public Service was beyond the control of ministers and was publicly unaccountable. As a result, the emphasis of the reforms, at least initially, was on an overall improvement in accountability. To this effect the role of Parliament as scrutineer was improved and the Public Service was brought under closer ministerial control. Departments are now required to provide Parliament with 'explanatory notes' which contain the information necessary to enable its members to make informed judgements. These notes are presented for each programme along with the annual budget and provide details of the specific objectives of each programme together with financial information and, wherever possible, quantitative information concerning performance. In programmes concerning policy advice, which do not lend themselves to quantification, a qualitative assessment is included instead. Departments have also been restructured into super-departments, a two-tier system of ministerial positions has been introduced, the procedures for appointing departmental heads has been changed to provide the government of the day with greater flexibility in appointment and deployment, and the appointment by ministers of non-Public Service advisers has become acceptable.

The first phase of Public Service reform took place within the context of extensive constitutional reform which involved public debate and participation, and, partly because of this, there was a degree of tension in the reforms—efficiency, democratic accountability, and equity not always being comfortable bedfellows. In particular, some saw an inherent conflict between 'the aim of inducing stronger compliance with ministerial direction, on the one hand, and, on the other, the intention to promote a more managerially-orientated public service.'[1] However, constitutionally important was the fact that the objectives of the administrative reforms were largely 'congruent'[2] with the restructuring and reform of administrative law which had already been undertaken. This also arose out of the constitutional debate and, like the political and administrative reforms, represented 'a political desire to make public officials accountable for their actions'.[3] This was coupled with a related desire 'to remove unnecessary secrecy in government, and to provide individuals with effective and accessible remedies for correcting defective public administration'.[4] There was also the belief that administrative law should play its part in making public administration more efficient and move to 'redress the balance of bureaucratic power' by bringing 'judicial power into administration'.[5]

Thus the 'new administrative law', as it has often been called, was seen as being 'geared to promoting good and efficient decision-making in government, and to meeting the interests of citizens in our ever more complicated society.'[6] Indeed, according to the Attorney-General of Victoria, 'It sets a framework for interaction between government and the citizen. It supplements the accountability of the administration to government and to the Parliament. It throws into relief the interaction between the Executive and the courts. In all this it makes a major contribution to the control of government.'[7] This suggests that administrative law has become an integral part of the State apparatus instead of an adjunct to it and as such should have a fundamental bearing on the principles of good administration.

The reforms necessary to provide administrative law with such a central position involved the setting up of an Administrative Review Council, the establishment of new institutions to increase the accountability of public officials and to provide the individual with additional mechanisms through which remedies could be sought, the passing of a Freedom of Information Act, and the reform of judicial review.

The Administrative Review Council was established under the Administrative Appeal Tribunal Act 1975. Its function is to monitor matters relating to the review of administrative decisions and to advise the Government. In its first Annual Report to the Commonwealth Parliament it set out a comprehensive scheme of administrative review which it saw as not just being concerned with correcting errors but also with the promotion of efficiency, justice, and correct decision-

---

[1] J. Boston, 'The Problems of Policy Co-ordination' (1992) 5 *Governance* 1 at 298.

[2] P. Bayne, 'Administrative law'(1988) 62 *Aust. Law Journal* 1043.

[3] J. Griffiths, 'Australian Administrative Law' (1985) 63 *Pub. Admin.* 4.

[4] Ibid.

[5] P. Wilenski, 'Administrative reforms—general principles and the Australian experience' (1986) 64 *Pub. Admin.* 4 at 268.

[6] G. D. S. Taylor, 'The new administrative law' (1977) 51 *Aust. Law Journal* at 811.

[7] J. Kennan MLC, 'The control of Government' (1987) 61 *Aust. Law Journal* at 523.

making. Such a scheme was therefore seen as improving the administrative process and, through 'the articulation it gives to administrative principle and justice', fostering principles of good administration.[8]

Nowhere is this articulation more apparent than in the decisions of the Administrative Appeals Tribunal (AAT). The AAT, like the Council, was established under the Administrative Appeals Tribunal Act 1975. The AAT can substitute its opinion for that of the administrator, and has 'a peculiar responsibility in the development of good administration'.[9] It is concerned with the review of administrative decisions on their merits and through this review with providing 'a model of decision-making and principles on which administrative decisions can be grounded'.[10] Not all decisions are subject to administrative review. A provision has to be included in the relevant legislation. However, the constitutional importance accorded administrative review is demonstrated by the fact that the Government is required by Parliament to justify why a statute omits review by the AAT.

The AAT has the power to determine the correct or preferred decision, regardless of whether or not this accords with departmental or ministerial policy. However, if it is to avoid the criticism that administrative review is detrimental rather than beneficial to the administrative process, the AAT has to be careful in the exercise of this power. Any determination which is contrary to departmental policy may justifiably be criticized on the basis that it was made in isolation, without regard to the overall impact on good administration. In an attempt to minimize this concern, the AAT has developed the practice of seeking guidance on issues of policy from departmental representatives.[11]

It has also sought to minimize concern about the political controversy that could arise should its preferred decision be contrary to a policy operated by a minister. In general the AAT has adopted the practice recommended by Mr Justice Brennan in *Drake* (No. 2).[12] Mr Justice Brennan considered, 'When the Tribunal is reviewing the exercise of a discretionary power reposed in a Minister, and the Minister has adopted a general policy to guide him in the exercise of the power, the Tribunal will ordinarily apply that policy in reviewing the decision, unless the policy is unlawful or its application tends to produce an unjust decision in the circumstances of the particular case.'[13] He continued, 'Where the policy would ordinarily be applied . . . cogent reasons will have to be shown against its application, especially if the policy is shown to have been exposed to parliamentary scrutiny.' Conflict is therefore generally avoided.[14]

The keynote of the AAT is flexibility. It is required to proceed with 'as little formality and technicality, and with as much expedition', as possible.[15] It is not

---

[8] Taylor (above, n. 6) at 805.   [9] Ibid. at 806.
[10] Kennan (above, n. 7) at 525.
[11] L. J. Curtis, 'Judicial review of administrative acts' (1979) 53 *Aust. Law Journal* 530 at 543.
[12] *Re Drake and Minister for Immigration and Ethnic Affairs* (No. 2) [1979] 2 ALD 634.
[13] Ibid. at 645.
[14] But see, e.g., *Re Becker and the Minister for Immigration and Ethnic Affairs* [1977] 15 ALR 696.
[15] S. 33(1)(b).

bound by rules of evidence but has the power to order the attendance of witnesses and the production of documents and, if an applicant is unrepresented, can adopt an inquisitorial role. In effect 'the tribunal steps into the shoes of the primary decision-maker to determine what is the correct or preferable decision'.[16] It is therefore in an ideal position to develop principles of good administration. However, 'decisions of the AAT are taken on the basis of the material before the tribunal which might be quite different to that which was available to the primary decision maker'.[17] This inevitably opens the way for accusations that the AAT has the advantage of hindsight when making its decisions and that this is unfair on the original decision-maker.

The AAT and the Administrative Review Council were not the only new institutions to be established under the administrative law reforms. In 1976 the office of the Commonwealth Ombudsman was set up by the Ombudsman Act. The Ombudsman has the power to investigate complaints regarding defective administration. However, in contrast to the position in Britain, he or she is not inhibited by an MP filter and, in addition, can undertake investigations on their own initiative. The Freedom of Information Act 1982 also presents differences from the British equivalent, the most significant being that it has the status of law rather than of a code. It was enacted in the belief that 'people and Parliament must have the knowledge required to pass judgement on the government'.[18] Like all such legislation, it contains exemptions to disclosure. These can be reviewed by the AAT.

In 1977 the Administrative Decisions (Judicial Review) Act ('the Judicial Review Act') was enacted.[19] This Act 'goes further than any other attempt to reform judicial review of administrative action in the common law world'.[20] Its objective is 'to ensure that decisions of public servants and others which affect the rights, prospects and property of citizens, are made after giving careful consideration to the questions involved in the particular case, so that it is more likely that the decision will be right and justice done to the persons affected by it.'[21]

It creates a single form of relief by way of an application for an order of review for which leave is not required. The court has the discretion to 'grant the application either unconditionally or subject to such conditions as it thinks fit; or refuse the application'.[22] The Act also provides a list of the grounds on which judicial review can be sought. These move away from the need for categorization on the basis of illegality, procedural impropriety, and irrationality or unreasonableness. Thus applications can be made for a breach of natural justice or mandatory procedural requirements, a lack of jurisdiction, the absence of statutory authority or

---

[16] Griffiths (above, n. 3) at 454.   [17] Ibid.
[18] PM Fraser (1978) quoted in P. Bayne, 'Freedom of Information' (1988) 62 *Aust. Law Journal* 538.
[19] Subsequently amended in 1978 and again in 1980, when it came into operation.
[20] Griffiths (above, n. 3) at 454.
[21] Lockhart J., *Toy Centre Agencies Pty Ltd* v. *Spenser and ors* [1983] 5 ALD 121 at 128.
[22] S. 12.

the improper exercise of statutory power, an error of law, a decision induced by fraud, the absence of evidence, or a decision otherwise contrary to the law.[23]

The Act goes on to provide guidance as to what constitutes 'the improper exercise of statutory power', a ground which is less specific than the others. It states that it 'shall be construed as including a reference to' taking an irrelevant consideration into account or failing to take account of a relevant consideration, exercising a power for a purpose other than the purpose for which the power is conferred or in bad faith, acting at the direction of another person, applying a rule or policy without regard to the merits of a particular case, exercising a power unreasonably, producing an uncertain result, or any other exercise of a power in a way that constitutes abuse of the power.[24]

The Act also provides a further ground—unreasonable delay—which applies where there is a duty to make a decision, and covers both situations where there is no stipulated time-limit[25] and where a prescribed time-limit has expired.[26] In addition, the Act provides that anyone entitled to apply for review of a decision may obtain a statement of reasons for the decision. This consists of 'a statement in writing setting out the findings on material questions of fact, referring to the evidence or other material on which those findings were based and giving the reasons for the decision.'[27] This right to reasons, which is also provided in the AAT Act, has been described as the lowering of 'a narrow bridge over the moat of executive silence'[28] and has been applauded by judges and legal commentators in the UK.

The codification of the grounds of review, as summarized above, has been portrayed as having an advantage not only for those wishing to make applications for judicial review but also for those engaged in public administration. It provides a much clearer indication than previously of the challenges that can be made to administrative decisions and thus some guidance as to the principles administrators should follow. The requirement that reasons should be given can also be seen as aiding the administrative process, according with the requirement of good administration that decision making should be reasoned and all decisions justifiable. There is some evidence to suggest that '[t]he requirement to give reasons has encouraged a more thoughtful and thorough approach to decision-making which is the subject of review.'[29] This approach is accompanied by a general presumption on the part of administrators 'that what they write may be reviewed or exposed to the light of day'. This inevitably affects the way they operate. It 'may . . . [cause] some to be more circumspect'.[30] However, there is support for the view that 'the effect generally has been to improve the quality of decision-making'.[31] Indeed, 'in certain cases, [departments] . . . have changed

---

[23] S. 5(1); abbreviated list taken from JUSTICE–All Souls, *Review of Administrative Law*, 18–19.
[24] S. 5(2) and see JUSTICE–All Souls (above, n. 23), 19.   [25] S. 7(1).
[26] S. 7(2).   [27] S. 13(1).
[28] Deane J., *Minister for Immigration and Ethnic Affairs* v. *Pochi* [1980] 44 FLR 41 at 63.
[29] Kennan (above, n. 7), at 525.   [30] Ibid.
[31] Ibid. and see, e.g., P. Wilenski, 'Administrative law and the public service' (1985) *Rupert Public Interest Journal*.

their procedures to accord with the purpose and spirit of the Judicial Review Act itself.'[32]

These observations suggest that the Act has an educative effect with public administrators developing a greater awareness of the legal requirements and of judicial expectations. Conversely, '[h]earing applications under the . . . Act brings the courts into touch, through the evidence, with the administrative practices of many government departments', resulting in judges being more sympathetic to the problems of administrators, and adopting an approach to review which is 'fair, practical and of common sense'.[33] Judicial familiarization with the principles and practice of public administration may therefore avoid the courts requiring perfection from decision-makers or imposing 'such onerous duties upon them as to cause them to be afraid to make decisions, lest they be challenged on trivial grounds, or to preoccupy them with minutiae.'[34]

However, despite greater judicial exposure to the administrative process and its problems, 'it has been a source of frustration to administrators that in focusing so heavily on the resolution of individual disputes, courts and tribunals have not taken the administrative consequences of their decisions fully into account.'[35] A decision may have 'enormous financial implications' or 'may undermine considerations of administrative precedent and broader public interest'.[36] If this is the case, then review which is intended to improve the administrative process may actually undermine it and be detrimental to good administration.

The new administrative law in Australia, like administrative law in Britain, centres upon the individual. With the exception of the Commonwealth Ombudsman, it is always the individual grievance that initiates judicial or administrative review or investigation. It is therefore perhaps inevitable that the focus is on resolving the individual dispute. However, the courts need to see this resolution in the wider context and consider its impact on public administration in general. Despite the criticisms this may be easier in Australia, where the Judicial Review Act and the Administrative Appeals Tribunal Act bring the courts more directly into the administrative process. The legislation has certainly enabled them to adopt a more proactive role than their English counterparts. This was evident in *Toy Centre Agencies* where Mr Justice Lockhart was critical of the procedures used by Customs and Excise and of the department's initial failure to identify the real decision-maker.[37] He noted that as yet 'the message ha[d] not got through' to the department that administrative procedures needed to be re-fashioned 'so as to recognize the role played by the Judicial Review Act (also the Administrative Appeals Tribunal Act 1975) in the area of administrative decision-making'.[38] He continued, 'It is time it did. I make this comment solely for the constructive purpose of ensuring that, in the future, administrative decisions will be taken by the Customs with due regard to the requirements of administrative legislation.'[39]

---

[32] Lockhart J., *Toy Centre Agencies* (above, n. 21) at 128.   [33] Ibid.   [34] Ibid.
[35] Kennan (above, n. 7) at 526.   [36] Ibid.   [37] Above, n. 21.
[38] Ibid. at 130.   [39] Ibid.

The assumed development of greater understanding between public administration and the courts presents the possibility of a cross-fertilization of the standards and values which inform good administration and, in the view of Mr Justice
Lockhart, a mutual recognition that '[t]here is no essential inconsistency between
the duty of decision makers to be fair to those who may be affected by their decisions and the advancement and efficiency of the Public Service.'[40] Much, of
course, depends on the extent and nature of any efficiency measures that are
implemented or, indeed, on the procedural requirements imposed by the courts in
the interests of fairness. As Mr Justice Lockhart suggested, '[e]xtremes of view
favouring one side or the other will not promote the plain objectives of administrative legislation'.[41] Thus while there may be no 'essential inconsistency', the
needs of fairness may limit efficiency as an end in itself and, conversely, efficiency
requirements may be detrimental to fairness. As ever, it is a question of balance.

Even as the new administrative law was being established, concern was
expressed that the balance was wrong and that the administrative legislation itself
tipped the balance between individual justice and efficiency too far in favour of
the individual. As a consequence, critics argued, it was 'unlikely that effective,
economical and expeditious public administration can be achieved and maintained
in the face of a continuing and disproportionate high number of reviews, particularly those that are especially demanding on an agency's resources.'[42] The need
to cater for review and the Freedom of Information Act was already being seen as
too costly by the mid 1980s and, despite attempts by departments to reduce the
need for external review by improved decision-making and internal procedures,[43]
the administrative law reforms have been subject to increasing criticism since the
second half of the 1980s.

This criticism has been from both a constitutional and administrative stand-
point. Firstly, there has been concern that judges on occasions have undermined
the intention of Parliament and taken over the decision-making responsibilities of
ministers.[44] Secondly, the financial implications of adverse review decisions, particularly in the area of social welfare, have become apparent, and there has been
Government concern at the potential effect upon public spending. Indeed, the
Minister for Finance went as far as to suggest that 'the legal system had taken de
facto control over spending a great deal of public money'.[45] Such spending is, of
course, the preserve of elected representatives.

Thirdly, extensive external review by courts and tribunals no longer accords
with political thinking on the role and management of the Public Service and with

---

[40] Ibid. at 128–9. [41] At 129. [42] Griffiths (above, n. 3) at 462.

[43] Griffiths indicated there was evidence of this happening (ibid.), while Kennan stated that in the
State of Victoria the Govt. had placed 'heavy emphasis on the achievement of fair
administration'(above, n. 7) at 528.

[44] See, e.g., the criticism surrounding *Conyngham* v. *Minister for Immigration and Ethnic Affairs*
[1986] 68 ALR 423.

[45] 'Administrative law: retrospect and prospect', (address to seminar) held at Faculty of Law,
National Univ. of Australia (1987)), cited in Bayne (above, n. 2).

the increasing requirement for efficiency, responsiveness, and cost-effectiveness. As in Britain and elsewhere, there has been a reassessment of the role of government and a new public management model of administration is in the ascendancy. This model centres upon cost-efficiency, economy and value for money, the management methods of the private sector, and performance targets. Like the British model it places 'less of a premium on the traditional concepts of equity, fairness, justice and consistency'.[46] As a consequence, 'the very notion that law should govern public administration is in question. It does not sit very easily with a goals-oriented administration.'[47] Nor does control by external review accord with a culture of innovation, for it encourages a cautious Public Service, whose main concern is to avoid review by not making mistakes, rather than an innovative one in which 'performance management assumes a relatively high degree of failure . . . [while seeking] to ensure that critical targets are met.'[48]

However, an even greater concern is that judicial and administrative review inhibit, even prevent, the achievement of policy targets and goals. If the goal is a reduction of cost, its achievement may be impeded by the need to account to a court or tribunal, for such accountability devices 'ensure that efficiency cannot be taken as an end in itself but has to be subordinated to other ends'.[49] This distrust of the courts and of the law with its soft unmeasurable concepts, such as reasonableness and justice, is a feature of the new public management model and is evidence of the influence of rational-choice thinking. However, its emergence in Australia sits particularly uncomfortably with the administrative law reforms which have given lawyers and the law a far more prominent place in public administration than previously was the case or is the case today in Britain. As Bayne suggests, 'the ideas that make up the new managerialism present those who promote and practise administrative law with a very different set of challenges to those of a decade ago.'[50]

One of those challenges arises from the cost-cutting exercises that have been undertaken both in relation to legal services and the running of public administration. As a result of the Freedom of Information charging regime, introduced in 1986, requests for documents, other than those relating to personal matters, are beyond the reach of ordinary citizens. Similarly, the introduction of a charge, except for the very poor, for review by the AAT has limited review. More generally the administrative law reforms have been affected by the cuts in public administration staff, such that the administration of the Freedom of Information Act is affected, as is the production of 'reasons statements'. These cuts have also affected the standard of compliance with the law whilst the Office of the Ombudsman also felt the squeeze in the late 1980s leading to complaints from Ombudsman Pearce of under-resourcing.[51]

[46] R. C. Mascarenhas, 'Reform of the Public Service in Australia and New Zealand' (1990) 3 *Governance* 1 at 76.
[47] Bayne (above, n. 2) at 1045.
[48] R. B. Cullen, 'Business, Government and Change' (1987) 46 *Aust. Journal of Pub. Admin.* 10 at 16.
[49] Sir William Cole, quoted in Bayne (above, n. 2) at 1043.
[50] Ibid., at 1045.   [51] *Canberra Times*, 31 Mar. 1989.

Thus the administrative law reforms, initially seen as an integral part of the reform of public administration and in accord with the desire in the 1970s and early 1980s for accountability and individual justice, are now a source of tension between the courts and the new model of public administration. It is against that background that the review cases featured below needs to be considered.

The Australian Courts and the Interests of Good Administration

An examination of Australian cases where reference is made to good administration, reveals, not surprisingly, the adoption of precedents from the English courts, particularly in relation to fairness and legitimate expectations where citations from *Re HK*, the *Hong Kong* case and *CCSU* are much in evidence,[52] as well as references to Lord Denning's judgments in *Breen* v. *Amalgamated Engineering*,[53] *Schmidt* v. *Secretary of State for Home Affairs*,[54] and *Nowest Holst Ltd* v. *Secretary of State for Trade*.[55]

As a result, also not surprisingly, many of the principles of good administration which the courts uphold, either explicitly or implicitly, accord with those recognized by the English judiciary. They also show the same balancing of good administration as a benefit to the individual and good administration as in the public interest and the interest of the administrators themselves. There are, however, interesting differences which arise largely from the reform of administrative law in Australia. Firstly, the enactment of the Administrative Decisions (Judicial Review) Act, amongst other things, lists the grounds for review and removes the need for justification in terms of illegality, procedural impropriety, or irrationality. In addition, it gives legal effect to the requirement for reasons and has therefore removed the need to express the importance of this requirement in terms of good administration, usually all the English courts can do. The giving of reasons can therefore be taken for granted as a requirement of good administration. Secondly, the Act removes the requirement for leave and simplifies the procedure by which applications for judicial review are made. It does not include provisions in any way similar to those contained in Order 53. As a consequence, the Australian courts are not so involved in the consideration of what might be detrimental to the interests of good administration. Rather, their perspective tends to be a positive consideration of what is in its interests, whether the benefit is to the individual or the public interest.

Thirdly, the passing of the Freedom of Information Act has resulted in consideration by the courts of the interests of good administration in relation to the disclosure of documents, and fourthly, the establishment of the AAT has opened the way for decisions to be altered if they do not accord with good administrative practice. Finally, as the cases below demonstrate, the Australian courts would

[52] [1967] 2 QB 617, [1983] 2 All ER 311, and [1984] 3 All ER 935, respectively.
[53] [1971] 2 QB 175.   [54] [1969] 2 Ch. 149.   [55] [1978] 1 Ch. 201.

seem to take a wider view of what is required in terms of good administration and at times to use these requirements as stepping-stones to their decisions.

In the interests of consistency, the cases are divided in the same way as those in the proceeding chapters, that is into those cases where good administration is seen as for the benefit of the individual and those cases where it benefits the public interest. However, the division is less clear-cut than the English cases with benefit more frequently accruing to both sides. Challenges under the Freedom of Information Act are considered separately.

Good Administration and the Interests of the Individual

A number of the cases where good administration arises in the Australian context are immigration cases and in these instances its interests have most usually been upheld in support of the individual. In *El-Sayed* one of the concerns of the applicant, who had been denied refugee status, was the length of time taken by the department to reach the decision.[56] The decision was upheld but the court was critical of the delay, stating that 'good administration demands reasonably prompt action'. Indeed, where there is a duty to make a decision, Australian law, in contrast to that in the United Kingdom, also demands it.[57] In *Wu Shan Liang* the decision of the department was also upheld.[58] The court considered that the failure of the department to implement its promise to follow a particular procedure was 'a failure of good administration [which] may occasion justifiable criticism'. However, it pointed out that this did not necessarily mean that the authority had acted unfairly towards any particular person and it did not find unfairness in the case before it.

These cases demonstrate that, as in the British context, good administration may require a higher standard than that upheld by law. This was also the position in *Re: Peninsula Anglican Boys School* where the matter before the court was whether the significance of a new policy should have been brought to the special attention of the applicant.[59] Mr Justice Wilcox suggested, '[s]ome might think that it would have been desirable, in the interests of good administration . . . [b]ut a departure from optimum administrative procedures is not necessarily the same thing as unfairness, in the natural justice sense.' Thus the standards of good administration can at times be infringed while the legal requirements are satisfied.

Such cases contrast with the situation in *Hamilton and McMurray* where a much closer link was made between good administration and fairness.[60] The

---

[56] *El-Syed* v. *Minister for Immigration, Local Government and Ethnic Affairs* Fed. Ct of Aust. [1991] 22 ALD 767.

[57] See Administrative Decisions (Judicial Review) Act, s. 7.

[58] *Wu Shan Liang* v. *Minister for Immigration and Ethnic Affairs* No. NG 501 of 1993, Fed. No. 381/94 (Lexis).　　　　　　　　　　　　　[59] Fed. Ct of Aust., [1985] 7 FCR 415.

[60] *Hamilton and McMurray* v. *Minister for Immigration, Local Government and Ethnic Affairs* No. NG 113 of 1993; Fed. No. 999/93.

applicant had not been provided with a set of explanatory notes which were produced by the department to assist immigrants in completing their application forms. In giving judgment the court reasoned, 'One of the fundamental requirements of good administration is consistency of decision-making . . . Likewise, as a general rule, consistency of treatment of persons the subject of administrative action is of primary importance in good administration. Indeed, consistency of treatment in like circumstances is probably best categorized as a constituent ingredient of consistent decision-making.' It then reasoned that when uniform procedures were introduced and formalized, presumably to promote consistency, 'procedural fairness requires that in normal circumstances persons have equal access to those procedures.' This, the court said, meant that the applicant, along with applicants generally, 'had a legitimate expectation that she would be provided with the explanatory notes', these notes being the instrument for providing the 'equal access' that fairness required. The failure of the department to provide them resulted in the court upholding the application.

The court was therefore supporting the principle that like cases should be treated alike and the view that good administration was concerned with consistency and equity. In the particular case this concern coincided with the requirements of fairness giving rise to a legitimate expectation. By implication this expectation could be extended to an expectation of good administration, an implication that was made in the *Teoh* case (discussed below). The coincidence between good administration and fairness was also found in *Cox* v. *O'Donnell* where a Vietnam veteran was questioning whether he might have been entitled to retire on medical grounds some twenty years previously.[61] His case had finally reached the Chief of General Staff who rejected the possibility just one day after receiving extensive medical documentation. The applicant had been led to believe that the decision would only be made after there had been an independent review of his medical condition at the time of his retirement. However, no such review had been undertaken. The court held that the applicant had a legitimate expectation of such a review and that 'it would be unfair to the applicant and inconsistent with good administration to allow the . . . respondent to do other than follow the agreed procedure.'[62]

In *Re Wan* the coincidence was of a statutory provision and good administration.[63] Like *Hamilton and McMurray*, the principles concerned were equity and consistency. The applicant was entitled to a 'Newstart' allowance, providing he was actively seeking employment, and he challenged the decision by the Department of Social Security to withhold the allowance for six weeks because he had failed to turn up for an appointment. He argued that he had not received proper notice of the appointment. The application was granted because details of the appointment had not been recorded on a standard form for the applicant. The AAT held that '[g]ood administration as well as the statutory content dictates that the

---

[61] Fed. Ct of Aust. [1992] 26 ALD 773.   [62] Ibid. at 74.
[63] *Re Wan and Secretary, Department of Social Security* AAT [1992] 30 ALD 899.

standards of notification should be uniform, i.e. the same irrespective of the person notified'.[64]

Perhaps surprisingly, there are occasions when the courts considered the requirements of law to be more rigorous than those of good administration. This was a matter discussed in *Quinn*.[65] The case concerned the reorganization of the court system, whereby, whilst ninety-five out of one hundred magistrates immediately got jobs under the new system, five had to apply for positions in open competition. The issue in question was whether they had a legitimate expectation to procedural or substantive fairness. Chief Justice Mason cited *Re HK*, the *Hong Kong* case and *CCSU*, noting, 'The duty to accord procedural fairness in connection with a claimant's legitimate expectations is sometimes said to be referable to a general duty of good administration'.[66] He continued, 'But the content of that broader duty is still defined by reference to the claimant's legitimate expectation. In the absence of such an expectation, there is no corresponding duty to accord fairness. For that reason, although in one sense it means nothing to say that a person entitled to fair procedures or good administration has a legitimate expectation of being accorded that treatment, it is still necessary to identify a relevant legitimate expectation and that legitimate expectation may consist of an expectation of a procedural right, advantage or opportunity. . . . The procedural right which forms the subject matter of the legitimate expectation may not necessarily be the same as the procedure which procedural fairness or good administration, the duty to accord which is enlivened by the expectation, will demand.'

Chief Justice Mason illustrated his point that a legitimate expectation may require more than good administration or procedural fairness with reference to the *CCSU* case, stating that 'the expectation of consultation with management through trade unions, which but for the issue of national security would have been a legitimate expectation, may not necessarily have sufficed to require that the procedures of consultation be maintained, procedural fairness or good administration may simply have demanded that there be hearing before the practice of consultation was abandoned.'[67] Thus, where a legitimate expectation gives rise to substantive fairness in the form of a procedural right, advantage, or opportunity, the requirement may be beyond that which arises from procedural fairness or good administration. However, '[i]n other cases the procedural benefit which is legitimately expected will in fact be that which fairness or good administration demands should be accorded.'[68]

Despite the fact that fairness and good administration may be seen as supporting the same standard, the courts recognize that '[g]ood administration cannot of itself offer a sufficient reason for the imposition of a duty to observe fair procedures and the imposition of a duty must ultimately rest upon fairness itself in all

---

[64] *Re Wan and Secretary, Department of Social Security* AAT [1992] 30 ALD 899 at 906.
[65] *Attorney-General* v. *Quinn* High Ct of Aust. [1989] 170 CLR 1.   [66] Ibid. at 20.
[67] Ibid. at 21.   [68] Ibid.

circumstances.'[69] However, such observations do not seem to prevent the reasoning of the courts from at times implying a legitimate expectation of a duty of good administration. This implication was evident in *Teoh* where good administration was used as a mechanism to give legal effect to the Convention on the Rights of the Child, a treaty which had been ratified by the Australian Government but not incorporated into domestic law.[70] The facts of the case were that the applicant, a Malaysian, was in prison for heroin offences and was to be deported after serving his sentence. He had a wife who was a drug-addict, a factor relevant to the commission of his crimes, and he was the actual or *de facto* father of seven children who had Australian citizenship. It was argued on his behalf that because Australia had ratified the Convention on the Rights of the Child, the best interests of the children should be a primary consideration in any deportation decision and that, despite the decision-maker having been aware of the hardship that would be caused to the children by deportation, their interests had not been considered. It was further argued that the applicant had a legitimate expectation that proper regard would be had to the requirements of the Convention and that this would necessitate an investigation by the authorities of the effect of deportation upon the children prior to making the decision to deport.

Chief Justice Black accepted that ratification of the Convention gave rise to a legitimate expectation that actions of the Commonwealth of Australia, which concerned children, would be conducted 'in a manner which adhered to the relevant principles of the Convention'.[71] Such adherence was, he considered, a duty of good administration and, as a consequence, created an expectation of good administration. He therefore reasoned, '[t]he degree of consideration given to the separate interests of the children, each of whom was an Australian citizen, was not adequate to meet the expectation of good administration raised by ratification of the Convention. It is apparent that the opportunity was not taken to assess how the best interests of the infant children could be identified and considered in the event that a decision was made that Teoh be deported.'[72] He continued, 'Proper exercise of the general duty of good administration to meet the legitimate expectation that the best interest of the children would be given a primary consideration, extended to effective representation of the interests of those children by providing the means for ascertaining how the interests of the particular children were to be assessed and duly considered.'

The court therefore held, 'The failure to exercise the decision-making power consistently with the legitimate expectations of persons affected by the decision involved an error of law, whether described as a breach of rules of natural justice in failing to accord procedural fairness in the decision-making process, or by failing to carry out a duty to effect good administration.'[73]

[69] Dawson J. in *Quinn* (above, n. 64) at 56, and see *Waters* v. *Acting Administrator of the Northern Territories and Anr* Fed. CA [1993] 119 ACR 557.

[70] *Teoh* v. *Minister for Immigration, Local Government and Ethnic Affairs* Fed. CA [1994] 32 ALD 420.

[71] Ibid. at 432.   [72] Ibid. at 434.   [73] Ibid. at 422.

The finding of the court that having regard to international treaties, in this case the Convention on the Rights of the Child, was a matter of good administration and a basis for a legitimate expectation went far further than the English courts have been prepared to go. They have limited themselves to a view that reference to the ECHR is on occasions a relevant consideration. The Australian court was not only prepared to find a legitimate expectation, it detailed the requirements that needed to be satisfied and seemed to give the duty to effect good administration legal force (although allowing itself a 'let out' by providing an alternative grounds—failing to accord procedural fairness).

The *Teoh* case also demonstrated a more open judicial attitude to good administration than is found in the English courts. Whilst English judges may refuse an application or a remedy on the basis that to do otherwise would be detrimental to good administration as per Order 53, they have not been prepared to uphold an application, even indirectly, because the duty to give effect to good administration has not been fulfilled. In addition, the content of good administration, as recognized by the Australian courts, would seem to be wider, taking in aspects that in Britain have only been referred to by the PCA.

The *Teoh* decision was itself controversial. Moreover, it raised the prospect that the courts might find a legitimate expectation that decision-makers must make their decisions in accordance with treaty obligations in any of numerous treaties that had been ratified by the Australian Government but not incorporated into Australian law. Such a move by the courts would effectively sideline Parliament's incorporation role. In seeming recognition of the constitutional implications of this development, *Teoh* expressed the view that a legitimate expectation might be displaced by statutory or executive intention and this was seized upon by the Minister for Foreign Affairs and Trade and the Attorney-General, who in a joint statement clarified the intention of the executive.

The statement accepted that ratified treaties could be taken into account by decision-makers in the exercise of their discretion but stated that the *Teoh* decision had created some uncertainty by apparently upholding the necessity of doing so. It continued: 'We state, on behalf of the Government, that entering into an international treaty is not reason for raising any expectation that government decision-makers will act in accordance with the treaty if the relevant provisions of that treaty have not been enacted into domestic Australian law. It is not legitimate, for the purpose of applying Australian law, to expect that the provision of a treaty not incorporated by legislation should be applied by decision-makers. Any expectation that does arise does not provide a ground for review of a decision.'[74]

Subsequently, the Government attempted to introduce legislation through the Administrative Decisions (Effect of International Instruments) Bill 1995. This was given a first reading but the Bill lapsed because of the national election in 1996. The effect of *Teoh* is therefore uncertain. However, Piotrowiaz suggests that

---

[74] Joint Statement by the Minister for Foreign Affairs and Trade and the Attorney-General, 'International Treaties and the High Court Decision in *Teoh*', para. 8.

'[g]iven the very public nature of the ministerial statement, purporting moreover to be couched in the manner required by the Court, the Government has a strong case for insisting that there are no grounds for seeking to rely on an unincorporated treaty as giving rise to legitimate expectations.'[75] A government's insistence is not, of course, the same as a legislative enactment. However, it may restrain future courts from developing the law further.

Whilst the courts recognize, both as a legal principle and as a principle of good administration, that if rules are prescribed, they should generally be followed, one of the grounds for review, the improper exercise of statutory power, makes reference to applying a rule or policy without regard to the merits of the case.[76] Thus the law and good administration require that exceptions be made. The courts also recognize a need for flexibility within the law to achieve sensible and fair results. Such flexibility was upheld by the Immigration Review Tribunal in *Re: Allan Nunez*.[77] The applicant had been refused a family permit. He had applied for a preferential family visa and was considered only in relation to this category, even though it was clear he was eligible for a concessional family visa.

The tribunal recognized that the legislation was complex and, following Mr Justice Wilcox in *Eremin*,[78] considered that 'where the law allows the decision-maker to consider the grant of a visa outside the "category" applied for, such consideration should take place as a matter of good administration. To do otherwise, would be to force many applicants to make serial applications at considerable cost in time and money, with a concommitant burden on decision-makers to process extra applications from the same individual. This cannot be reasonable or just.' Subsequently, the principle would seem to have become established that the Immigration Review Tribunal, in reconsidering a decision to refuse a visa, will look at the application in all categories that might be applicable.[79] This 'is both in accordance with the law and consistent with good administration'.[80]

Flexibility within the administrative system was thus seen as a benefit to the individual and the administrators, saving time and money all round. Most significantly, the statement that good administration requires additional action to be taken to remedy injustice caused by a simple adherence to the law was given considerable force by its expression within the legal context and its linkage with unreasonableness. In Britain such statements have been confined to the reports of the PCA.[81] However, the requirement of flexibility may be contrary to that of cost-effectiveness. If the law is drafted with the intention of mechanizing decision-making through categorization, then the policy it enacts is undermined by the need to consider applications more widely. In addition, despite the court's belief that

---

[75] R. Piotrowiaz, 'The *Teoh* case' (1996) *PL* 194.

[76] Administrative Decisions (Judicial Review) Act, s. 5.

[77] IRT Ref. V90/00073 [1990] (Lexis).

[78] *Eremin* v. *Minister for Immigration, Local Government and Ethnic Affairs* (1990), unreported.

[79] see *Re: Hinojosa* IRT ref. V91/00311 [1991] and *Re: Kiymet Evirgen* IRT Ref. No. V91/00744; Fed. No. 1027 [1992].

[80] *Re: Kiymet Evirgen* (Lexis transcript used).   [81] See ch. 4.

re-categorizing applications would benefit the administration because it would prevent officials having to deal with multiple applications, re-categorization would mean spending more time on each application for no additional fee, hardly efficient in terms of cost. Multiple applications, on the other hand, all have to be paid for.

Still within the immigration field there was criticism by the Immigration Review Tribunal of 'the Department's practice in adopting profiles of standards based on statistics in reaching decisions relating to the granting of close family visitor visas. . . . Such stereotyping per se has no place in good administration as it effectively amounts to the taking into consideration of irrelevant factors.'[82] Once again, however, the view of the court as to what constitutes good administration, as well as what is relevant, may conflict with the requirements of cost-efficiency, stereotyping being an effective mechanism for speeding up the process and thus cutting costs.

However, despite any possible conflict with the needs of efficiency and cost-saving, the Australian courts would seem determined to encourage a caring administration. This was evident in *Sloane* where Mr Justice French dismissed an application finding no error in law, but, nevertheless, took the opportunity to observe the requirements of good administration in relation to the case.[83] These, he said, required that the applicant be told that the material he had provided on his mother's psychological state was insufficient without supporting evidence from a qualified psychiatrist. Similarly, in *Re: Mu Jiang* the Immigration Review Tribunal was critical of the department's 'unnecessary rigid application of the "common sense" onus rule'.[84] This it considered made 'applicants in third world countries who may be illiterate in their own language and who must proceed through translators to complete forms . . . scapegoats of the system'. This was contrary to good administration which 'will on occasions require decision makers to make further enquiries rather than to simply refuse an application because forms were incomplete or apparently misleading'.

Likewise the Tribunal was critical of the department in *Re: Melekiola*.[85] The applicant had become an illegal immigrant because he had overstayed his leave. His solicitor had written to the authorities expressing a wish to regularize the applicant's status and seeking advice as to how best to do this. The Department did not reply. The Tribunal found that 'it was under no legal obligation to do so'. However, it considered that 'the requirements of good administration might seem to have warranted at least the courtesy of a reply'.

Good administration would therefore seem to require consideration, courtesy, and compassion. Moreover, whilst those courts concerned with the legality of the decision are unable to give such principles effect, the AAT is not so restricted.

---

[82] Fadjiar J, *Re: Marissa Ferreras*, IRT Ref. W91/00815 [1991] (Lexis).
[83] *Sloane* v. *Minister for Immigration, Local Government and Ethnic Affairs* Fed. Ct of Aust. [1992] 28 ALD.
[84] IRT Ref. V91/01253, Fed. No. 910 [1992] (Lexis).
[85] IRT Ref. V92/01512; Fed. No. 1634 [1993] (Lexis).

Indeed, the AAT in its examination of the merits of a decision would seem to be informed by what it considers to be the principles of good administration.[86] In *Re Taylor* the issue before the AAT concerned the overpayment of benefit to an applicant who had no assets and could therefore only make repayments out of income.[87] The Tribunal considered that it 'was not good administrative practice, except in clear cases of fraud or dishonesty, for the respondent to seek to recover small sums of money, per week over a very long period, that could impose an undesirably heavy burden upon the payer.'[88]

The view of the AAT on repayments was reasserted in *Re VXY* (1993).[89] Moreover, the Tribunal was not influenced by the fact that benefits had been paid on the understanding that they might have to be repaid. Rather it took account of 'the confusion which has already been caused by conflicting advice to Mr VXY by officers of the department, and . . . the respondent's ill health', coming to the conclusion that 'good administration seems to suggest that payments which have been made to the respondent pursuant to the decision of the SSAT [Social Security Appeals Tribunal] should not have to be repaid.'[90]

Good Administration in the Public Interest

Unlike the British position with regard to judicial review,[91] Australian rules, as contained in the Administrative Decisions (Judicial Review) Act, provide no grounds for refusing an application on the basis that it is detrimental to the interests of good administration. As a consequence, the Australian cases contain no explicit reference to such detriment. There are, however, instances where the courts, either explicitly or implicitly, uphold the requirement for efficiency and effectiveness and thus the public interest and the interest of the administrative process in good administration.

This was apparent in *Elbourne* where Mr Justice Davies suggested that an illegal immigrant should have been advised that she had no chance of staying in Australia but could apply for a limited entry permit.[92] He recognized that there was no legal duty to provide such advice and that it was not a requirement of good administration. However, he observed that 'good administration does not preclude the giving of help and assistance when it appears to be needed'.[93] The use of good administration in this context suggests a recognition that the principles it encompasses go beyond those relating to the individual interest to considerations of efficiency and effectiveness. In this case giving assistance was unlikely to have interfered with the administrative process or to have placed an unwarranted

---

[86] See *Re Sec., Department of Social Security and VXY*, AAT [1993] 30 ALD 681.
[87] *Re Taylor and Director General of Social Security* AAT [1984] 6 ALD 500.
[88] Ibid. at 501.   [89] [1993] 30 ALD 681.   [90] Ibid. at 683.
[91] As contained in Ord. 53 and Supreme Court Act 1981.
[92] *Elbourne* v. *Minister for Immigration, Local Govt and Ethnic Affairs* [1991] 22 ALD 211.
[93] Ibid. at 212.

burden on administrators. If it had done so, Mr Justice Davies's observations might have been different. An inference can be drawn that unless there is a requirement of fairness, the level or amount of help given should not interfere with the efficiency of the administrative process.

Efficiency was also a factor in *Pashmforoosh*.[94] The court held that fairness did not require the Immigration Department to disclose information which was considered to be irrelevant to the decision of whether to grant a permanent entry permit. Such disclosure would have meant that the department 'would have been called upon to deal with extraneous matter which was not being taken into account' and the court considered that 'such a course would have been the antithesis of good administration'.[95] The implication was that it would interfere with the requirement of efficiency.

In *Smiles* the need for public administration to be effective was given support by the court.[96] Mr Smiles was a Member of Parliament whose case had been referred by the Australian Taxation Office to the Director of Public Prosecutions for a decision whether to prosecute for tax offences. Mr Smiles argued that the decision to prosecute was made to achieve an improper purpose or collateral advantage, namely publicity. Mr Justice Davies accepted that the prosecution of all offences would not be in the public interest and that suitable penalties were available by way of additional tax payments. However, he continued, 'It is not wrong to take account of the publicity likely to arise from and the deterrent effect of a prosecution when considering whether or not a prosecution for a taxation offence should be instituted. I see no element of abuse of power in that consideration, rather good administration.'[97] He therefore seemed to consider that the prosecution of a public figure would serve the public interest in good administration by acting as a warning to others who might be tempted to evade their taxation obligations.

The public interest also requires that public administration should not be unduly hindered by the over-application of the rules of natural justice. This was a consideration in *Haoucherv*, a case in which Mr Justice McHugh was concerned with their application in licence cases.[98] He considered that there was 'no sense, let alone justice, in the common law rules of natural justice giving protection to an existing licence but denying it to a legitimate expectation of the renewal of a licence'. However, he accepted that if a person, seeking the renewal of a licence, were entitled to be put in possession of all considerations affecting its renewal, 'public administration would be seriously impaired'. He thus concluded that 'in

---

[94] *Minister for Immigration, Local Govt and Ethnic Affairs* v. *Pashmforoosh and anor* Fed. Court of Aust. [1989] 18 ALD 77.

[95] Ibid. at 78.

[96] *Smiles* v. *Fed. Commissioner of Taxation and ors*, Fed. Ct of Aust. [1992] 107 ALR 439.

[97] Ibid. at 454.

[98] *Haoucherv* v. *Minister for Immigration, Local Govt and Ethnic Affairs* High Ct of Aust. [1990] 169 CLR 648.

such cases, it may not even be possible, consistently with good administration, to give a hearing to the person affected'.[99]

Similarly, the private interests of an individual may have to take second place to the requirements of consistency. Consistent decision-making and the consistent application of a policy is considered by the Australian courts in the same way as those in Britain, as one of the keystones of good administration. In *Hamilton and McMurray* the public interest in consistency coincided with the private interest.[100] However, this was not the situation in *Re Bundy*.[101] Mrs Bundy claimed she had been advised by the Department of Housing and Construction on the telephone that the calculation of her grant would take into account certain payments she had made. It had not done so.

The Tribunal accepted that there may be circumstances where an administrator would feel it appropriate to use his discretion to take account of advice that had been given. However, in this situation, it considered that 'the interests of good administration in the consistent application of that policy outweighed any private interests of the applicant whose hope for a larger grant may have been wrongly bolstered by the information she received.'[102] The case arose before the Judicial Review Act came into force and before the development of the concept of legitimate expectations. Whether a later tribunal would have found differently probably depends upon the merits of the case and whether the applicant had suffered detriment because of her reliance upon the advice or, as indicated by the judgment cited above, just had her hopes dashed.

Making exceptions supports the requirement for the fair and just treatment of individuals at the expense of consistency. It may also be detrimental to 'speedy finality'. As in Britain this is seen as necessary so that administrators know their position and can function effectively and third parties can organize their affairs accordingly. In Australia it is underwritten by legislation which imposes time limits for appeals to tribunals. The purpose of these were recognized by Mr Justice Martin in *Jones* v. *Motor Accidents*.[103] He considered 'that when the legislature enacted the current provisions governing references to the tribunal it intended that there should be relative speedy finality to claims against the fund, as an aid to good administration of it, and so that the level of contributions to the fund could be fixed from time to time.'[104] As a result he refused an appeal made out of time. Closely related to being out of time is delay in making an appeal. Such delay can be against the interests of good administration particularly if it leads to the belief that the case has been disposed of. This was the situation in *Ward* v. *Nicholls* where the applicant had deliberately delayed in appealing against a decision not to award him extra war pension.[105] The court had 'considerable sympathy for the argument

---

[99] Ibid. at 681.
[100] Above, n. 59.
[101] *Re Bundy and Sec., Dept of Housing and Construction* AAT General Admin. Division, No. 12030 of 1979.
[102] A. N. Hall, Senior Member, at 755.
[103] AT [1988] 17 ALD 287.
[104] Ibid. at 291.
[105] Fed. Ct of Aust. [1988] 16 ALD 353.

based on delay and the possibility of administrative inconvenience', although on the facts, it found the case to be exceptional.

Generally there is clear reluctance by the courts to grant an extension of time 'without good cause or when the grant of the extension will inhibit effective on-going administration.'[106] These stipulations have much in common with Order 53 and the Rules of the Supreme Court. Moreover, as far as the Australian courts are concerned, 'prompt and efficient decision-making' is 'an integral part of good administration'.[107] However, the desirability for promptness may on occasions give way to the need to give best effect to a policy or scheme.

This was the case in *Gerah Imports* where a scheme for dealing with tenders for the right to import goods at a concessional duty rate had a time limit for the pro-vision of securities by successful tenderers.[108] The administrator of the scheme extended the time by a week, an extension which was challenged in the court by an unsuccessful tenderer. Mr Justice Davies accepted 'that in a Scheme such as this, which affects an industry, clear rules and fair dealing with all parties within those rules is important. Members of an industry will quickly lose confidence in a scheme if terms of the Scheme, clearly stated, are not complied with.'[109] However, he considered that the administrator 'acted lawfully to all parties and in a way most calculated to achieve the implementation of that which the Scheme had in mind'.[110] He continued, 'It appears to me that what was done accorded with good administrative practice and was sound in law'. An additional factor in *Gerah Imports*, which distinguishes it from other cases involving the extension of time-limits, was that the extension had no detrimental effect on the wider public. Indeed, the court considered that it was in the public interest, as well as in the interests of successful tenderers, for the scheme to be implemented to best effect. As indicated by dicta from the British courts, good administration is therefore con-cerned with giving best effect to the legal requirements.

In many of the above cases it is apparent that the courts are balancing aspects of good administration and the interests of individuals against the public interest in efficient administration. This balance was reflected in *Baker* v. *Campbell* when the court considered that '[t]he dictates of good administration of complex social and commercial legislation may require increasing resort to compulsory proced-ures'.[111] Here good administration was concerned with the effective implementa-tion of Government policy and the implication was that whilst compulsory procedures may benefit the efficiency of the administrative process, they may be detrimental to the individual interest in equity, a consideration of the individual case, and a 'human' side to public administration.

At times the balance is between the individual on the one hand and the admin-istrative process and third party interests on the other. In *Re Liddle* Deputy

---

[106] Davies J, *Baker* v. *Sec., Dept of Social Security* Fed. Ct of Aust. [1991] 23 ALD 305 at 306.
[107] Ibid.
[108] *Gerah Imports Pty Ltd* v. *Minister for Industry, Technology and Commerce* Fed. Ct of Aust [1987] 14 ALD 351.
[109] Ibid. at 365.   [110] Ibid.   [111] High Court of Aust. [1983] 153 CLR 52 at 52.

President Forgie dissented from the majority decision to allow the late election by a public servant to preserve his benefit rights, considering 'that a late election should be recognized only if it would benefit the person making it while, at the same time, not adversely affecting the payment of pensions and benefits to other beneficiaries under the Act and not impeding the efficient and proper administration of the . . . scheme . . . It may be that what would benefit the individual may not be consistent with the interests of the other beneficiaries and of good administration.'[112] This reasoning was subsequently adopted in *Re: Parsons*[113] and in *Green*,[114] cases which concerned the same issue and the same consideration of individual interest versus administrative and third party interests.

Freedom of Information Act

The Australian context provides a further situation in which the courts are concerned with good administration, namely challenges under the Freedom of Information Act 1982. In one such challenge, *Re Downie*, which concerned the disclosure of documents from the Housing Department, the AAT accepted the view that the 'public interest in sound, efficient, effective and fair administration of public housing funds in the Australian Capital Territory . . . [was of] greater importance than the ordinary public interest in good administration where there were . . . "objective" indications of discord and evidence of deficiencies within the administration and evidence of high and mounting losses to the public revenue.'[115] The AAT reasoned that this gave rise to 'a strong public interest in the disclosure of information about the operation of an agency', overriding arguments that disclosure would damage the confidentiality of the relationship between ministers and advisers, undermine the integrity and validity of the decision-making process and prejudice candour. The AAT was also concerned about the practice of partial disclosure, suggesting that there was 'a public interest in ensuring that the material already released does not represent a distorted selection of the totality of the material on this issue.'[116] This is an even greater concern in Britain where departments and agencies are involved in releasing information rather than documents and thus have considerably more opportunity for partial disclosure.

The arguments employed above for non-disclosure are familiar in the freedom of information context and are usually expressed in terms of the public interest. Here they might be equated with the 'ordinary public interest in good administration'. This interest, which was not sufficient to prevent disclosure in *Re Downie*, was upheld in *Re Guy*[117] on the basis that disclosure would damage

---

[112] *Re Liddle and Commissioner for Superannuation* AAT [1991] 25 ALD 307 at 322.
[113] *Re: Parsons and Commissioner for Superannuation* No. A92/48 AAT; Fed. No. 8254 (1992).
[114] *Green* v. *Commissioner for Superannuation* No. A92/117 AAT; Fed. No. 8855 (1993).
[115] *Re Downie and Dept of Territories* AAT [1985] 8 ALD 496 at 500.
[116] Ibid.   [117] *Re Guy and Dept of Transport* AAT [1987] 12 ALD 358.

State–Commonwealth relations. Disclosure of a telex between Queensland and the Commonwealth was sought but it was argued that intergovernmental relations often required a quick response by telex to an earlier communication and if 'such a response had to be considered with a view to the effects of its being made public, this [would] . . . introduce an undesirable delay not conducive to good government and good administration.'[118]

In *Re Dyrenfurth* the concern was whether information on the assessment of applications for appointments in the Senior Executive Service should be disclosed.[119] The AAT initially held that it should because the information did not meet the criteria for exemption contained in the Freedom of Information Act. The tribunal was concerned at this apparent lack of exemption and at the effect of disclosure on good administration. It said, 'it might have been preferable for criteria for the handling and release of documents in relation to selection and promotion to have been evolved and determined in the first place in terms of what is good administration and management, without too much looking over the shoulder at the FOI Act.' It was the belief of the Tribunal that, this done, 'such criteria might then have been able to be accepted in the FOI context. Material put before us however suggests that the FOI tail is wagging the management dog.'[120]

This would seem to be an indication that effective management, recognized by the Australian courts as an important aspect of good administration, was giving way to a competing requirement, consideration of the FOI Act. The decision on disclosure made by the AAT was subsequently overruled by the Federal Court of Australia on the basis that the information was of a personal nature.[121] It agreed with the Tribunal that forced disclosure in the area of personnel assessment would have serious consequences for good administration.

Conclusion

The Australian courts operate in the context of a coherent system of administrative law with detailed statutory grounds for judicial review, review on merits, the requirement that reasons are given and a Freedom of Information Act. As a consequence, many of the requirements that the British courts can only cite as principles of good administration can be upheld by the Australian courts as law. Most obviously this applies to the giving of reasons, the release of information and, where there is a statutory duty, unreasonable delay in making a decision. This may explain why the principles of good administration upheld by the Australian courts would seem to include 'softer' elements, such as consideration, compassion, and courtesy, although such a view of how public administrators should operate may be a reaction to the public disquiet about the public service in the 1970s. Either

---

[118] *Re Guy and Dept of Transport* AAT [1987] 12 ALD 358 at 361.
[119] *Re Dyrenfurth and Dept of Social Security* AAT [1987] 12 ALD 577.
[120] Ibid. at 588.   [121] [1988] 15 ALD 232.

way, the principles supported by the courts are very much in accord with a public service model of good administration. Moreover, there is little evidence that they have changed during the later 1980s and beyond to accommodate considerations of cost-effectiveness and value for money. The lack of an Order 53 requirement that the courts should consider whether an application is detrimental to good administration deprives public bodies of an automatic defence to an application being granted. This no doubt accounts for the sparsity of cases where good administration is used negatively, as a reason for dismissing an application. These mainly concern cases of delay or being out of time, or cases where the concern is to give best effect to a policy and its administration. Such dismissals support the principles of consistency, speedy finality, and efficiency in terms of doing the best possible.

There is another important difference which concerns the use by the Australian courts of good administration as a stepping-stone in legal reasoning. This was most evident in the *Teoh* case, where good administration was used as a mechanism for giving legal effect to the Convention on the Rights of the Child,[122] and in *Re: Allan Nunez* where it supported the need for flexibility.[123]

In the Australian context good administration is most usually seen as being in the interests of the individual. However, this does not necessarily conflict with the public interest and the interests of public administration. Indeed, it is frequently portrayed as a mutually shared interest. The assumption would seem to be that public servants have an interest in operating a caring system that steps beyond its legal obligations to be fair, considerate, and compassionate to the individual and that such a system is in the public interest. This view of the interests of good administration would seem to reflect the values expounded more generally by the courts during the 1990s, a period which, in common with Britain, has been one of judicial intervention. In support of their decisions, judges have used a number of closely-related reference points. These have included 'the contemporary values of the Australian people', 'the contemporary values of the community', 'the relatively permanent values of the Australian community', 'enduring values [and] unequivocally accepted values', and 'contemporary notions of justice and human rights'.[124]

There seems to be little judicial consideration of issues relating to resourcing or cost. This suggests that the Australian courts, like their British counterparts, are supporting a model of good administration which, in many respects, conflicts with that of the new public management. Indeed, in the Australian context some of the values underlying it are so far removed from the requirements of cost-effectiveness and value for money that the notion of balancing competing principles would seem unsustainable. In addition, as far as Australia is concerned, the

---

[122] Above, n. 69.   [123] Above, n. 76.
[124] From *Mabo* v. *Queensland* (No. 2) (1992) 175 CLR 41 at 42; *Dietrich* v. *The Queen* (1992) 177 CLR 292 at 319; ibid.; Mason CJ in an interview on *Four Corners*, ABC, 3 Apr. 1995, respectively. All cited by P. H. Lane, 'The changing role of the High Court' (1996) 70 *Aust. Law Journal* 3.

whole system of external control as operated through administrative law would seem to be contrary to the requirements of those engaged in the current wave of administrative reform and must have a limiting effect on what can be achieved.

Australia may therefore present a more obvious conflict between the model of good administration supported by the courts, which reflects the public-service model, and the model supported by the new public management. However, that said, the reforms of public administration, whilst in many ways similar to those in Britain, have from the start been tempered by considerations of public accountability both in the political arena and in the courts. The courts may therefore justifiably claim public support and legitimacy for their actions. Moreover, they can take refuge behind authorizing legislation, which demonstrates Parliamentary intent, in a way that is denied British judges.

10

CONCLUSIONS

A Change of Values?

The preceding chapters have examined the concept of good administration against a background of fundamental change in the structure and operation of the Civil — or Public — Service and increased tension between the executive and judicial branches of government. The change in the public service is the manifestation of a market philosophy, supported by rational-choice thinking, which centres upon efficiency, effectiveness and economy, when all the 'Es' are quantifiable, and which views the private-sector as the preferred medium for the delivery of public services. The result is the reduction and fragmentation of the public sector as government functions are privatized, contracted-out, market-tested or consigned to quangos or Next Steps executive agencies, and the incorporation of private-sector methods into the management and operation of these agencies and their parent departments.

The new public management model of the Civil Service that emerges is very different from the traditional public service model and inevitably supports a different view of what constitutes good administration. However, many see the principles it supports as inappropriate for the public sector. In particular, the new public management is goal-driven with the means by which the goals are achieved having little or no intrinsic worth. It is their effectiveness in achieving the ends that is of importance. The new public management therefore 'shift[s] attention away from the traditional focus on procedural integrity to concentrate much more upon efficiency and performance methods'.[1] This devaluing of processes is particularly relevant to good administration which relies upon procedures and rules to uphold principles such as equity and consistency, and which values these principles in their own right, not just as a means to an end.

The emphasis on goals and performance also encourages a concentration on self and narrow organizational interests rather than the broader interests of the public service and society. Moreover, in the fulfilment of a function or delivery of a service the focus is on the individual rather than the public at large, and narrowed further to the individual as customer. Thus the new public management model of good administration is concerned with customer satisfaction, as determined by the meeting of Charter standards, rather than process rights, such as fairness, and notions of serving the public, dominant in the public service model, are largely

---

[1] L. Pratchett & M. Wingfield, *Public Service Ethos in Local Government*, 34.

missing. This suggests that the public service ethos,[2] traditionally seen as the 'glue' holding the Civil Service together and giving it a common purpose and culture,[3] is therefore changing, being given only a narrow construction in the new public management model.

The notion of change is supported by the findings of the Oughton Report which, after a survey of 4,250 civil servants, reported that the public service ethos was 'being eroded'.[4] It is also given substance by the survey of local government officials undertaken by Pratchett and Wingfield.[5] This found an impatience with bureaucratic rules and procedures, which seemed to get in the way of effective and efficient management, and a requirement for greater discretion and freedom to meet set objectives. It also found that 'many of the respondents identified with only a narrow definition of the public service ethos, and operated within a very limited conception of it'. Thus only professionalism, honesty, impartiality and integrity were supported as 'key principles' and even these were seen as 'being under threat'.[6]

Pratchett and Wingfield concluded that 'a new set of dominant values' were emerging with a resulting ethos which emphasized a 'competitive, contracted, insular and adversarial culture'.[7] This conclusion suggests that an over-arching culture based on public service is no longer sustainable and has implications for the way in which public services are delivered. Indeed Pratchett and Wingfield comment, 'the real concern is whether the evolving set of values are those that are appropriate for local government' and whether they will result in the loss of 'the cohesive force' which has held local government together.[8]

Local government is in many ways different from central government. Its very nature means that it has never been subject to the centralized control and common purpose of the Civil Service and thus it may have been more susceptible to the impact of fragmentation and the diversification of interests. It has in any case felt the brunt of CCT and the move from government as provider to government as enabler.[9] However, the evidence regarding the erosion of the public service ethos would seem to have application to central government and relevance to the notion of good administration, for the principles it supports feed into ideas of how public administration should operate and thus sustain good practice. Moreover, although rebuttals by Government of any suggestion that the public service ethos is being eroded are no doubt made in good faith,[10] they may be misguided.[11] As Pratchett and Wingfield warn in relation to local government, 'of all the changes

---

[2] For discussion on public service ethos see Chs. 1 and 2 and see W. Plowden, *Ministers and Mandarins*.

[3] Sir Robin Butler, 'Future of the Civil Service', lecture to FDA (1991).

[4] Efficiency Unit, Cabinet Office (1992); see also J. Smith, 'The Public Service Ethos' (1991) 69 *Pub. Admin.* 4.

[5] Above, n. 1.   [6] Ibid., 34.   [7] Ibid.   [8] Ibid.

[9] On effects on local government of reforms, see J. Stewart & G. Stoker (eds.), *Future of Local Government* (London, 1989); A. Cochrane, *Whatever Happened to Local Government?*

[10] Sir Robin Butler in evidence to TCSC HC 390–II, (1992–3), Q102, Q201 (see ch. 1).

[11] See Oughton Report (above, n. 4) and PAC, HC 154, (1993–4), (see ch. 1).

that have occurred . . . over the last fifteen years . . . the changes in the public sector ethos threaten to be the least conspicuous but most profound in their impact.'[12] The same seems likely to be applicable to central government and the Civil Service.

It is not only the values underlying good administration which would seem to be changing or at the very least being given a different emphasis. The purpose that good administrative practice is seen as serving may be different in the new public management model. The public service model supports a view of good administration being above politics. It may be concerned with the implementation of government policies according to the values underlying these policies, but it has the additional concern of protecting the system from corruption and of preventing the arbitrary exercise of power. It is therefore more than a reflection of prevailing political philosophy. Rather it has constitutional status and is a confirmation that the Civil Service not only owes a loyalty to the government of the day but also to the public at large, 'officials exist[ing] in the end for the public they serve', acting as 'the trustees, the fiduciaries of the public'.[13] Thus good administration serves the public interest and acts for the public good. To this end, it upholds the principles of equity and consistency and ensures that the individual is treated fairly.

The new public management model has a different view of the purpose and benefit of good administration. This arises in part because of different, or additional, loyalties: namely, the loyalty owed by an official to his or her own career prospects, which are largely dependent upon meeting performance criteria, and the loyalty owed to the particular client group or individual through the Citizen's Charter.[14] Good administration is therefore concerned with meeting performance and Charter standards and thus, either directly or indirectly, its purpose is efficiency and customer satisfaction. Once more ideas of there being a public interest in good administration, or even an individual interest, other than a pseudo-contractual one, are missing.

As the preceding chapters have demonstrated, the new public management model of good administration is at odds not only with the public service model but with the perspective of the PCA and that of the courts. These perspectives recognize, and at times uphold, the public interest in good administration, even though their emphasis is on the individual interest. Moreover, the principles they support, and the purpose they see good administration serving, are in accord with the traditional model. This partly accounts for the usually successful co-operation between departments and the PCA in determining appropriate remedies. It also accounts for the non-interventionist stance of the courts for most of the twentieth century. Judges have worked on the premise that civil servants, and indeed politicians, operate according to mutually accepted principles.

This can no longer be assumed and neither can judicial non-intervention. Indeed, the shift to the new public management has been accompanied by an

---

[12] Above, n. 1 at 34.　　　　[13] C. P. D. Finn, 'Integrity in government' (1991) 3 *PLR*.
[14] See J. Greenaway, 'Having the bun and the halfpenny' (1995) 73 *Pub. Admin.* 3 at 363.

unusual degree of judicial activism, demonstrated directly through judicial decisions, writings, and comments, and indirectly through the relaxation of the rules relating to *locus standi* and the gradual reduction in those areas considered to be non-justiciable. In some respects the emergence of an interventionist judiciary at the same time as changes within public administration has been coincidental, the degree of activism of any court in part being determined by the personalities and philosophy of its members. Moreover, the reasons for the courts wishing to assume a greater public law role are complex, with constitutional and European influences at play. However, there is evidence to suggest that judicial intervention is also a response to Government policies and practices, in particular the move away from the liberal values associated with the post-war consensus and the public service model of administration, and concern about the principles that now inform public administration.[15]

This coincidence of an interventionist judiciary and the new public management has produced a tension that at times is barely containable. This has been demonstrated by judicial–executive disagreements over sentencing policy and efficiency measures within the legal system and by adverse court decisions and Government reaction to them. Underlying the tension is the philosophy of the new public management, which, informed by rational-choice thinking, plays down external control by courts and tribunals. It focuses instead upon internal review and on external control by the PCA and the C & AG, both of whom recognize the efficiency restraints under which Government operates, and is resentful of judicial decisions which may impact upon policies, have resource implications and be framed in terms of soft, unmeasurable concepts, such as fairness and reasonableness. As far as the new public management is concerned, the courts are seen as seeking to impose a value system which is no longer relevant to modern government and a market economy.

Judges, for their part, are unlikely to be persuaded by arguments based on the market economy, the management methods of the private-sector, or value for money. Rather they see their obligation as being 'to protect values which no democratic politician could honestly contest, values which . . . may be described as apolitical, since they stand altogether above the rancorous but vital dissentions of party politics.'[16] A statement of responsibility, couched in terms that are unquantifiable and, indeed, may be difficult to qualify, gives the judges considerable leeway, thereby confirming new public management concerns about the role of the courts. However, in the context of good administration many consider that there are such values[17] and that in the 1990s they need protection from cost-cutting and value for money programmes and from the new public management culture which may minimize their importance.

---

[15] See ch. 6.   [16] J. Laws, 'Law and democracy' (1995) *PL* 72 at 93.

[17] As demonstrated by the Resolution and Recommendation from the Council of Europe and recommendations from JUSTICE (*Administration Under Law*) and JUSTICE–All Souls, *Review of Administrative Law in the United Kingdom* (see ch. 1).

Possible Judicial Developments

The examination of cases where the interests of good administration have been raised demonstrate that the courts do not uphold good administration directly as a legal concept.[18] However, they do support it through the principles of judicial review, which, according to Sir John Laws, 'constitute ethical ideals as to the virtuous conduct of the state's affairs'.[19] Thus legal requirements will often coincide with the requirements of good administration. Thereafter good administration extends beyond the law, providing the courts with an additional set of principles which, although having no legal force, can allow judicial criticism of, or support for, administrative practice and decision-making. It enables the courts to encourage the giving of reasons and greater openness, neither of which are given legal effect in Britain, and to express views about how the individual should be treated by the administrative process.

Thus the means by which the courts have fostered principles of good administration have been mainly indirect. However, it is possible that, in view of the concern that these principles are being undermined, the courts will adopt a more direct approach. Judicial reasoning in previous cases in both Britain and Australia may pave the way for a number of developments. Firstly, the failure of public administration to comply with the standards required by good administration could be seen by the courts as evidence that Government has not exercised its powers properly. There were indications of this approach in Mr Justice Woolf's judgment in *ex parte Greenwich*, where he noted that conventions could 'provide guidance as to what are the proper standards' and non-compliance with a convention 'may be an indication that the government has not exercised its powers properly'.[20] The compliance, or otherwise, with the requirements of good administration could likewise be a factor taken into account by the court.

Secondly, the courts could adopt the 'hard-look' review developed by the American courts. This requires a degree of openness such that the basis of a decision is clear and it is apparent what factors have been taken into account. Sir John Donaldson showed support for this approach in *ex parte Huddleston* where he expressed the opinion that sufficient reasons should be given to enable the courts to determine the legality of a decision with regard to the factors considered,[21] as did Mr Justice Brooke in *ex parte Connell* when he held that there should be an open consideration of ministerial Guidance, required by the authorizing statute to be taken into account.[22]

Thirdly, the courts could look to the standards in the Citizen's Charter as incorporating some aspects of good administration. The distinction made by the PCA

---

[18] See chs. 7, 8 & 9. [19] Above, n. 16 at 80.
[20] [1984] The Times, 16 Aug. (see ch. 7).
[21] *R. v. Lancashire County Council, ex p. Huddleston* CA [1986] 2 All ER 941 (see ch. 7).
[22] *R. v. Independent Review Service ex p. Connell* CO/18111/94 (Lexis) (see ch. 7).

between 'mandatory' standards and 'persuasive indicators'[23] could be utilized with the non-fulfilment of a mandatory standard, such as a right to a decision, being a factor used by the courts in determining whether there are grounds for a remedy. They could also draw upon the Code of Practice on Access to Government Information and on its aim 'to protect the interests of individuals and companies by ensuring that reasons are given for administrative decisions, except where there is statutory authority or established convention to the contrary'.[24] Thus a failure to give reasons, in a situation not covered by a legitimate exemption, could likewise be seen as a failure of good administration and as a factor to be considered by the court when determining the legality or otherwise of a decision.

The courts would still not be directly upholding good administration, unless its requirements coincided with a legal obligation, but their support for the principles that govern its operation would be more apparent. More controversially, they could utilize the concept of legitimate expectations, such that mandatory charter standards are seen as giving rise to a legitimate expectation at least of fair treatment.[25] In many ways this is a simple progression from finding that published policy criteria give rise to a legitimate expectation.

The utilization of legitimate expectations moves on to the fourth possibility and the consideration by the courts of developments in Australia. These developments centre on the link made in *Teoh* between legitimate expectations and good administration[26] which implied a duty of good administration which may give rise to a legitimate expectation. The reasoning suggested that where good administration requires a particular consideration to be taken into account or acted upon there may be a legitimate expectation. In *Teoh* the court considered that it was the duty of good administration to act in accordance with the Convention on the Rights of the Child and that this gave rise to a legitimate expectation that the interests of the children would be paramount.

The decision was controversial in Australia because the court was seen as giving effect to an unincorporated treaty. However, the ratification by a government of a treaty of this nature is a commitment to the principles enshrined within it. It would therefore seem appropriate that, when relevant, these principles should be taken into account by public administration, as British civil servants are advised by the publication *Judge Over Your Shoulder*. The problem with *Teoh* would seem to be the court's view that the principles of the Convention should determine the decision rather than inform it. In Britain a similar view in relation to the Convention on the Rights of the Child, to which we are also a signatory, or of other non-incorporated treaties, such as the European Convention on Human Rights, would be equally controversial. Indeed, even a decision that held a treaty obliga-

---

[23] See ch. 4.   [24] Para. 1.2.

[25] Wade & Forsyth note, 'Where the Charter leads the citizen legitimately to expect service of a certain quality, this may have legal consequences' (*Administrative Law*, 106, n. 17).

[26] *Teoh* v. *Minister for Immigration, Local Government and Ethnic Affairs* Fed. CA [1994] 32 ALD 420 (see ch. 9).

tion to be a relevant factor which should have been considered, may be seen as unacceptable judicial interference.[27] Yet the argument that the Government's duty to comply with international human rights law may give rise to a legitimate expectation is a persuasive one and may prove to be 'the trumpcard of the future'.[28]

Less controversially, a legitimate expectation of the duty of good administration may also arise in relation to the concern of good administration to give best effect to legal requirements and provisions. Thus if there is a legal requirement that notice be given, there could be a legitimate expectation that notice will be given in the most effective way.

The possible developments outlined above relate to the individual interest in good administration. However, the ideas put forward by Mr Justice Sedley in *ex parte Hamble Fisheries* were also concerned with the public interest.[29] Mr Justice Sedley suggested that policies could contain thought-out exceptions 'which may well be exhaustive of the obligation [to make exceptions]' and which 'may well set up an unanswerable case of partiality or arbitrariness' in relation to making other exceptions. This would reduce the inefficiencies associated with having to make unforeseen exceptions and thus benefit the public interest in good administration whilst still providing protection for the individual.

A Code of Good Administration

The problem with any judicial development which aims to give the principles of good administration a higher profile and greater protection is that the courts have little authority for their actions other than public confidence.[30] In Britain judges lack even the legislative authority for judicial review which the Australian courts can at least cite as a basis for public support and which provides a useful framework for upholding many of the principles of good administration, including, to the envy of the British courts, the duty to respond to a request for reasons.[31] The only legislative authority the British courts have in relation to good administration is the Supreme Court Act, section 31 of which, together with Order 53, is concerned with detriment to the interests of good administration. Thus it is frequently

---

[27] But see criticism (e.g. I. Loveland, *Constitutional Law,* 599) of the House of Lords view that the Home Secretary was not required to take the ECHR into account (*R. v. Sec. of State for the Home Department, ex p. Brind* [1991] 1 All ER 720).

[28] John Wadham, Director of Liberty, at Sweet & Maxwell Conference on Judicial Review, Dec. 1996 and see Lord Lester, 'Government's compliance with international human rights law' (1996) *PL* 187 and G. J. Szabolwski, 'Administrative discretion and the protection of human rights' in Chapman (ed.) *Ethics in Public Service.*

[29] *R. v. Minister for Agriculture, Fisheries and Food, ex p. Hamble Fisheries Ltd* [1995] 7 Admin LR 637 (see ch. 7).

[30] See G. Brennan, 'The purpose and scope of judicial review' in M. Taggart (ed.), *Judicial Review of Administrative Action in the 1980s.*

[31] Administrative Decisions (Judicial Review) Act 1977, s. 13(1).

a negative perspective with which the courts are involved rather than with positive aspects of good administration.

This suggests that if the principles of good administration are to be protected—
and many believe this to be necessary—they need to be codified. Codification
would provide an authorative source and a working brief for the courts, either as
a basis for judicial review or as a reference or interpretative document. It would
also ensure that civil servants continue to know what is expected of them. Whether
or not the public service ethos is being eroded, it would seem essential for the
principles under which the Civil Service work to be recorded. This would guard
against the possibility of those appointed from outside the Service being unaware
of the values that inform the public sector and the probability that the fragmentation of the Civil Service will make sustaining an over-arching culture impossible.
In addition, codification would provide a blueprint for private organizations who
are contracted to carry out public functions, for the principles that inform good
administration are also relevant in this context. A code would also empower the
public. They would know the principles upon which administrative decision-
making and action should be based, thereby facilitating their ability to complain
to the agency concerned, the PCA or the courts, if these principles were not followed.

Somewhat paradoxically, in view of the belief that principles need protecting
from the methods and philosophy of the new public management, the codification
of expected standards of administration accords with the thinking behind the
Citizen's Charter and with the greater openness encouraged by the Code of
Practice on Access to Government Information. The difference is that whereas the
expectations of the Citizen's Charter are quantifiable, and because of this may
present superficial standards, those of good administration are less easy to measure and may require subjective judgement on whether they have been fulfilled.
Despite this difference, there are common principles. Charters are not just concerned with how much or how many, but may incorporate rights, such as the right
to a decision and the right to appeal, which any code of administrative practice
would recognize. Similarly, notions of good administration extend to modes of
behaviour, such as courtesy and politeness, which are also present in the Citizen's
Charter. This suggests that a code of good administration could work alongside the
various Charters, providing the general standards for administration whilst
Charters concentrate on those standards which are relevant to the function of the
agency or department concerned.

There are a number of codes or laws which could inform a code of good administration. Of considerable note are the statements of the Council of Europe, contained in the Resolution (1977) and Recommendation (1979) of the Committee of
Ministers.[32] These had a bearing on the grounds for judicial review provided by
the Australian Administrative Decisions (Judicial Review) Act 1977 (as amended

[32] See ch. 1.

in 1978 and 1980) of which the JUSTICE–All Souls Committee commented, 'It is obvious from even a cursory reading of the grounds . . . that very many of them could be established only by proving a breach of one of the principles of good administrative practice adopted by the Committee of Ministers.'[33] Similar comments could be made about the Administrative Justice Act 1980 of Barbados which has much in common with the Australian legislation.[34] There are, in addition, examples from the United States. The JUSTICE–All Souls Report points to the Administrative Conference, an advisory body established in 1968, whose purpose is to 'identify causes of inefficiency, delay and unfairness in administrative proceedings affecting private rights and to recommend improvement to the President, the agencies, the Congress, and the courts'.[35] It is thus concerned with formulating 'recommended good administrative practice'.[36]

There are other examples of codes of American, Canadian, New Zealand and Australian origin relating to ethics and principles of public service which, whilst not directly concerned with good administration, support principles upon which it is founded. In the United States senior appointees of the Executive Branch of the public service are required to sign 'ethics pledges'[37] and it is a mandatory requirement for agencies to produce an ethics statement or policy which is then subject to monitoring. They also have to appoint an officer to be responsible for ethics and give guidance to others. As Lewis and Longley point out this is similar to the responsibility placed upon Chief Executives in local government[38] which requires them to act as monitory officers and to report any action or decision which may be in contravention of the law or result in maladministration or injustice.[39]

In Britain the draft Statement of the Principles of Good Administration, published in 1971 by JUSTICE,[40] provides a useful model, as does *Good Administrative Practice; Guidance on Good Practice,* a booklet produced in 1993 by the Commission for Local Administration.[41] The *Guidance* is 'not an exhaustive statement of good administrative practice. It is, however, a broad indication of the most important principles',[42] some of which are an incorporation of the recommendations of the Committee of Ministers of the Council of Europe. The main concern of the Guidance is 'to assist councils in the promotion of good administrative practice for all services and functions and the achievement of high standards for their customers.'[43]

The structure of local government is obviously different from central government, notably in the controls upon it and in the relationship between officers and members as opposed to that between civil servants and ministers.[44] However,

---

[33] At para. 2.21.   [34] JUSTICE–All Souls Report, App 9.
[35] Ibid., para. 2.16.   [36] Ibid.
[37] Exec. Order 12834, 58 Fed. Reg., 22 Jan. 1993, cited in N. Lewis & D. Longley, 'Ethics and the public service' (1992) *PL* 596 at 606.
[38] Ibid.   [39] Local Government and Housing Act 1989.   [40] See ch. 1.
[41] Commission for Local Administration in England, *Good Administrative Practice; Guidance on Good Practice 2.*
[42] Ibid., 28.   [43] Ibid., 3.
[44] See M. Loughlin, *Constitutional Status of Local Government.*

there are also many points of commonality, particularly relating to public service, and of the '42 principles or axioms of good administration'[45] included within the *Guidance*, many are as relevant to central government and its agencies as they are to local government.

The *Guidance* reiterates the common requirements of legality, objectivity, consistency, equity, fairness, integrity, rectitude, and justifiability. It also echoes the support of the PCA for the proper dissemination of information, the giving of reasons, effective complaints or grievance mechanisms, appropriate remedies, and politeness and consideration. The *Guidance* divides the axioms of good administration into categories which include the law, policy, decisions, actions prior to decision-taking, administrative processes, customer relations, impartiality and fairness, and complaints. Thus good administration requires an understanding and fulfilment of legal obligations[46] and the formulation of, and compliance with, policies which have clear and relevant criteria.[47] Such policies 'help to ensure that there is a systematic consideration of relevant factors . . . and consistent decision-making'[48] and, because of the requirement that they be made public,[49] they also 'ensure that the public or participating individuals involved can understand how decisions are made and see that the process is fair and consistent.'[50]

As far as decision-making is concerned, good administration requires that the relevant policy, or established practice, is followed[51] whilst at the same time taking account of relevant codes of practice or other advice received[52] and allowing for the exceptional case.[53] The *Guidance* stresses the importance of not taking account of irrelevant considerations whilst ensuring that 'adequate consideration is given to all relevant and material factors',[54] giving reasons in writing for an adverse decision,[55] and ensuring that decisions are taken within a reasonable time.[56] It also records the need for appropriate consultation,[57] the maintenance of adequate procedures,[58] and the keeping of adequate records.[59]

In the section entitled 'Customer Relations', officers are warned to 'avoid making misleading or inaccurate statements to customers' and to 'formulate undertakings with care and discharge any responsibility towards customers that arise from them'.[60] In addition, they are instructed that customers should be provided with 'adequate and accurate information, explanations and advice',[61] receive 'courteous' replies to letters and other enquiries within a 'reasonable period',[62] and be kept 'regularly informed about the progress of matters which are of concern to them'.[63]

The *Guidance* also sets out the principles of impartiality and fairness and the need to inform individuals of any rights of appeal, and, with regard to complaints,

[45] Above, n. 41, 5.
[46] Ibid., paras. 1 & 2.
[47] Ibid., paras. 3 & 4.
[48] Ibid., 6.
[49] Ibid., para. 5.
[50] Ibid., 6.
[51] Ibid., para. 7.
[52] Ibid., para. 10.
[53] Ibid., para. 8.
[54] Ibid., paras. 11, 12 & 19.
[55] Ibid., para. 16.
[56] Ibid., para. 17.
[57] Ibid., para. 21.
[58] Ibid., para. 26.
[59] Ibid., para. 28.
[60] Ibid., para. 31.
[61] Ibid., para. 35.
[62] Ibid., para. 33.
[63] Ibid., para 34.

states that there should be 'a simple well publicized complaints system'.[64] Where faults are identified, the *Guidance* advises that remedial action should be taken 'both to provide redress for the individuals concerned and to prevent recurrence of the problem in future'[65].

Good Administrative Practice provides a useful over-view of good administration as it benefits individuals or 'customers'. The main thrust of the document accords with the public service model of good administration. It makes no mention of cost efficiency or value for money, nor of other new public management principles. It does, however, 'welcome the current emphasis on customer care, quality assurance and the quest for excellence', considering that the 'accent on quality promotion is timely'.[66] Moreover, the requirements for openness and the disclosure of information and for effective grievance procedures accord with new public management thinking, a further indication that a code of good administration has some relevance to reformist strategies.

The formulation of such a Code for central government and its agencies would need to be informed by the PCA[67] and by judicial decisions concerned with good administration. It should also take account of the Citizen's Charter, the Code of Practice on Access to Government Information and the Code of Conduct for civil servants, drafted by the Treasury and Civil Service Select Committee.[68] Its structure could be similar to the model proposed by Kernaghan for a Code of Conduct[69] which starts with a statement of general principles, follows with an explanation of their purpose and practical operation, and concludes with a provision which allows individual departments or agencies to add their own statements on the operation of the principles. In a Code of Good Administration this last section could incorporate charter principles.

The arguments against a Code of Good Administration, which have in the past mainly centred on an absence of need together with concerns about flexibility and increased judicial intervention, seem even less persuasive in the 1990s than previously. The Civil Service culture which finds expression through the public service ethos is unlikely to continue to protect the principles underlying good administration. The fragmentation of government, together with the wholesale importation of private-sector methods and values, makes the notion that an unwritten set of principles will suffice unsustainable. Moreover, a change of government is unlikely to alter the situation. Indeed, Labour has demonstrated support for, or at least a lack of opposition to, the Civil Service reforms, and is committed to value for money and cost-cutting exercises within the public-sector. It has, however, shown signs of being more constitutionally aware than Conservative governments have been and thus may be more easily persuaded of the need for a Code of Good Administration.

[64] Ibid., para. 41.   [65] Ibid., para. 42.   [66] Ibid., 3.
[67] The PCA is at present compiling guidance for civil servants which might form the basis for a code.
[68] See TCSC, HC 390, (1992–3), (see ch. 1).
[69] K. Kernaghan, 'Promoting public service ethics' in Chapman (ed.) (above, n. 28).

Whatever party is in office it is important that a Code is balanced, concerned not only with the interest of the individual in good administration but also with the public interest. Thus the requirements it imposes should not be such as to overly burden the administrative process or to impede decision-making. It should be concerned with good decision-making and could in many respects improve efficiency, as the Citizen's Charter aims to do. However, in the final analysis, it may need to be accepted that in a democracy there are times when efficiency has to give way to other concerns such as acceptable standards of public administration and the appropriate mechanisms of accountability to ensure that these standards are met. These mechanisms include the courts, which, in the light of the failures in political accountability, have assumed a steadily increasing role. The formulation of a Code of Good Administration, whether or not given legislative effect, would not reduce this role. Nor would it necessarily reduce the underlying tension between administrators and judges who would still from time to time pull in different directions. It would, however, make the principles of good administration explicit and provide a base line for administrators and judges. Most significantly, it would be a recognition of the constitutional importance of good administration.

BIBLIOGRAPHY

Books and Articles

Bagehot, W., *The English Constitution* (London 1963).

Baldwin, R., *Rules and Government* (Oxford 1995).

Baldwin, R. and McCrudden, C. (eds.), *Regulation and Public Law* (London 1987).

Barker, A. (ed.), *Quangos in Britain* (Basingstoke and London 1982).

— — 'The impact of judicial review: perspectives from Whitehall and the Courts' (1996) *Public Law* 612.

Bayles, M., *Procedural Justice: Allocating to Individuals* (Dordrecht 1990).

Bayne. P., 'Freedom of information: democracy and the protection of the processes and decisions of government' (1988) 62 *Australian Law Journal* 538.

— — 'Administrative law' (1988) 62 *Australian Law Journal* 1043.

Beetham, D., *Bureaucracy* (Milton Keynes 1987).

Bellamy, R. and Greenaway, J., 'The New Right conception of citizenship and the Citizen's Charter' (1995) 30 *Government and Opposition* 4.

Benn, T., *Diaries*, Vols. 1–5 1963–1990, (London 1987–92).

Birkenshaw, P., *Grievances, Remedies and the State* (2nd edn., London 1995).

Blom-Cooper, L., 'Lawyers and public administration' (1984) *Public Law* 215.

Boston, J., 'The problems of policy co-ordination: the New Zealand experience' (1992) 5 *Governance* 1.

Boyle, A. E., 'Sovereignty, accountability and the reform of administrative law' in Richardson & Genn (eds.), *Administrative Law and Government Action* (Oxford 1991) at 81.

Bradley, A., 'The Parliamentary Ombudsman again; a positive report' (1995) *Public Law* 345.

Brennan, Sir Gerard, 'The purpose and scope of judicial review' in Taggart (ed.), *Judicial Review of Administrative Action in the 1980s* (New Zealand 1986) at 18.

— — 'Judicial review and good administration' (1991) 65 *Australian Law Journal* 32.

Breyer, S. and Stewart, R. B., *Administrative Law and Regulatory Policy* (3rd edn., Boston, Mass. 1992).

Bridges, L., Meszaros, G. and Sunkin, M. *Judicial Review in Perspective* (London 1995).

Brown. P., 'The Ombudsman' in Richardson & Genn (eds.), *Administrative Law and Government Action* (Oxford 1991) at 309.

Brown, R. G. S. and Steel, D., *The Administrative Process in Britain* (2nd edn., London 1979).

Browne-Wilkinson, Lord, 'The infiltration of a Bill of Rights' (1992) *Public Law* 397.

Butler, Sir Robin, 'The Future of the Civil Service', Lecture to First Division Association (London 1991).

— — 'The evaluation of the Civil Service—a Progress Report' (1993) 7 *Public Administration* 3.

Cabinet Office *Departmental Evidence and Response to Select Committees* (London 1994).

Cane, P., *An Introduction to Administrative Law* (3rd edn., Oxford 1996).

Castle, B., *The Castle Diaries 1974–76* (London 1980).

Castle, B. *The Castle Diaries 1964–70* (London 1984).

Chapman, R. (ed.), *Ethics in Public Service* (London 1993).

Citizen's Charter Complaints Task Force *Access to Complaints Systems* (Discussion Paper 1, London 1994).

— — *Effective Complaints Systems: Principles and Checklist* (London 1995).

Cochrane, A., *Whatever Happened to Local Government?* (Buckingham 1993).

Commission for Local Administration in England *Good Administrative Practice; Guidance on Good Practice (2)* (London 1993; reissued 1995).

Cotterall, R., 'Judicial review and legal theory' in Richardson & Genn (eds.), *Administrative Law and Government Action* (Oxford 1991) at 13.

Craig, P., *Public Law and Democracy in the United Kingdom and the United States of America* (Oxford 1990).

— — 'Legitimate expectations: a conceptual analysis' (1992) 108 *Law Quarterly Review* 79.

— — *Administrative Law* (3rd edn., 1994).

Cranston, R., 'Reviewing judicial review', in Richardson & Genn (eds.) *Administrative Law and Government Action* (Oxford 1991) at 45.

Cullen, R. B., 'Business, government and change: managing transition in the public and private sectors' (1987) 46 *Australian Journal of Public Administration* 10.

Curtis, L. J., 'Judicial review of administrative acts' (1979) 53 *Australian Law Journal* 530.

Davis, K. C., *Discretionary Justice* (Urbana, Ill. 1979).

Dearlove, J. and Saunders, P., *Introduction to British Politics* (Cambridge and London 1984).

Dicey, A. V., *An Introduction to the Study of the Law of the Constitution* (10th edn., Basingstoke and London 1959).

Doig, A., 'From Lynskey to Nolan: the corruption of British politics and public service?' (1996) 23 *Journal of Law and Society* 1.

Drewry, G. and Harlow, C., 'A cutting edge: the Parliamentary Commissioner and MPs' (1990) 53 *Modern Law Review* 745.

Dworkin, R., *A Matter of Principle* (Oxford 1985).

Efficiency Unit, *Report to the Prime Minister: Improving Management in Government; the Next Steps* (London 1988).

— — *The Oughton Report* (London 1992).

Feldman, D., 'Judicial Review: a way of controlling government?' (1988) 66 *Public Administration* 3.

— — 'Public Law values in the House of Lords' (1990) 106 *Law Quarterly Review* 246.

Finn, C. P. D., 'Integrity in government' (1991) 3 *Public Law Review*.

Flynn, N., *Public Sector Management* (London 1993).

Forsyth, C., 'The provenance and protection of legitimate expectations' (1988) 47 *Cambridge Law Journal* 238.

D. Galligan, 'Judicial review and the textbook writers' (1982) 2 *Oxford Journal of Legal Studies* 257.

— — (1986) *Discretionary Powers* (Oxford 1986).

Greenaway, J., 'Having the bun and the halfpenny: can Old Public Sector Service ethics survive the New Whitehall?' (1995) 73 *Public Administration* 3.

Greenwood, J. and Wilson, D., *Public Administration in Britain Today* (2nd edn., London 1989).

Gregory, R. and Drewry, G., 'The Barlow Clowes affair' (1991) *Public Law* 192, & ibid. 408.

Gregory, R. and Pearson, J., 'The Parliamentary Ombudsman after twenty-five years' (1992) 70 *Public Administration* 4.

Griffith, J. A. G., *The Politics of the Judiciary* (4th edn., London 1991).

Griffiths, J., 'Australian administrative law: institutional reforms and impact' (1985) 63 *Public Administration* 4.

Hailsham, Lord, *Elective Dictatorship* (London 1976).

— — *The Dilemma of Democracy* (London 1978).

Harlow, C., 'Administrative reaction to judicial review' (1976) *Public Law* 116.

— — 'The Ombudsman in search of a role' (1978) 41 *Modern Law Review* 446.

Harlow, C. and Rawlings, R., *Pressure through the Law* (London 1992).

Harrow, J. and Gillett, R., 'The proper conduct of public business' (1994) 14 *Public Money and Management*.

Hartley, T. C., *The Foundations of European Community Law* (3rd edn., Oxford 1994).

Hawkins, K. (ed.), *The Uses of Discretion* (Oxford 1992).

Hennessy, P., *Whitehall* (London 1990).

Holmes, M. and Shand, D. 'Management reform; some practioner perspectives on the past ten years' (1995) 8 *Governance* 4.

Hood, C. 'A public management for all seasons' (1991) 69 *Public Administration* 1.

Howe, Sir Geoffrey, 'Procedure at the Scott Inquiry' (1996) *Public Law* 445.

Johnson, N., 'Change in the Civil Service; retrospect and prospects' (1985) 63 *Public Administration* 4.

Jowell, J. L., *Law and Bureaucracy* (Port Washington, NY. 1975).

— — 'The Rule of Law today' in Jowell & Oliver (eds.), *The Changing Constitution* (3rd edn., Oxford 1994) at 3.

Jowell, J. L. and Lester, A., 'Beyond Wednesbury: substantive principles of administrative law' (1987) *Public Law* 368.

Jowell, J. L. and Oliver, D. (eds.), *The Changing Constitution* (3rd edn., Oxford 1994).

JUSTICE, *Administration under Law* (London 1971).

— — *Our Fettered Ombudsman* (London 1971).

JUSTICE and All Souls, *Review of Administrative Law in the United Kingdom; Administrative Justice; Some Necessary Reforms* (Oxford 1988).

JUSTICE and Public Law Project, *A Matter of Public Interest; Reforming the law and practice on interventions in public interest cases* (London 1996).

Kennan, J., 'The control of government' (1987) 61 *Australian Law Journal* 523.

Kernaghan, K., 'Promoting public service ethics' in Chapman, R. (ed.), *Ethics in Public Service* (London 1993).

Kerry, Sir Michael. 'Administrative law and judicial review—the practical effects of developments over the past twenty-five years on administration in central government' (1986) 64 *Public Administration* 2.

Lacey, N., 'The jurisprudence of discretion' in Hawkins, K. (ed.), *The Uses of Discretion* (Oxford 1992) at 361.

Lane, P. H., 'The changing role of the High Court' (1996) 70 *Australian Law Journal* 3.

Law Commission, *Administrative Law, Judicial Review and Statutory Appeals* (Consultation Paper No. 126; London 1993).

Laws, Sir John, 'Law and democracy' (1995) *Public Law* 72.

Lawton, A. and Rose, A., *Organisation and Management in the Public Sector* (2nd edn., London 1994).

Lester, Lord, 'Government's compliance with international human rights law: a new year's legitimate expectation' (1996) *Public Law* 187.

Lewis, N. and Birkenshaw, P., *When Citizens Complain; Reforming Justice and Administration* (Buckingham 1993).

Lewis, N. and Longley, D., 'Ethics and the Public Service' (1992) *Public Law* 596.

Loughlin, M. *The Constitutional Status of Local Government* (London 1994).

Loveland, I., 'Housing Benefit; administrative law and administrative practice', (1988) 66 *Public Administration* 57.

— — *Constitutional Law; A Critical Introduction* (London 1996).

McAustlan, P., 'Public law and public choice' (1988) 51 *Modern Law Review* 699.

MacDonald, O., *The Future of Whitehall* (London 1991).

Mackenzie, W. J. M. and Grove, J. W., *Central Administration in Britain* (London 1957).

Mascarenhas, R. C. 'Reform of the public service in Australia and New Zealand' (1990) 3 *Governance* 1.

Mashew, J., 'Administrative due process: the quest for a dignitary theory' (1981) 61 *Boston University Law Review* 885.

— — *Bureaucratic Justice: Managing Social Security Disability Claims* (New Haven, Conn. 1983).

— — 'Dignitary process: a political psychology of liberal democratic citizenship' (1987) 39 *University of Florida Law Review* 433.

Mowbray, A., 'The Parliamentary Commissioner and administrative guidance' (1987) *Public Law* 570.

— — 'A right to official advice: the Parliamentary Commissioner's perspective' (1990) *Public Law* 68.

Oliver, D. 'Is the *ultra vires* principle the basis of Judicial Review?' (1987) *Public Law* 543.

— — 'The Lord Chancellor's Department' (1994) *Public Law* 163.

Osborne, D. and Gaebler, T., *Reinventing Government: How the Entrepreneurial Spirit is Transforming the Public Sector* (Reading, Mass. 1992).

O'Toole, B. J., The loss of purity: the corruption of public service in Britain' (1993) 8 *Public Policy and Administration* 2.

Piotrowiaz, R. 'The *Teoh* case' (1996) *Public Law* 194.

Pliatzky, L., 'Mandarins, ministers and the management of Britain' (1984) 66 *Political Quarterly* 1.

— — 'Quangos and agencies' (1992) 7 *Public Administration* 4.

Plowden, W., 'What prospects for the Civil Service?' (1985) 63 *Public Administration* 4.

— — *Ministers and Mandarins* (London 1994).

Ponting, C., *Whitehall: Changing the Old Guard* (London 1989).

Posner, B., *Economic Analysis of Law* (2nd edn., Boston, Mass. 1972).

Pratchett, L. and Wingfield, M., *The Public Service Ethos in Local Government* (Report by The Commission of Local Democracy and the Institute of Chartered Secretaries and Administrators London, 1994).

Purchas, Sir Francis, 'Lord Mackay and the judiciary' (1994) *New Law Journal* 6644, 22 Apr.

Raine, J. W. and Willson, M. J., 'New public management and criminal justice' (1995) 15 *Public Money and Management* 1.

Rawlings, H., 'Judicial review and the control of Government' (1986) 64 *Public Administration* 2.

Richardson G., 'The legal regulation of process' in Richardson & Genn (eds.), *Administrative Law and Government Action* (Oxford 1991) at 105.

Richardson, G. and Genn, H. (eds.), *Administrative Law and Government Action* (Oxford 1994).

Richardson, G., and Sunkin, M., 'Judicial review: questions of impact' (1996) *Public Law* 79.

Sainsbury, R., 'Internal reviews and the weakening of Social Security claimants' rights of appeal' in Richardson & Genn (eds.), *Administrative Law and Government Action* (Oxford 1991) at 287.

Sedgemore, B., *The Secret Constitution* (London 1980).

Sedley, Sir Stephen 'The sound of silence: constitutional law without a constitution' (1994) 110 *Law Quarterly Review* 280.

— — 'Governments, constitutions and judges' in Richardson & Genn (eds.), *Administrative Law and Government Action* (Oxford 1991) at 35.

— — 'Human rights: a twenty-first century agenda' (1995) *Public Law* 386.

Smith, J., 'The public service ethos' (1991) 69 *Public Administration* 4.

Stewart, J. D., 'Management in the public domain' (1989) 15 *Local Government Studies* 5.

— — and Walsh, K., 'Change in the management of public services' (1992) 70 *Public Administration* 4.

Stewart, J. D. and Stoker, G. (eds.), *The Future of Local Government* (London 1989).

Sunkin, M., 'The judicial review case-load 1987–89' (1991) *Public Law* 490.

Szabolwski, G. J., 'Administrative discretion and the protection of human rights' in Chapman (ed.), *Ethics in Public Service* (London 1993).

Taggart M. (ed.), *Judicial Review of Administrative Action in the 1980s* (New Zealand 1986).

Taylor, G. D. S., 'The new administrative law' (1977) 51 *Australian Law Journal* 804.

Treasury Solicitor, *Judge over your Shoulder* (1st edn. 1987; 2nd edn. London 1995).

Wade, H. W. R. and Forsyth, C. F., (1994) *Administrative Law* (7th edn., Oxford 1994).

Waldegrave, W., *The Reality of Reform; Accountability in Today's Public Service* (CIPFA; London 1993).

Wilenski, P., 'Administrative law and the public service' (1985) *Rupert Public Interest Journal* March.

— — 'Administrative reforms—general principles and the Australian experience' (1986) 64 *Public Administration* 4.

Woolf, Sir Harry, *The Protection of the Public: A New Challenge* (London 1990).

Woolf, Lord, 'Droit Public—English style', (1995) *Public Law* 57.

Official Publications

Comptroller and Auditor-General, *20th Report*, HC 172, (1991–2).

— — *48th Report*, HC 558, (1992–3).

Foreign Affairs Select Committee, *Public Expenditure: the Pergau Hydro-Electric Project*, HC 271, (1993–4).

Home Affairs Select Committee, *Murder: the Mandatory Life Sentence*, HC 111, (1995–6).

Bibliography

Parliamentary Commissioner for Administration, *Annual Report for 1976*, HC 116, (1976–7).

Parliamentary Commissioner for Administration, *Finding by the PCA that an Injustice had not been remedied*, HC 666, (1977–8).

—— *Annual Report for 1978*, HC 205, (1978–9).

—— *Annual Report for 1980*, HC 148, (1980–1).

—— *Annual Report for 1981*, HC 258, (1981–2).

—— *Annual Report for 1982*, HC 257, (1982–3).

—— *Investigation of a complaint about delay in reviewing a conviction for murder (the Preece case)*, HC 191, (1983–4).

—— *Annual Report for 1985*, HC 275, (1985–6).

—— *Annual Report for 1986*, HC 248, (1986–7).

—— *Annual Report for 1987*, HC 363, (1987–8).

—— *Annual Report for 1988*, HC 301, (1988–9).

—— *Annual Report for 1989*, HC 62, (1989–90).

—— *The Barlow Clowes Affair*, HC 76, (1989–90).

—— *Annual Report for 1991*, HC 347, (1991–2).

—— *Annual Report for 1992*, HC 569, (1992–3).

—— *Annual Report for 1993*, HC 290, (1993–4).

—— *Annual Report for 1994*, HC 307, (1994–5).

—— *Investigation of complaints against the Child Support Agency*, HC 135, (1994–5).

—— *Access to Official Information; Selected Cases*, Vol. 2, HC 14, (1994–5).

—— *Access to Official Information: the First Eight Months*, HC 91, (1994–5).

—— *The Channel Tunnel Rail Link and Blight; Investigation of complaints against the Department of Transport*, HC 193, (1994–5).

—— *Access to Official Information; Selected Cases* Vol. 3, HC 606, (1994–5).

—— *Access to Official Information; Selected Cases* Vol. 4, HC 758, (1994–5).

—— *Access to Official Information; Selected Cases* Vol. 5, HC 762, (1994–5).

Public Accounts Committee, *Payment to meet legal expenses incurred by the Chancellor of the Exchequer*, HC 386–i, (1992–3).

—— *The Proper Conduct of Public Business*, HC 154, (1993–4).

—— *Pergau Hydro-Electric Project*, HC 155, (1993–4).

Public Service Select Committee, *Ministerial Accountability and Responsibility*, HC 313, (1995–6).

—— *Government's Response to the Second Report from the Public Service Select Committee (session 1995–96) on Ministerial Accountability and Responsibility*, HC 67, (1996).

Scott, Sir Richard, *Report of the Inquiry into the Export of Defence Equipment and Dual-Use Goods to Iraq and Related Prosecutions*, HC 115, (1996).

Select Committee on Parliamentary Commissioner for Administration, *Second Report*, HC 350, (1967–8).

—— *First Report*, HC 385, (1968–9).

—— *Second Report*, HC 480, (1975–6).

—— *First Report*, HC 544, (1977–8).

—— *Second Report*, HC 615, (1977–8).

—— *First Report*, HC 593, (1979–80).

—— *Fifth Report*, HC 322, (1983–4).

—— *Non-Departmental Public Bodies*, HC 619, (1983–4).
—— *Fourth Report*, HC 368, (1990–1).
—— *Implications of the Citizen's Charter for the work of the PCA*, HC 158, (1991–2).
—— *First Report*, HC 387, (1992–3).
—— *Powers, Work and Jurisdiction of the Ombudsman*, HC 33, (1993–4).
—— *Government replies to Reports from Select Committee on the Parliamentary Commissioner for Administration*, HC 46, (1993–4).
—— *Second Report*, HC 64, (1993–4).
—— *Maladministration and Redress*, HC 112, (1993–4).
—— *Third Report*, HC 345, (1993–4).
—— *The Channel Tunnel Rail Link and Exceptional Hardship*, HC 270, (1994–5).
—— *Open Government*, HC 290, (1994–5).
—— *Government's Response to Report from Select Committee on Parliamentary Commissioner for Administration, Maladministration and Redress*, HC 316, (1994–5).
—— *The Operation of the Code of Practice on Access to Government Information*, HC 84, (1995–6).
Social Security Select Committee, *The Operation of the Child Support Act*, HC 69, (1993–4).
Treasury and Civil Service Select Committee *Efficiency and Effectiveness in the Civil Service*, HC 236, (1981–2).
—— *Developments in the Next Steps Programme*, HC 348, (1988–9).
—— *The Role of the Civil Service, Interim Report*, HC 390, (1992–3).
—— *The Role of the Civil Service*, HC 27, (1993–4).

Command Reports

(listed in chronological order)

Report of the Committee on the Civil Service, Cmnd. 3638 (1966–68) (the Fulton Report).
Report on Non-departmental Public Bodies, Cmnd. 7797 (1980).
The Citizen's Charter, Cm. 1599, (1991).
Competing for Quality: Buying Better Public Services, Cm. 1730, (1991).
Open Government, Cm. 2290, (1993).
The Civil Service: Continuity and Change, Cm. 2627, (1994).
Reply by the Government to the Report of the Select Committee on the Parliamentary Commissioner for Administration on the Child Support Agency, Cm. 2865, (1994–5).
Standards in Public Life, Cm. 2850–1, (1995) (the Nolan Report).
Legal Aid, Targeting Need: the Future of Publicly Funded Help in Solving Legal Problems and Disputes in England and Wales, Cm. 2854, (1995).
Review of Prison Service Security in England and Wales, Cm. 3020, (1995).
Striking the Balance: the future of Legal Aid in England and Wales, Cm. 3305, (1996).

INDEX